# Praise for Jane Hyun's
## *Breaking the Bamboo Ceiling*

"In *Breaking the Bamboo Ceiling*, Jane Hyun meaningfully advances the dialogue around diversity as it relates to Asian Americans. It is a must read for any CEO or aspiring CEO who believes in building a culture of inclusion."
—Douglas R. Conant, President and Chief Executive Officer, Campbell Soup Company

"I am delighted that a qualified expert like Jane Hyun has written a book to help Asian Americans realize their dreams and aspirations in the American business world. This book is long overdue and will be of great benefit to those Asian Americans who want to take advantage of the experiences of others who have gone before them. Asian Americans (as all Americans) have a great deal to offer to their organizations and to our country—and this book will show them how they can harness the strengths of their unique cultural values to be fully engaged in the corporate environment and in the community at large! Her book should be required reading for both Asian and non-Asian readers who want to avoid costly misunderstandings that prevent many from realizing this potential."
—Dennis Ling, senior vice president, Global Finance and treasurer, Avon Products, Inc.

"*Breaking the Bamboo Ceiling* is a terrific combination of theory and practice, skills coaching and life wisdom, sociology and practical behaviors. It defines career strategies, self-assessment, and action steps for Asians while teaching practical, applied diversity to everyone. Only a trainer who is also a coach could have written a work so usefully rich."
—Gus Lee, author of *China Boy, Chasing Hepburn,* and *Moral Courage*

"Jane Hyun has written a sage, sensible, and long overdue book. With pragmatism and warmth, Jane shows how cultural values can adversely impact workplace behavior, and provides tips for overcoming those differences. *Breaking the Bamboo Ceiling* is an important book for employees and managers, as well as every career coach, leadership consultant, and human resources professional. I have known and worked with Jane for years; she is the *leading authority* in coaching Asians who want to succeed in Fortune 500 companies. She understands cultural differences and she is an expert career coach!"

—Kate Wendleton, president, the Five O'Clock Club, a national career coaching and outplacement organization, and author of *Targeting a Great Career*

"Hyun says 'This book is a call to action for both Asian Americans and organizations.' She's right—the case studies are excellent examples of career do's and don'ts, infused with a cultural flavor. This much-needed work has particular applicability to Asian employees, but will be hugely valuable to anyone who's interested in achieving cultural fluency in the workplace—and given today's competitive environment, that should include all of us."

—Patrice A. Hall, managing director and head of Diversity, Investment Bank, JPMorganChase

"We at Deloitte have long been the beneficiary of Jane's experience, insight, and counsel as it relates to our vision of being the place where the very best talent chooses to spend their careers. Now, all companies have the opportunity to take full advantage of her wisdom as they, too, strive to attract, retain, and develop their talented Asian workforce. The business imperative demands no less. *Breaking the Bamboo Ceiling* is a practical guide to realizing this vision."

—James H. Wall, Deloitte Touche Tohmatsu, global managing director, Human Resources

"In *Breaking the Bamboo Ceiling,* Jane Hyun confronts the dilemma of how to be an Asian in America, and what it means to be 'American' in a diverse America. Her culturally appropriate examples, revealing exercises and relevant stories, extend beyond ethnicity and present a working model for retaining one's culture, values, identity, and heritage while being an effective participant in this country. A truly valuable and insightful resource for Asian Americans who want to be challenged in their conventional thinking and for those who want to better understand the Asians with whom they interact."

—J. D. Hokoyama, president and CEO, Leadership Education for Asian Pacifics (LEAP)

"In a clear personal voice, Hyun provides Asian professionals and anyone who works with them real tips and tools to use in everyday business interactions. You will find numerous 'quick hits' that can be implemented on Monday. Real life examples combined with analysis and recommendations illustrate the obstacles to advancement and offer suggestions on how to achieve personal career success and optimal workplace interactions. *Breaking the Bamboo Ceiling* is right on the mark."

—Jeannie Diefenderfer, senior vice president,
Network Services, Verizon Communications

*"Breaking the Bamboo Ceiling* is the book Asian Americans in the workplace have needed for decades. Jane Hyun combines research, interviews, and her own years of experience as a corporate trainer and coach to give us very practical and seasoned help. The self-assessment exercises—if taken seriously—are worth the price of the book. Hyun takes her insights in both the Asian American experience and corporate America and melds them seamlessly."

—Paul Tokunaga, national Asian American ministry coordinator,
InterVarsity Christian Fellowship and author of *Invitation to Lead*

"A powerful piece of work! This book speaks words of wisdom that are profound and yet extremely practical. Hyun has a vivid style that will capture your intellect and appeal to your common sense. The book delivers on the promise of presenting specific techniques so that you can successfully 'break the bamboo ceiling' (or help someone else do it)! Hyun presents valuable strategic and tactical next steps that Asian professionals can implement to advance their careers. She 'gets it' and so will any person who picks up this book!"

—Philip Berry, vice president, Global Workplace Initiatives,
Colgate-Palmolive

"Hyun's book will help you unlock the barriers to better business communications with your Asian American coworkers. It is a clear, straightforward guide to easing cultural barriers between Asian Americans and their non-Asian counterparts. What's in it for the non-Asian colleague is increased efficiency and a more productive work environment. You must read this book!"

—Luke Visconti, partner and cofounder, DiversityInc.

"Knowing yourself and the values that you hold are integral steps to developing leadership competencies. *Breaking the Bamboo Ceiling* is a must read for everyone who wants to better understand how cultural influences (among other factors) affect workplace persona so they can better manage their careers and learn the skills necessary to thrive in today's multicultural workplace. The book effectively addresses these influences and their effect on Asian professionals' behavior, attitude, and performance. Tactical strategies for self-assessment and external feedback should help readers improve work relationships, achieve cultural competency, and increase chances of upward mobility."

    —Jim Loehr, principal, LGE Performance Systems, author of *Power of Full Engagement,* and creator of the Corporate Athlete Training System

*"Breaking the Bamboo Ceiling* is an excellent resource to help demystify business practices for Asian Americans striving to reach the top of corporate America. More critically, this book addresses dimensions of culture in such an integrated way as to be just as useful for companies to understand a more complete picture of diversity. It will be exciting to see more Asian Americans break through the 'bamboo ceiling' in the years to come and that these successes become more of the norm, rather than the exception. This book will be a key part of this evolution."

    —David L. Kim, director, Sales Development and Community Relations, Anheuser-Busch, Inc.

"Kudos to Jane Hyun for a provocative, thoughtful, and engaging book. It offers useful insights and practical strategies for all persons of Asian descent striving for career advancement and success. I only wish I had had the benefit of this book when I began my career—it would have saved me a lot of time by addressing some mystifying questions that took years of experience to answer."

    —Diane Yu, chief of staff and deputy to the president, New York University

*"Breaking the Bamboo Ceiling* is a workplace must read. Jane Hyun nailed it with this essential guide—a well-written, easy-to-read, and thorough com-

pendium for every Asian who wants to move up the ladder. Because her grasp on workplace issues has widespread practical application, I recommend this book to everyone who wants to build a solid and successful career."

—Susan RoAne, the nation's undisputed networking expert, keynote speaker, and author of *How To Create Your Own Luck* and *How To Work a Room*

"There is much in this book for diversity officers, including the cultural backdrop Hyun offers for understanding workplace interactions, and the long-term, big-picture strategies and proposals for immediate implementation. I strongly recommend this book to anyone who is committed to diversity and inclusion."

—Dr. Johnnetta B. Cole, president, Bennett College for Women

"The recommendations found in Hyun's book are immediately applicable to not only Asians living and working in the U.S. but also to those working for U.S. multinational corporations in Asia. I have seen far too many cases of well-qualified executives who have been passed over for promotions because of their inability to be assertive or to communicate in a style that translates into 'leadership' in a U.S. corporate culture. Read this book and find out how best to manage your career in today's multicultural workplace."

—Kyung H. Yoon, vice chair, Heidrick and Struggles

"Hyun's book provides clarity and insight into the issues confronting Asian professionals in their pursuit of success in corporate America. Academic success and hard work alone will not get you the corner office. She advises us in the most effective way—by empowering individuals to take charge of their careers and giving them the tools to navigate the corporate structure. Every student, professional, and parent of Asian descent should read this book!"

—David Chu, founder and former president and CEO, Nautica, Inc.

"Bravo to Jane Hyun for advancing the critically important conversation about Asian Americans in the workplace. By giving us a set of practical maps to define, measure, and envision our professional lives, Hyun reveals truths that too often remain unspoken."

—Phoebe Eng, creative director, The Opportunity Agenda and author of *Warrior Lessons: An Asian American Woman's Journey into Power*

"Hyun's book offers valuable insights into the Asian culture."

—Peggy Klaus, workplace communication and leadership coach and author of *BRAG: The Art of Tooting Your Own Horn Without Blowing It*

"Inspiring and engaging, this book is a winner! Every Asian professional and student, in addition to anyone who works with them (HR, diversity professionals, trainers, professors, and career counselors), should read this book. It is a call to action for all of us who want to achieve our personal best in the workplace."

—Jino Ahn, president and founder, Asian Diversity, Inc.

"Finally! A book that addresses the truth and shatters so many myths and misconceptions about Asian Americans in the workplace. Jane Hyun's book is a practical handbook for today's Asian American professionals wondering why they are not being promoted like their non-Asian counterparts despite their educational background and seemingly great performance evaluations. Read this book to understand a new concept called 'cultural barriers' and how it is unknowingly affecting your success in corporate America."

—Vincent Yee, national president, NAAAP (National Association of Asian American Professionals)

"*Breaking the Bamboo Ceiling* addresses an issue that most of corporate America and diversity experts have been silent about. Why is it that despite being one of America's most well-educated ethnic groups, Asian Americans are the most absent demographic in Fortune 500 boardrooms and executive suites? Hyun's answers are based on sound research and have implications for both corporate HR practices and how Asian Americans choose to present themselves in the workplace. This important work should be read by all who are committed to creating inclusive and high-performing organizations."

"Practical, personable, and strategic, Jane Hyun is the workplace mentor every Asian American would like to have. Accessible stories and concrete suggestions fill this book. Read it, and find clarity about who you are and what you want to become."

# BREAKING
### THE BAMBOO
# CEILING

Collins

An Imprint of HarperCollinsPublishers

# JANE HYUN

# BREAKING THE BAMBOO CEILING

## CAREER STRATEGIES FOR ASIANS

THE ESSENTIAL GUIDE TO GETTING IN,
MOVING UP, AND REACHING THE TOP

HarperCollins books may be purchased for educational, business, or sales promotional use. For information please write to: Special Markets Department, HarperCollins Publishers, 10 East 53rd Street, New York, New York 10022.

FIRST EDITION

Designed by William Ruoto

Library of Congress Cataloging-in-Publication Data
Hyun, Jane.
Breaking the bamboo ceiling : career strategies for Asians / by Jane Hyun.
    p.    cm.
Includes bibliographical references and index.
ISBN 0-06-073119-2
1. Career development—United States.    2. Asian Americans—
Employment.    3. Vocational guidance for minorities—United States.
I. Title.
HF5382.5.U5H98 2005
650.1'089'95073—dc22
2004054055

09   10   11   12   DIX/RRD   10   9

For my mom and dad,
Wha Ja and Min Hwan Kim,
my first mentors in life

# – ACKNOWLEDGMENTS –

This book would not have been possible if it were not for the dozens of friends, clients, mentors, and colleagues who read multiple drafts and provided expert opinions, feedback, and suggestions for improvement. Thanks to all the individuals who agreed to be interviewed, quoted, and challenged.

To everyone at HarperBusiness, for supporting this first-time author. Edwin Tan, editor extraordinaire, who truly "got it" the first time we spoke and continues to be a great cheerleader. You have been the gentle nudge, while also challenging me to produce more than I ever expected. Thanks to the production editorial team, consisting of production editor Jessica Chin and copyeditor Katharine O'Moore-Klopf, and the sales force and marketing group at HarperBusiness.

Stephanie Rostan and the team at Levine Greenberg Literary Agency, thanks for believing in me and for understanding the subtleties of the book early on. Thanks to Soyung Pak, for prompting me to write this in the first place seven years ago and for making the valuable introductions.

Jane Rohman—I am thrilled to be working with such a pro.

*The artistic team:*

Writing a book is one thing, but making it presentable for others to view is another. Dan Koh—your expert eye and natural artistic abilities created a cover that everyone loved. Randy Jones created a beautiful Web site and updated all the print material—I never knew that a few short meetings at Starbucks would create such superb results!

*Various subject matter experts:*

A special thanks to Roger Daniels, professor emeritus at University of Cincinnati, for his encouraging words and for providing access and permission to use the Asian Assimilation Model from the book he coauthored with Harry Kitano, *Asian Americans: Emerging Minorities.* Thank you to Jeannette Yep, for permission to use the adapted version she originally created for InterVarsity. A special thank-you to Greg Jao, for his sharp wit and insights that helped refine the ideas for the book.

Thank you to the LEAP leadership—J. D. Hokoyama, Linda Akutagawa, and others—for their assistance: Your active involvement with the Asian community inspires many to action.

Thanks to Belinda Huang, Sunny Park Suh, Ezer Kang, Jino Ahn, Jean Sun Shaw, Angela Oh, Wendy Horikoshi, and Kurt Takamine for advice and counsel about Asian diversity issues.

Eric Liu provided eloquent feedback and opened my eyes to the "hidden" audience for the book. Judy Provost trained me well in the MBTI. And Katherine Giscombe at Catalyst provided rich insights. To the "Connectors" who made the valuable introductions to corporations, influencers, and decision makers, your generosity knew no bounds. You were the influencers who made the proper introductions at key junctures in the process: Marian Rose, Martha Patton, Anne Marie Yarwood, Annie Wong, Elizabeth Nieto, Paul Tokunaga, Greg Jao, Dennis Ling, Lisa Choi, Matt Fong, Sonny Whang, Andy Hahn, Patrice Hall, David Chu, Kyung Yoon, Sharon Foo, Kim Ng, Cherry Fay, and Anthony Wong.

To all my friends and advisors at EPC, including Amy Quan, Jae O and Carolyn Bae, Audrey Lee, Charlie and Jeannie Drew, Kathy and Scott Strickman, Sandi and Nick Darrell, Selena and Tim Hia, Daijin Kim, Evelin and Earl Tai, Yilo Cheng, Mike and Sarah Kuo, Lauren Franklin, Kathy and John Chao, and Jan Kang, you have provided a wonderful sense of community during the most grueling writing periods.

Susan RoAne was immediately supportive and continued to be an early cheerleader.

Liana Loh: Your friendship has given this first-time writer strength during the hardest times of this journey. She and Bob Steadman read through rough drafts, offered numerous suggestions, and helped me meet my deadlines.

To Lynne Bernstein, Amy Root, Anna Hillengas, Sandi Darrell, and Kevin Kuo, who tirelessly helped me fact-check and revise my manuscript during many late nights, your advice was timely and always appropriate!

Bob and Mae Hong, Helena Yoon, Andy and Abby Wen, and Sang Ahn were other valuable "critiquers" during the earlier stages of writing.

Peggy Klaus's energy was contagious.

Caroline King, Charlie Lan, and Deloitte's Asian American Alliance added much value and asked the right questions. David Kim at Anheuser-Busch showed great support, Bobbi Silten provided candor and insight, and Guy Kawasaki challenged my thinking. Thomas Tseng confirmed last-minute stats with his keen knowledge of the multicultural market.

To the team at JPMorganChase—Ken Fong, Patrice Hall, Alice Wang, Janice Won, David Rottman, and Anne Marie Yarwood—you are all champions of the cause!

To the IBM Asian Diversity Task Force leadership—Karen Fukuma, Wes Hom, Satish Gupta, and Vijay Lund—for sharing their experiences. Phil Webber provided rich insights. Jackie O'Sullivan and Jim Sinocchi shared their perspectives.

The InterVarsity leadership: Paul Tokunaga, your invitation to lead inspired me, and Jeannette Yep, you are a courageous woman leader! Thank you for modeling inclusive leadership and for your vision for Asian American ministry.

To Kate Wendleton, for inviting a young career counselor to join the guild in 1997. You have taught me much and I will always be grateful. You have provided expert guidance, mentored me, and believed in me. Richard Bayer and David Madison at the Five O'Clock Club—I'm honored to have worked with such a gifted and dedicated team. To Rich Hille, Mary Keller, John Bradley, and Jane Lassner, former managers and mentors, who showed me the ropes early on. Bea Perdue and Dr. Johnnetta Cole at Bennett College's Diversity and Inclusion Institute, you have played a vital role in this writing journey. Thanks for your support. To Liz Fernandez, for sharing her diversity knowledge.

*All the friends and colleagues who supported and inspired:*

Sue Yim—thank you for your constructive feedback and endless supply of creative ideas. To Susie Case, for providing shelter before a manuscript deadline and for urging me to continue. Mary Harding Cist, for the e-mails that edified and encouraged. Special thank-yous to Moon Sung, longtime friend and confidante, for her prayers. To Sue Ryeom and Michele Cole at BSF, for spiritual support and friendship. To Nancy Corona, Christine Rogers, and Stephanie Lofgren, for their wise advice.

To Rochelle Yu, Evelin Tai, B. J. Noh, Mee Soo Jin, and Hee Jung Moon—my Tuesday afternoon accountability group and the Sonship crew—for loving me for who I am; those trips to K-Town will never be forgotten. Cathy Yoo Durham was an early cheerleader.

*My wonderful family:*

My husband, David, for encouraging me to do this when it was merely an "idea." I am proud to be your life partner.

To Abigail and Timothy, who have allowed me to practice my coaching techniques on them. You've made my life so rich; I often forget what life was like before you entered it. To Mom and Dad, for sharing the richness of the Asian culture with me from the very start, and for instilling that achievement is not limited by gender or race. I will always remember your unconditional love. Susan, my one and only sister, thank you for your steadfast support. Mom and Dad Hyun (Jewel and Gene Hyun), who have always encouraged me to do this book, you are the best in-laws, and I'm thankful for your consistent support. To Alyce, Rob, and Straka, for always being there for me, and for being a stable force for us in New York City.

To the Almighty God, who knew me before I was born and had a specific calling for my life.

## DISCLAIMER —

Except where affiliated with obviously identified corporations or organizations, all names and identities used in the case examples throughout the book have been changed.

Asian professionals are referred to as any Asian employee working in the U.S. labor force. Though most Asian professionals tend to be Asian American, it is noted if specific individuals are expats from an Asian country or recent immigrants.

Although *Asian American, Asian/Pacific Islander,* and *Asian Pacific American* are often used interchangeably to describe Asians in the United States, *Asian American* is used for simplicity.

*Minority professionals* and *professionals of color* are terms used to describe African Americans, Latinos/Hispanic Americans, Asian Pacific Americans, and Native Americans in the workplace.

Not all elements of Asian culture will apply to every person; some generalizations were necessary. These generalizations should not be used to stereotype Asian Americans, as the values are not exclusively Asian.

## NOTE—

In this book, I've used the terms *assimilation* and *acculturation* thusly: Assimilation is adopting the dominant culture's behaviors, values, perspectives, and characteristics at the expense of one's own cultural characteristics. Acculturation is adapting to new cultural patterns of the dominant culture while continuing to maintain values, perspectives, and features of one's native culture. As America has become more diverse, the melting pot model has evolved into a "salad bowl" or "mosaic" concept.

# – CONTENTS –

## Is There a Bamboo Ceiling for Asians in Corporate America? —

A career book about Asian Americans? Aren't they doing fine on their own? Does being Asian really make a difference in the workplace? Believe me, there was a time when I couldn't imagine writing a career book focused purely on Asians in corporate America. Early in my years as a human resources (HR) executive and recruiter for an investment banking firm, I considered writing a guide for up-and-coming professionals that provided tips on upward mobility and career management. However, as I was exposed to a wide variety of issues that involved cultural differences, manager–employee misunderstandings, and conflicts in the workplace, I realized very quickly that Asian American professionals tend to operate on an entirely different plane because of their unique cultural lenses. Many find it difficult to implement the prescribed management strategies commonly found in mainstream leadership books and corporate training programs because of their cultural values, which are often at odds with what it takes to get ahead in corporate America.

While I was working with various U.S. corporations, dozens of fellow Asian professionals urged me to coach them in their careers and show them a blueprint for success. Specifically, they asked for help with selling and presentation skills, managing their boss, navigating the political landscape, and managing teams. Non-Asian workers and managers also asked me for assistance in understanding their Asian coworkers' cultural differences. Clearly, teaching the same management and leadership techniques to all professionals without regard for ethnicity, cultural heritage, and deeply held values could very well be counterproductive. I sensed a pronounced need for a more specific book that would help Asian Americans better understand the effects of their cultural values on career advancement. It would identify how Asians' deeply rooted cultural influences impact workplace behaviors and present tactical strategies for managing those differences.

## REALITY CHECK: THE NUMBERS ARE IN —

Without a doubt, corporate America has always been a tough terrain for professionals of color to navigate. Various studies confirm the low percentages of minorities in the executive suites of U.S. companies. In 1995, the Federal Glass Ceiling Commission stated that of the top 1,000 industrial firms and 500 largest businesses in the United States, only 3% of senior managers were professionals of color. Contrast that with a 2003 U.S. Department of Labor report which stated that women and minorities make up two-thirds of new labor force entrants annually. A 2003 Catalyst study focusing on Asian women in the workforce revealed that although Asian women represent an important and growing source of talent, they are not well represented in senior management ranks. (Catalyst is a nonprofit advisory organization seeking to advance women in business.) In fact, they make up less than 0.5% of corporate officers at the 429 Fortune 500 companies that provided these data: Out of 10,092 Fortune 500 corporate officers in 2002, only 30 (0.29%) were Asian women. According to Catalyst, Asian women have difficulty moving into senior management positions because Asian cultural values, whether learned or reinforced by family, work against their ability to successfully navigate the corporate landscape. A 1997 study of Caucasian, African American, and Asian American engineers by Joyce Tang using the U.S. National Science Foundation's survey revealed that both Asian Americans and African Americans were significantly disadvantaged in terms of career mobility. Even in Silicon Valley, where Asian Americans comprise 30% of technology professionals, a 1993 study by the Pacific Studies Center found that Caucasians hold 80% of managerial positions, versus 12.5% for Asian Americans. These findings challenge the model-minority myth—that Asian Americans are doing "just fine" and need no career assistance—in professions where one might expect Asian Americans to be well represented. Their virtual absence in influential leadership roles demonstrates that Asians face challenges to mobility much like other ethnic and racial minority groups. According to the Committee of 100, a nonprofit, nonpartisan organization formed to improve China–United States relations and to provide a perspective for issues concerning Asian Americans, the percentage of Asian Pacific Americans holding seats on U.S. corporate boards is a mere 1%. Given the educational achievements of Asian Americans, there's clearly a disconnect. According to 2002 data from the U.S. Census Bureau, 44% of Asian Americans over age 25 have graduated from college, the highest percentage for any racial group, compared with the 27% average for the U.S. population. And according to feedback from recruiters and HR directors, there is significant representation of entry-level Asian talent in corporations. There is also a need for more updated statistics on Asians and their career mobility. According to an article written by Tojo Thatchenkery at the International Association of Business Disciplines National Conference in 2000, a Korn Ferry International survey revealed that between 1971 and 1997, there were 8,403 studies on women and career development, 101 studies on African Americans and career advancement, and just 4 studies on Asian Americans and career advancement!

So why don't Asian Americans make it to senior management? What's happening between the training program and the corner office? One can point to natural attrition, lack of adequate leadership training, and corporate politics as partial explanations for the small numbers of Asian corporate leaders, but this book uncovers the myth of Asians as the "Model Minority" who are "doing just fine" and don't require any special attention. There is actually a desperate need for practical measures to help Asian Americans (and all other minorities) reach their full potential in the workplace. Jino Ahn, president and founder of Asian Diversity, Inc., the first organization to offer job fairs targeted to Asian Americans, remembers attending a diversity conference a few years ago where all the breakout session topics excluded Asian Americans. There were workshops geared toward an array of workplace diversity programs, ranging from issues affecting women to gays and lesbians, older workers, workers with disabilities, African Americans, Latino Americans, and Native Americans, but absolutely nothing for the Asian American constituency. When he raised his hand to inquire about the absence of Asian Americans in diversity discussions, the nearly hostile response from one of the panelists was: "Is there a need for this? I thought Asians are doing better than the whites! Why in the world would they need any more help?" But clearly, Asians *are* still minorities in all but the entry levels of American companies.

The title *Breaking the Bamboo Ceiling* was selected because it acknowledges that Asian Americans do indeed face obstacles in the workplace and it asserts that there are cultural barriers that play a role in impeding career advancement. Asian Americans must take an active role in combating the problem. To shrug helplessly and say, "They didn't give me that promotion" or "There are no Asians at the top, so I won't make it, either" is not an empowering approach to career management. While biases in the workplace do exist, this ceiling is not always imposed by others. As with many challenges, Asians should acknowledge that barriers could also stem from self-limiting cultural influences on their behavior, attitude, and performance in various social and professional settings.

In my initial discussions with both non-Asian and Asian professionals about cultural issues impacting interpersonal dynamics in the workplace, I noticed an uncanny trend: Members of both groups were often ignorant about the cultural issues at play in their work environment. Because of the varied acculturation levels and immigration history of each Asian American group, there are inevitably some who may be uneducated about Asian culture. Some Asian Americans indicated that they didn't require any special treatment or assistance. Some even thought a career strategies program for Asians would bring negative attention to themselves; they didn't want to be singled out as part of a minority group because they felt that the less they rocked the boat, the better. Yet, when I probed further into the anatomy of their careers, those same Asians were overlooked for promotions and rarely selected for special corporate task forces—the same projects and task forces that lead to increased exposure to senior management. At the same time, few, if any, of the non-Asian managers had any idea what Confucian influence is or that culturally Asian ways of operating can affect well-educated, English-proficient Asians living and working in the United States.

It takes time and effort to understand your workplace persona, to identify what behaviors and communication styles you have to adjust for your particular situation, and then to actually implement that change! Achieving that finesse in relating takes time, practice, and candid feedback such as you will find in this book.

We can't successfully develop Asian leaders by educating only the Asian employees. We must include non-Asian managers, clients, coworkers, and mentors in identifying and resolving problems. This book, then, is for Asian American professionals (and students); their bosses, clients, and coworkers; HR and diversity managers; and anyone doing business with the Asian community. Clearly, an all-around understanding increases the chances of healthier business relations.

*Breaking the Bamboo Ceiling* should be an indispensable part of your career tool kit that you refer to repeatedly. Think of it as a real-time executive career coach in book form. You may find that you will go to one section in the book that is relevant to you and then tackle the other chapters at a later date. This book can also be used in diversity programs, career development offices at universities and graduate schools, and academic programs in Asian studies, organizational behavior, or cultural studies to help structure role plays and exercises that illustrate cross-cultural scenarios.

This career guide not only offers practical ideas for engaging managers, clients, coworkers, and subordinates about personal effectiveness and career mobility, but it also discusses the organizational processes that have been effective for Asian employees. I describe real workplace case studies that highlight concrete strategies. Case studies and stories of Asian professionals between ages 20 and 40 are presented. They are recent immigrants and first-, second-, and third-generation Asian Americans working in U.S. companies. The most challenging aspect of this project was the difficulty in being completely pan-Asian in scope. Toward that end, I present stories of individuals from a variety of Asian ethnicities, but it should be noted that not all elements of Asian culture will apply to every person; some generalizations were necessary. These generalizations should not be used to stereotype Asian Americans, as the cultural values are not exclusively Asian. All of the stories and case studies included are true, but the individuals' identities, unless specifically noted, have been changed to protect privacy.

## WHO SHOULD READ THIS BOOK? —

This book is not just for Asian Americans. For change to take place, *diversity* can no longer be just a corporate buzzword or a trendy HR term limited to appearances in annual reports. Managing diversity and successfully leading Asian, African American, Latino American, and other minorities are imperative for thousands of U.S. companies that are looking for a competitive advantage. For companies that want to be successful in the global marketplace, it is a business mandate. Many U.S. companies are seeking innovative ways to lead minority employees and develop their skills, and they are gradually becoming aware that doing so entails more than just a basic diversity-awareness campaign.

Asian Americans can use this book to first identify how their cultural lenses may affect the way they operate in a corporate setting, then examine how they might use some of the techniques explained here, and, finally, facilitate an ongoing dialogue between Asian and non-Asian workers.

## HOW TO READ THIS BOOK —

This book is divided into three major parts, each offering tips, case studies, and advice for a particular career phase. Part I, "Understanding Asian Cultural Influence and Its Impact," paints an introductory landscape of Asians in the United States and establishes a foundation for understanding the unique bicultural experience of many Asian Americans. There, you'll learn about Confucian influence, which is characterized by filial piety, the importance of family, respect for authority, communal decision making, the priority of duty over personal rights, and suppression of feelings. You'll see how these cultures can be in direct conflict with Western corporate culture and explore how these traditions, family pressures, and cultural influences can affect individual behavior and group interactions.

Part II, "Career Choices and Getting in the Door," tackles cultural influences and their potential impact on career choices and job search strategies. Modern Western culture dictates a self-directed, individualistic approach to career decisions, where you are in the driver seat when choosing your career. However, for many Asians, the Confucian influence of respecting and obeying elders (especially parents) may take them off their desired career path. As a result, they change careers later in life or spend protracted periods of time in "acceptable" careers with which they are unhappy. You'll read case studies of Asian Americans who have struggled with this issue. You'll also learn how an Asian's behavioral tendencies and face-to-face presentation can be misperceived by interviewers and hiring managers during the job search process.

In Part III, "Getting Ahead on the Job," you'll learn how to find the right mentor as well as how to be an empowering mentor. You'll learn the warning indicators of career immobility and discover ways to identify stagnation. And you'll find out how to navigate compensation reviews and promotion discussions.

This book is not the final word on this relatively new subject matter. I believe that only by sharing more of these stories can we begin to piece together our unique road maps to success. If you have a personal story you want to share, I want to hear from you. Contact me at info@janehyun.com.

# PART I

# UNDERSTANDING - ASIAN - CULTURAL INFLUENCE AND ITS IMPACT

# ONE

# YOUR ASIAN AMERICAN ROOTS AND YOU

*My first impression upon meeting Trinh was that she was far more Chinese than I: engaged with the (Asian) community, fluent. Also, less polished, less assimilated than I. But there are some who would consider her very un-Chinese. She speaks up, she fights, she exposes hypocrisy. She cares less about race than about basic moral courage. . . . The irony, then, is this: I am perhaps more Americanized. She is perhaps more American.*

—Eric Liu, *The Accidental Asian*

## ASIAN AMERICANS: A MOSAIC OF BACKGROUNDS —

The 2000 U.S. Census reported that there are 11.9 million Asians in the United States, a 72% increase since the previous census. Compare that to the total U.S. population growth of 13% for the same period. Even though Latino Americans are the largest minority group in raw numbers, Asians are the fastest-growing minority group, and the population is expected to double by 2020 and triple by 2030. Forty-four percent of Asian Americans over age 25 have graduated from college, the highest percentage for any racial group. These numbers imply a success story. However, these statistics don't always tell the whole story of what really happens to Asian Americans once they leave the halls of academia for corporate America.

Who are Asian Americans? Far from being homogeneous, we are of varied Asian ancestry. We represent multiple nationalities and languages as well as many social and political viewpoints. At last count, there were over 80 distinct Asian languages spoken in the United States. Even within each specific Asian group, there is considerable variability in education, class, and acculturation level. In addition, there is a long history of war, political unrest, and resulting prejudices in many Asian nations. What further complicates matters is that non-Asian Americans often think of Asians as a homogeneous group of people. Companies tend to view us as the Asian Pacific American constituency and do not necessarily categorize us by our specific nationalities.

## THE MANY FACETS OF PERSONAL IDENTITY —

An Asian American woman who works at a large distributor of home appliances notes: "I used to be quite involved with Asian networking group activities. But lately, I find a much deeper sense of community with the multicultural women's networking group. As a new mother attempting to juggle home and a very demanding job, I identify myself as a woman and mother first, then take my ethnicity into consideration next." You can define yourself along a continuum of factors, your cultural heritage being one of them. Most people describe themselves differently throughout the stages of their lives, such as oldest daughter, father, mother, Catholic, manager, Asian American, cancer survivor. Yet we know these tags don't fully define us or what we are capable of. We're each composed of so many qualities, skills, ideas, emotions, values, and behaviors that a few descriptors won't do anyone justice. We also know these self-ascribed tags aren't necessarily how we are perceived by others, especially those who don't know us well or who know us in other contexts.

## WHEN PERCEPTION BECOMES REALITY —

In workplace scenarios particularly, perception is often reality. As a result, what they don't know *can* hurt you. An assessment of your character and how you perform is based not solely on the quality of your "work deliverables" but also on how you interact with your colleagues. It's not what you say but how you say it. How confident do you sound? How articulate are you? How well do you motivate others on your team? Do you take the time to chat with colleagues, whether it's to discuss a project more thoroughly or to just socialize? Other cues that may brand you can be as superficial as how you dress, how you carry yourself, and what your facial expressions are. Behavior is often misinterpreted by people from different cultures, because it is visible, unlike motivations, feelings, intentions, and thought processes. At the most basic level, an underrepresented group like Asian Americans will stand out more.

To manage your career then, you must manage your personal brand—your image, how you come across. And knowing yourself is the first step in shaping the impression you make and in achieving your professional goals. You must understand your personality, strengths, weaknesses, and internal driving forces to guide how this all plays out in a work environment.

You may already know that your Asian background is integral to your identity. But not fully realizing how that background manifests itself in your attitudes and behaviors may cause misunderstandings in a Western corporate setting. Your Asianness doesn't have to work against you, however. In the process of deciphering your Asian cultural values and integrating them into your workplace persona, you can leverage your natural talents and maybe even learn new skills. You will learn the tools to help break the bamboo ceiling without compromising yourself. Training in selling, presenting, negotiating, and assertiveness can tap and channel your knowledge to enhance your presence and capabilities.

Keep in mind that professional upward mobility requires action on your part. It's unrealistic to expect that your managers and colleagues will automatically want and *know how* to unearth the true you and understand all you are capable of offering. People miscommunicate and misunderstand one another all the time; there will always be inaccurate perceptions of under-represented emplyee populations. You have to take the initiative in clarifying the issues to effect change.

The corporate world is also recognizing that it's up to them as well. By 2050, the majority of Americans will come from non-Caucasian backgrounds. When a managing director from a top financial services institution went to a Harvard recruiting luncheon in 2002 to identify candidates for the investment banking training program, she was surprised to see more than 50% of the students who attended were of Asian descent, including a majority that were students who resided in Asia. She realized then that if this was the future of her company, she had better start understanding Asians better as her new recruiting targets—as the pipeline of potential bankers at her firm.

Diversity programs were introduced at some companies as early as the 1980s. More recently, they have been developing and promoting more formal, nuanced programs that strive for inclusive environments and equip professionals to realize their full potential. Businesses are no longer implementing these programs because it's the right thing to do or because it makes for good public relations. Comprehensive diversity programs make good business sense; groups of people with diverse backgrounds and experiences are now commonly acknowledged as repeatedly producing rich ideas and solutions. Cultural competency has become an increasingly important skill for the savvy executive. Furthermore, as cited in the 2003 Catalyst report *Advancing Asian Women in the Workplace,* "Biculturalism and bilingualism are important business skills. Asians who have experience in Asian countries and Asian cultures can act as 'connecting points' to other countries, which is crucial for global companies."

A February 2004 *Wall Street Journal* article by Carol Hymowitz asserts that the very traits that make women in general good students—diligence, organization, and the ability to follow instructions—may not be sufficient to help them move up the career ladder and could even hold them back. Says Hymowitz, ". . . What counts a lot more than conscientiousness is daring, assertiveness and an ability to promote oneself—all qualities men more typically demonstrate." As we'll see, Asian values tend to echo these traditionally female traits, which also holds them back in the workplace.

## ASIAN AMERICANS —

So who are Asians? Beyond being able to check off the "Asian or Pacific Islander" category on the U.S. Census form, how do we define *Asianness*? As recently as 1970, the U.S. Census did not count Asians as part of a specific ethnic designation. Asian Indians were classified as whites, and Vietnamese were noted in the "other" race category. How far we have come! The 2000 U.S. Census provides the following breakdown: Chinese, Japanese, Korean, Asian Indian, Bhutanese, Burmese, Cambodian, Filipino, Hmong, Indochinese, Indonesian, Iwo Jiman, Laotian, Malaysian, Maldivian, Nepalese, Okinawan, Pakistani, Singaporean, Sri Lankan, Taiwanese, Thai, and Vietnamese. The largest group is the Chinese (2.4 million), followed by Filipino (1.9 million), Asian Indian (1.7 million), Vietnamese (1.1 million), and Korean (1.1 million).

## HOW CONFUCIAN INFLUENCE AFFECTS ASIAN AMERICANS —

Yet overall, Asians do share similar traits. The teachings of Confucius, a Chinese philosopher and scholar (551–479 BC), had a profound impact on Asian religion, government, and social structure that is in evidence even today. This influence differs dramatically from the Western school of thinking, particularly in the approach to interpersonal relations. Confucian influence emphasizes the importance of order, self-control, study, and education. To this day, many Asian countries still emphasize rote memorization and study as a significant vehicle for learning. Confucian values emphasize a sense of order, harmony, and decorum in human relationships over conflict and discourse. There is also a strong emphasis on respect for elders, both in the immediate family and at school and at work. Finally, there is a very high value placed on self-control versus self-expression, perhaps even to the extent of keeping feelings private. Other Asian philosophers have also emphasized similar ideas, holding self-restraint in high regard.

## ASIAN CULTURAL VALUES —

In a 1999 study by University of California, Santa Barbara, psychologists Bryan S. K. Kim, Donald R. Atkinson, and Peggy H. Yang, 14 Asian values were identified. Though these researchers stated that we must recognize that Asian Americans comprise an extremely diverse group and that significant differences within Asian ethnic groups do exist, they found that traditional Asians tend to emphasize the following values:

- Collectivism
- Maintenance of interpersonal harmony
- Reciprocity
- Placing others' needs ahead of one's own
- Deference to authority figures
- Importance of family
- Avoidance of family shame
- Educational and occupational achievement
- Ability to resolve psychological problems
- Filial piety
- Conformity to family and social norms
- Self-effacement
- Self-control/restraint
- Respect for elders and ancestors

The study also revealed that these values were not found to differ significantly across generations since immigration. There is a remarkable gap in Asian Americans' *behavioral acculturation*—regarding such issues as food, clothing, and language use—and *values acculturation* when transitioning to a new culture. Asian immigrants may seem to readily adopt Western ways of living, but their deeply ingrained Asian values, many inherited from Confucian values, are so fundamental to who they are that they and future generations are very slow to change.

This may explain why even more acculturated second- and third-generation Asian Americans feel burdened by the values of their parents and grandparents and proclaim themselves "bananas" (Asian on the outside, Caucasian on the inside—Asian Americans who have little or no identification with their Asian heritage). In many ways, this theme of conformity versus individuality is at odds with the objectives of America's founders. Because culture, Asianness, and Americanness are difficult to measure with precision, and because many cultural values are shared by diverse groups, Asian Americans may have difficulty deciphering which of their values are "American" and which are specific to their Asian background. Managing these bicultural and sometimes conflicting values can be so stressful that some Asian Americans wind up rebelling against or resenting one of their cultures.

Confucius also said, "A young man should serve his parents at home and be respectful to elders outside his home." Even if someone is just a few minutes older, he or she commands respect and authority in some Asian cultures. Asian children are sometimes taught to speak softly and not raise their voices, especially to those in authority. Respecting elders also affects body language, as it is customary in many Asian countries to cast your eyes downward in deference; direct eye contact is not always favored. In the United States, however, lack of eye contact may connote dishonesty, shiftiness, or lack of assertiveness.

In many Asian countries, the children or grandchildren care for their parents and grandparents, and quite often, that tradition is carried on by Asian Americans. This unwavering devotion to elders and superiors can be transferred to the workplace, regardless of how malevolent or incompetent superiors may be.

## RESPECT FOR ELDERS

A nationwide survey by the Population Resource Center found that Asian Pacific Islander families provided more care for their older relatives than did other groups: 42% of Asian Americans surveyed helped care for or provided financial support for their parents, compared with 34% of Latino Americans, 28% of African Americans, and 19% of Caucasians.

Teachers and professors in Asia are enormously respected because they represent higher learning. It is common to ask a new personal or business acquaintance where he or she attended school because this helps place the person. Yet in American companies, education isn't everything; what's valued more is what Dan Goleman, in *Working with Emotional Intelligence,* calls emotional intelligence. Many people have succeeded in the corporate arena without having attained bachelor's degrees.

In most Asian countries, there isn't any flexibility for "finding yourself" and figuring out your career path. The route is straight and narrow: You must select your major before you even sign up for one college-level class and then stick it out until you graduate and get a job in that industry. Changing your major isn't an easy option. What you study dictates your profession. And it is very difficult to change careers after you start down a certain career path. If you're accepted at a top university, you're virtually guaranteed a slot in one of the large companies upon graduation. But in the United States, even if you have excellent grades from an Ivy League institution, you won't be automatically deluged with job offers from prestigious companies.

## AMERICAN CULTURAL VALUES —

The United States was founded on the principle of freedom, including freedom of the press, freedom of religion, and freedom from political persecution. The country has long operated on the basis of free-market economics, which encourages competition, individual gain, and entrepreneurship. It is the land of opportunity, regardless of one's parents' social status. Moreover, education is considered important, but not always necessary to succeed in corporate America.

### Confucius versus Socrates

In *The Geography of Thought,* which presents an interesting perspective on how Asians and Westerners think differently, Richard Nisbitt describes the absence of argumentation and discourse in Asia that seems to be second nature to Westerners: "North Americans begin to express opinions and justify them as early as the show-and-tell sessions of nursery school. In contrast, there is not much argumentation or trafficking in opinions in Asian life." Indeed, at age 3, my American-born daughter was taught in a show-and-tell lesson to cite 10 reasons why chocolate was her favorite ice cream flavor. In contrast, the Asian culture lives closer to the adage "The loudest duck gets shot." Americans tend to live the adage "The squeaky wheel gets the oil." In the corporate world, this translates into interpersonal abilities that aid career advancement. Working really hard and hoping someone will notice and reward you will never be enough.

## ASIAN AMERICAN IDENTITIES —

*We worked at the dry cleaning store for 20 years, working 7 days a week, but my children, they all study hard and go to big Ivy schools—Yale and Princeton. I am proud that my hard work has helped them achieve their dreams.*

—Jung Ja Hong, Korean American parent

In Amy Tan's novel *The Joy Luck Club,* a character expresses the hopes of numerous immigrant Asian parents for their offspring: "Over there in America nobody will look down on her, because I will make her speak only perfect American English." But clearly, even perfect English won't obviate personal and professional obstacles. Though some Asian Americans grow up attending American schools and playing with non-Asian friends, they might come home to Asian food on the table and a family that speaks Chinese, Korean, Japanese, Tagalog, Hindi, or Vietnamese. Their parents may still subscribe to local Asian newspapers and expect them to continue living by Asian standards at home, yet they become more Americanized by the system outside of home.

For some Asian Americans, managing these two worlds can be difficult, and a few even report having a stressful relationship with the challenge of managing this dual-culture life. One may assume that first-generation immigrants are the only ones who are saddled with parental influences from the motherland. Yet, even more acculturated second- or third-generation Asians who are self-proclaimed bananas (Asian on the outside, white on the inside) report that they feel burdened by the cultural influence of their parents and grandparents.

Not only are Asian Americans raised with this contrasting perspective in the home, they continue to see the remnants of its effect on their behavior long after they leave home, start their first jobs, and begin their own families. Second- and third-generation Asian Americans report that their families *still* operate under a system of values they learned from their ancestors. And it's not just about language and food. It goes beyond external perceptions of Asians as foreigners. Asians who grew up straddling two very different worlds may face internal conflicts in the workplace as they maneuver through their careers. These strong cultural influences still manifest in certain behaviors in the workplace, including collegial or consensus decision making, a strong work ethic, and deference to elders.

Here are a few of the many variations of Asian Americans you may encounter in the workplace:

### The Acculturated Asian Immigrant

An immigrant who came to the United States at the age of 12, speaks English fluently, and has adapted quite easily to the American culture. She has forgotten most of her mother tongue because she was raised speaking only English in her home.

### The Second- or Third-Generation Bicultural Asian

A third-generation woman who may speak perfect American English and easily navigates diverse social circles, Asian or otherwise, but still feels strongly Chinese, Indian, Korean, Japanese, or Filipino.

*The Asian Unaware of Culturally Influenced Behaviors*

A second-generation Chinese American who grew up in a New England suburb may see himself as an apple-pie American and tends to operate in mostly non-Asian social and professional circles. However, his colleagues and clients frequently view him as an Asian person, and thus he may be pigeonholed at work and assigned, for example, leadership roles in the Asia/Pacific region.

## WHEN YOU LOOK THE PART —

## PROFILE OF A SECOND-GENERATION CHINESE AMERICAN

Kevin Lee doesn't identify culturally with his Asianness, though he may still exhibit some culturally influenced behaviors in the work setting. Though he is thoroughly American psychologically, his Asian appearance has caused some misunderstandings in certain work relationships.

Because he is one of few Asians at his company, he is consequently labeled the "Asian person" in the workplace by his colleagues. This is very insidious because he lacks strong self-knowledge and an accurate picture of how he is perceived by others. Members of senior management feel that as one of two Asian Americans in middle management, Kevin could be instrumental in furthering the company's growth efforts in Asia. They are constantly offering him opportunities to lead the Hong Kong or Singapore operations, much to Kevin's dismay—he has no interest in taking his career to Asia. His long-term career goal is to head one of the business units at headquarters, which requires additional experience in a different U.S. sales territory. Plus, after some business trips to Asia, he knows that he would be seen there as the Chinese person from the United States and not readily accepted by the locals.

### The Asian Adoptee

The Asian adopted by a non-Asian American family doesn't feel Asian at all because he grew up in a town with very little Asian diversity, though he is always perceived to be very Asian by outsiders, who continue to ask him if he speaks an Asian language.

Sandra Darrell, Korean-born and adopted into a Dutch Reformed family, doesn't speak Korean. If anything, she feels that her Dutch upbringing influenced her the most. That doesn't stop people who she meets from asking her about where she's from or assuming that she's culturally Korean. Because she is physically Asian, people assume that she must be culturally Asian as well. "Growing up in my family, I was never treated as if I were any different from my non-Asian siblings," says Sandra.

### The Asian of Mixed Heritage

Biracial and mixed-heritage Asians (representing more than one Asian country) are becoming more commonplace in the United States. Asian culture can remain intact in many biracial individuals.

### Asian by Association

The non-Asian spouse married to or partnered with an Asian for an extended period of time may adapt much of Asian culture and customs. Over time, he or she may show culturally Asian behaviors.

## COMFORTABLY BICULTURAL

Mary Wang, a 25-year-old second-generation Chinese American, recalls: "Growing up in Southern California, I never really lost touch with my Asian culture and rarely felt like a visible minority. My parents always spoke Chinese to me at home, and I always felt comfortable with my Chinese identity. I was born here, but I always felt more Chinese in many different contexts. When I started my first job in Boston, I was struck by the lack of understanding most of my Asian work colleagues had of their Asian culture. Many of them had grown up as the only Asian in their social circles, where they had to either ignore or suppress their Asianness."

## *Where Are You From? The Perpetual Foreigner Syndrome*

Asian Americans, by virtue of their physical features, face the challenge of being considered foreigners in social and professional circles—outsiders in the land they call home. My friend and colleague who is fourth-generation Japanese and does not speak any Japanese is asked all the time by new acquaintances whether he misses Japan and intends to go back to live there. To his knowledge, he has no living relatives in Japan and has lost contact with his extended family in Asia.

Critics may say that once you are more established in a company, people will see beyond your race and reward you justly for your work, so that after a reasonable time, the perception of foreignness should not be a problem. But in the corporate world, you're always meeting new people and making first impressions, and your Asian face will always be a part of you, so you remain the perpetual foreigner. This makes it hard to gain credibility quickly, which can pose problems in today's fast-paced, highly competitive work environment.

And sometimes, the perpetual foreigner syndrome can be combined with prejudice: Suresh Patel, an Indian American partner in a high-tech company providing Internet capabilities to other companies, recalls: "I was working on this deal with a potential investor who lives in another state. After some productive conference calls and pleasant exchanges over the phone, we thought it was beneficial for us to meet to talk through the deal in person. When I walked into that boardroom to shake his hand, the guy's jaw literally dropped. He said, very blatantly with an obvious look of disappointment, 'I had no idea that you were not white.' " Suresh's Indian face wasn't necessarily a deal breaker in this case, but the meeting's start wasn't ideal, and the other man's initial reaction made Suresh think twice about working with him over the long term. It was obvious that this potential investor was taken aback by the color of his skin.

---

June, a Korean American professional with over 25 years of experience in financial services and technology, shares her humorous answer to the "So where are you from?" question of a colleague she met at a seminar:

**Senior executive:** That was some really interesting material you just presented. Where are you from?

**June:** A northwest suburb of Boston.

**Senior executive:** Actually, I meant, where are you really from?

**June:** How far do you want to go?

**Senior executive:** As far back as you'd like!

**June:** Okay, then, I come from the Garden of Eden.

---

A 2001 Yankelovich study by the Committee of 100, an organization formed by prominent Chinese Americans, including Henry Tang, Yo-Yo Ma, and I. M. Pei, to improve United States–China relations, revealed that about one-third of all Americans feel that Chinese Americans are probably more loyal to China than to the United States. Almost one-half believe that Chinese Americans pass secret information to China, and one-quarter think that Chinese Americans are taking too many jobs from other Americans. The report said that these findings could be generally applied to other Asian nationalities, because it turns out that few Americans distinguish between Chinese Americans and other Asian Americans anyway.

The perpetual foreigner syndrome means that even second- and third-generation Asian Americans are met with a surprised look when their colleagues realize how perfect their English is. A close friend and colleague of mine, a second-generation Chinese American who teaches undergraduate humanities at a university in New York City, recalls: "Once, when talking to a fellow faculty member, I was asked, 'So, what do you teach?' When I answered, 'English,' the response was a chuckle and 'Ha—isn't that funny?' Apparently, the idea that a foreign-looking person could teach English to college students was humorous to him, as I did not fit neatly into his paradigm of the world." My friend had grown up speaking English his entire life, had attended top U.S. graduate schools, and is highly regarded by his employer. This dynamic demonstrates clearly how some non-Asians who often have little or no information about Asian culture assume difference between Asians and Caucasians that don't exist. This phenomenon adds another layer of challenges to assimilation in corporate America.

## A Brief Primer on Ethnic Identity —

The media and the general public presume Asian Americans as a group are well educated and haven't experienced discrimination. But there's a definite history of racism and discrimination toward Asian Americans and their ancestors. Perhaps one of the most tragic accounts involves the death of Vincent Chin, a Chinese American who was clubbed to death in a Detroit bar at his bachelor party in 1982. He had been mistakenly thought to be Japanese by two Caucasian men who blamed the Japanese for the decrease in U.S. auto manufacturing jobs. And then there is Wen Ho Lee, a Chinese American who, in 1999, was falsely accused by the FBI of being a spy because of his ethnicity. It is important to bear in mind that we form our identity from a variety of factors in addition to ancestry, including gender, sexual orientation, disability, and health status.

### *The Impact of Asian Culture*

Asian Americans have the same capacity for achieving career success despite cultural differences. Many Asian cultures tend to emphasize the importance of higher education and graduate degrees, and they may not focus enough on business and management skills that are *not* taught in schools—skills that propel professionals to more senior positions and help them succeed in those positions. In addition, the Confucian influence found in many Asian cultures places a tremendous emphasis on respect for elders, which can profoundly reduce assertiveness in Asian employees when dealing with their bosses, coworkers, and clients. It can also affect how this behavior is interpreted by their colleagues. But to achieve success, it is fundamentally important that you understand how the different cultural lenses affect the way you do business, the way you sell to a client, the way you interact with your manager and colleagues, and the way you compete every day.

---

My parents and many of my friends' parents and grandparents survived World War II and the Korean War. My grandmother often recounted the story of how she moved her family to the southern part of the country to escape war-torn Seoul. During such wartimes, the country's economy was in turmoil; sheer survival was at stake. To the war generation, studying hard became imperative because the goal for every young Korean was passing the examinations to get into the best colleges in the country, an automatic ticket to success—lifetime employment. Graduating from a good school meant that employers were at your door, giving you positions virtually guaranteeing lifetime employment in prestigious companies.

---

One of the enjoyable ways to manage cultural differences is to share the richness and nuances of your Asian culture with your colleagues. You don't have to leave your culture behind. A significant realization came to me recently during a conversation with two friends, one a Chinese American and the other a Caucasian who had recently adopted a baby from China. The new mother had more insights and knowledge about Chinese culture and history than my Chinese American friend! Later, as I wandered through a mainstream bookstore, I noticed dozens of books about Chinese culture written for adoptive parents. While my Asian American friend was busy acculturating to American ways so as to better fit into his work environment, my Caucasian friend was soaking up Asian culture. The increase in the numbers of biracial children and adoptions from Asia means that information about Asian cultures is being quickly disseminated in forums.

Examine your unique identity. Take stock of your ethnic culture, gender, personality, religion, sexual orientation, and personal values. Your Asian background may be only a small part of your identity. One executive director of a large Asian organization recalls:

When I was a student in Korea, I was given grades based on how I performed on tests. I was always an A student. When I went to college, I was in for a rude awakening! In my marketing class, I noticed that my peers were raising their hands to make very minor, at times irrelevant, comments about the subject matter of the day. It came to a point where I only raised my hand if I had something hugely important to add or some new insight into something. I did well on my papers and tests, so I was totally shocked when I got a C+ in the class. When I asked my professor about the grade, she told me that I rarely participated in class and it was difficult to determine how engaged I was in the topic from the evidence of my participation in discussions. The way I was taught in the Korean elementary and middle school system did not work very well in the American college system. There is a saying in Korea: "The most mature rice stalk bends the least," which implies that the more learned person keeps his opinions to himself, holds back his emotions, and is respected because of it. That was my critical incident, my aha moment. I had to drastically change my paradigm of working and studying if I wanted to thrive here in the States.

### Diversity Within Asian Cultural Values

Though the Asian cultural commonalities identified by the researchers at the University of California, Santa Barbara, are useful (see page 8), it's equally important to recognize the cultural distinctions between the various Asian American cultures. Even though more non-Asians today may be aware of the many countries from which Asian Americans' families originate, such distinctions can be ambiguous beyond nationalities and languages.

### Behavioral Change May Not Necessarily Imply a Shift in Cultural Values

The case studies sprinkled throughout this book illustrate that though Asian Americans may act "American," their Asian cultural values are still in play. This juxtaposition can come as a surprise to career counselors, HR professionals, and managers.

John Eng is a U.S.-born Chinese American with immigrant parents who grew up speaking only English in a suburb in Michigan. He has had difficulty setting limits with his clients, whom he views as authority figures, a group he was taught to respect deeply. When they frequently approach him with unrealistic deadlines, he does not push back or ask for additional resources.

### *What Colleagues May Say About Asian Americans*

In a recent workshop I conducted called "Managing a Diverse Workforce," I asked a group of 40 young professionals, ages 23 to 35, both Asian and non-Asian, from industries such as management consulting, investment banking, advertising, and education, to name stereotypes of Asians, whether or not they believed them to be true. Not surprisingly, the list included descriptions such as

- Quiet/don't speak up
- Submissive
- Good at math/science
- Good producers/hardworking
- Smart
- Well educated
- Don't ask a lot of questions
- Not involved with the community
- Cliquish with other Asians
- Not fluent in English/perceived as foreigners
- Loyal/don't do a lot of job-hopping

Although some of those characteristics could be considered positive, they can also be hurtful, especially if used to exploit Asian workers. For example, if a company's senior managers think all Asians are uncomplaining, industrious workers, Asian American employees run the risk of doing all the grunt work without getting credit for it. When asked, however, if they knew *why* Asians were perceived that way, half the group at my workshop stared blankly—so I phrased the question differently. When asked what specific visible behaviors and nonverbal cues caused them to have those perceptions, they made candid statements:

- They tend to not speak up in meetings or to wait their turns in meetings.
- They rarely complain about policies or work initiatives.
- They form Asian cliques.
- They are soft-spoken and don't make much eye contact.
- They're not good at self-promotion and marketing themselves.
- They tend to be risk averse.
- They are always busy working and never have time to socialize after hours.

It was clear that they made these judgments on the basis of behaviors, without learning more about the talented person within. For example, those who think that Asians are quiet and don't speak up in meetings may assume that they don't care about the subject matter or don't know the answer.

It's unreasonable to expect that your colleagues will think to probe enough to discover the true you. Invest time in obtaining feedback from your coworkers, boss, mentor, and clients about how you are perceived—by them and by others. Depending on your situation, you may sometimes need to clearly explain your cultural values and the effects they have on your interactions. But be sure to present those values not as a deficiency but as simply a part of you.

### *The Power of the Media*

But we can't chalk up all the stereotypes to behavior, either. The mainstream media, including movies and television, certainly help perpetuate inaccurate perceptions of Asians.

How many South Asian CEOs do we see portrayed on TV? How many Asian American third-graders see images of Korean politicians or firefighters portrayed in their school texts? Asians are more commonly the foreigners, the villains, the geeky scientists or professors, the martial arts fighters, or the exotic, mysterious, submissive women.

## Underlying Values

**COLLEGIAL DECISION MAKING AND COMMUNITY OVER INDIVIDUALISTIC THINKING**    Asians tend to place the group's interests over individual interests, often crediting the team rather than taking all of the credit themselves for a job well done. These Asians shy away from standing out too much or making big waves, particularly in a large group setting. In addition, they prefer collegial decision making and consensus building for the good of the group over individualistic thinking. Ask a random group of Asian Americans to pick a movie to see and chances are great that they'll solicit everyone's opinions before deciding on a movie. Ask the same question of a non-Asian group and you'll typically get lots of different answers.

**SELF-CONTROL, MODESTY, DUTY, OBLIGATION, AND HUMILITY OVER PERSONAL RIGHTS**    In the Asian culture, there is a strong emphasis on self-control, dogged perseverance, and hard work and a general dislike of self-promotion or anything that could draw attention. Working hard for the sake of the family, putting your head down and producing a lot—without complaining about how much work it is—is considered the norm. We all have seen the Asian immigrant family working 16-hour days, 6 days a week, 365 days a year at a dry cleaner, newspaper stand, fish market, or deli to put their children through college. Though some may complain about the hard work, many of them say that such sacrifices are necessary to help their children get the right kind of schooling for the right kind of careers, to provide security for future generations. Sarah Ming, a Chinese American, reports: "I am great at what I do. But no one in my company outside my department knows about it. My colleagues are tooting their horns all the time, but I feel really uncomfortable with the concept of self-marketing. It goes against everything I was raised with, and I feel like I'm coming up against this huge wall that is impossible for me to climb. My mom and dad always emphasized that I should be modest about my accomplishments—just work hard, get good grades, and I will be rewarded. Obviously, they were wrong! I'm not going to move anywhere inside my firm, let alone outside, if I continue on this road of self-effacement and modesty."

**FAMILY PRIVACY AND HARMONY: THE IMPORTANCE OF AVOIDING SHAME AND CONFLICT** Asian Americans rarely go to psychiatrists and psychologists, because they were raised to believe it is immodest to hang their personal issues out to dry. Because they want to maintain harmonious relationships, they can sometimes run away from conflict or potential confrontation. These twin desires make it difficult for them to engage in the collegial self-revelation and candor so crucial to building a career network.

**EDUCATION: THE MORE, THE BETTER** The majority of corporate professionals in Asia have several higher degrees attached to the end of their names, because education is revered; and knowing what school the other party attended helps place that person immediately in the order of things. In many parts of Asia, students are expected to be diplomatic communicators, not impudent debaters. They expect to be shot down for being audacious, disrespectful, or loud. Yet in the United States, sometimes having too much education can make you ill equipped for corporate maneuvering. I have worked with many Asian Americans who, when making a career change, opt first to go to graduate school instead of trying their hand at a new job. The better alternative is to find a company or an industry where you can develop your management skills.

**DUTY AND DILIGENCE: THE WORK ETHIC** Working hard is something that most immigrants can relate to. Yet for Asians, it takes on an entirely new dimension. Of course, a strong work ethic is admirable, but not at the expense of career success because you're too busy to network and showcase your accomplishments.

**RESPECT FOR AUTHORITY** Because family is critical to Asians, they may give up their career dreams to enter professions acceptable to their parents and grandparents. They often provide for their parents and grandparents, and their unwavering devotion to elders or superiors often carries over to workplace relationships. The boss gets respect regardless of temperament or competence. Asian children, taught to speak softly and not raise their voices, especially to those in authority, can grow into adult employees who don't speak up. The Asian practice of casting the eyes down in deference to elders may unfortunately be misconstrued by U.S. employers as indicating dishonesty, shiftiness, or, at the very least, lack of assertiveness.

### Differing Values

The following table was developed by Leadership Education for Asian Pacifics (LEAP), an organization cofounded by president and CEO J. D. Hokoyama that provides leadership training for companies as well as community organizations.

## A COMPARISON OF ASIAN AMERICAN AND MAINSTREAM AMERICAN VALUES —

| MAINSTREAM (WESTERN) VALUES | ASIAN AMERICAN VALUES |
|---|---|
| **Spontaneity/casualness** | **Self-control/discipline** |
| ■ Importance of social skills, informal relationships<br>■ Small talk<br>■ Acceptable to show full range of emotions<br>■ Flexibility | ■ Speaking only when spoken to<br>■ Inner stamina/strength to tolerate crisis<br>■ Hiding emotions |
| **Acceptability of questioning authority** | **Obedience to authority** |
| ■ Anticipation of problem areas, opportunities; initiation of appropriate actions<br>■ No fear of challenging or opposing authority; ability to push the envelope with parents, professors, bosses, clients | ■ Respect for those who lead<br>■ Loyalty<br>■ Trustworthiness<br>■ Follow-through on assignments |

**Promotion of personal accomplishments**

- Visibility (individual) is acceptable
- Rewards individual for outstanding actions
- Power perceived as individual power

**Humility**

- Low individual visibility
- Power shared with others

**Tough, individualistic, and authoritative leadership**

- Individual leadership
- Individual responsibility and ownership
- Independence
- Creativity and innovation

**Collective decision making**

- Proving the sources (accuracy and attention to detail)
- Collective responsibility and ownership
- Interdependence
- Strong sense of teamwork

**NOTE:** These are generalizations and may not totally reflect the values of specific Asian Americans or specific Asian groups. As we review these values and corresponding actions, it becomes clear that an organization rewards those who hold the dominant cultural values at the managerial level. Values of both groups are important. Many of those who have lived several generations in the United States may find themselves holding values from both cultures.

Adapted from material written by Leadership Education for Asian Pacifics, Inc., with permission from J. D. Hokoyama.

---

If they identify with many of the values in the table's right-hand column, it's no wonder that new Asian immigrants often experience culture shock when they join an American company! And even second-generation Asian Americans appear to have threads of these values demonstrated in their attitudes and behaviors. It is hard enough starting a new job or entering a new profession, but if your fundamental views of your boss and work colleagues are different from the corporate norms, you will face some adjustment as you become familiar with the new "rules of the game." Studies are beginning to attest to this fact. As you progress in your career, you'll have to sometimes put aside some of your natural tendencies.

Elaine Chao, U.S. secretary of labor, who immigrated to the United States at the age of 8 from Taiwan, agrees: "Earlier in my career, as I was developing as a leader, I had to learn to overcome my natural cultural inclination to not speak plainly; I was more prone to be indirect. Over time, I had to learn to communicate clearly what I wanted. In a diverse country as America, clear communication is essential to being a good leader."

## COMPANIES DOING THEIR SHARE —

Companies are gradually recognizing the importance of managing and promoting a diverse workforce. By 2050, the majority of Americans will come from non-Caucasian backgrounds, and senior management must understand how to work effectively with a multicultural employee population.

Says an HR vice president, "There are many positive aspects of team-based, collegial decision making. We don't always have to be so super-aggressive. Although the Asian professional may seem meek and mild-mannered, I have seen Asians who have, by virtue of their own styles and persistence, managed to perform as well as or better than their non-Asian counterparts. We Americans can often be too brash and inconsiderate of our colleagues. If we can teach Asians how to be assertive about sharing their opinions, they can teach us some good principles for respecting each other and creating a thoughtful balance in work relationships!"

- TWO -

# "But I Didn't Mean It That Way!": How Cultural Values Can Help or Hinder You at Work

*I was keenly aware of the unflattering mythologies that attach to Asian Americans: that we are indelibly foreign, exotic, math and science geeks, numbers people rather than people people, followers and not leaders, physically frail but devious and sneaky, unknowable and potentially treacherous. These stereotypes of Asian otherness and inferiority were like immense blocks of ice sitting before me, challenging me to chip away at them.*

—Eric Liu, *The Accidental Asian*

## How Asian Values Affect Individual Behavior and Workplace Interactions

The differences between Asian and mainstream Western values have serious implications for Asian American professionals. Yet I do believe that Asian Americans have the same capacity for achieving success in the workplace even if they may have been culturally trained to show these traits in manners fundamentally different from that of Westerners. The corporate ladder can seem daunting for professionals of any color to climb. Even when corporations have fully accepted the idea of workplace diversity with all the right intentions, senior managers may be unsure which strategies or programs will be the most effective in tapping the best-quality performance from their growing minority employee population. Even the most well-intentioned executives may subconsciously hold biases or prejudices about other races. The selection criteria as you reach higher rungs on the ladder become more subjective and less firmly based on technical abilities. Emotional intelligence becomes paramount because you must mobilize and lead others. And to get that chance to lead, you need to know how to promote your own achievements to build a cadre of mentors and sponsors who will readily toss your name into the candidate pool for highly desirable fast-track positions.

## A Diversity Timeline —

It was not until 1964, under Title VII of the Civil Rights Act, that the Equal Employment Opportunity Commission (EEOC) was born, outlawing discrimination on the basis of race, gender, or creed. Although its powers were relatively minimal then, the EEOC had applied to all private-sector companies (50 or more employees) doing business with the federal government. In addition, the Immigration and Nationality Act of 1965 opened the doors for many Asians with professional backgrounds (mainly medicine and engineering) to enter the United States. This sweeping revision to U.S. immigration policies, made under President Lyndon B. Johnson, played a large part in the growth of the U.S. Asian population. Later, in 1972, under President Richard Nixon, the EEOC gained the authority to bring suits against corporations violating antidiscriminatory policies.

In 1987, *Workforce 2000: Work and Workers for the Twenty-First Century*, produced by the Hudson Institute, predicted that by the year 2000, only 15% of the people entering the workforce would be U.S.-born white males, compared to 47% in 1987. Many people deduced that managing diversity had now become a bottom-line issue: Companies had to seriously consider the importance of hiring, developing, and promoting a diverse workforce.

In the early 1980s and 1990s, companies began instituting diversity recruiting practices, such as attending minority job fairs, promoting the use of INROADS (a selective minority internship program that recruits high-potential minorities for valuable summer internship positions in U.S. companies) and SEO (Sponsors for Educational Opportunity) programs to diversify their entry-level population by hiring more minority interns, and even requiring that all employees attend diversity and inclusion workshops. In 2002, Asian Diversity, Inc. launched its first annual job fair and conference in New York City, which was astoundingly successful: Over 6,000 enthusiastic Asian Americans from the Northeast registered for the event.

## THE CHALLENGE OF IMPLEMENTING A DIVERSITY STRATEGY —

Diversity management is a monumental undertaking for a simple training program or a recruiting strategy. Because prejudices and stereotypes are deeply held, consciously and unconsciously, and are acquired over many years, they are very difficult for people to shed just by attending a workshop or conference. To make new ideas filter down to the grassroots level, where positive change can effectively occur and maintain its momentum, training programs and workshops should be heavily buttressed by positive reinforcement and accountability measures. In other words, the performance management and reward systems need to be synchronized to reflect these values.

## THE IMPORTANCE OF INDIVIDUAL EFFORT IN THE CONTEXT OF CORPORATE DIVERSITY INITIATIVES —

An approach requiring both individual effort and management support has been effective for some of the companies profiled in this book. The networking and advocacy groups provide professionals of color at all levels with tools for mentoring, access to leadership training, and other career development forums. If the corporate diversity council in your company is modeling inclusive leadership and providing every employee access to top jobs, things could be headed in the right direction, ensuring that progress is being made. The CEO and the senior management team can play a major role in modeling inclusive leadership. Once the senior diversity champions at your company realize this dynamic, they can implement programs at the lower and middle-management levels to monitor and reinforce the progress of the company's diversity programs.

The buzzword today is *inclusive leadership* as a critical leadership competency for senior management members. Says Patrice Hall, managing director of diversity for investment banking at JPMorgan Chase, "There is no silver bullet to the challenge of managing diversity. If the business managers are not practicing active inclusive leadership with their staff, then the message of diversity has not been driven down far enough. To be effective, diversity has to be folded into the broader business initiatives of a company."

There is some indication (though minuscule) today that with the right mix of individual effort and appropriate organizational mechanisms, the bamboo ceiling can be broken. Though their numbers are few, some Asian Americans hold top management seats. For example, Andrea Jung is the chairman and CEO of Avon Products, Indra Nooyi is the president and CFO of PepsiCo, and Chris Poon heads up the pharmaceuticals division of Johnson & Johnson. Two members of the current presidential administration are Asian American: Elaine Chao, secretary of labor, and Norman Mineta, secretary of transportation. And in 1996, Washington State elected the first Asian American governor on the mainland, Gary Locke, who was re-elected in 2000.

## RACE, ETHNICITY, AND CULTURE ARE NOT THE ONLY FACTORS THAT AFFECT CAREER MOBILITY —

Diversity isn't about race alone. It's the unique combination of characteristics that differentiate one person or group of people from another, including gender, culture, ethnicity, age, class and socioeconomic level, religious beliefs, physical and mental disabilities, sexual orientation, and work style. It's often difficult to unravel which of these many aspects are influencing your career. And depending on the expert advisors or self-help book you consult, you may also be told that your personality, level of physical attractiveness, height/weight, political astuteness, and timing—and even good fortune—can affect how your career fares.

To say, then, that your Asian cultural heritage is the most critical determinant of your success or failure is being extremely shortsighted. But your race or your cultural values can play an active part in determining your success or lack of success on the job and access to senior management positions. Behaviors based on deeply ingrained cultural values passed down for generations may be tough to alter quickly enough to make a difference in a current job situation. This is precisely why diversity strategies intended for all women and minorities may not always be the best for you as an Asian professional. To do a complete job of defining individual success, you'll need to thoroughly assess yourself. This includes understanding which of your behaviors might be culturally influenced and how they could positively or negatively impact your job performance and understanding others' perceptions of you.

Additional problems arise when non-Asian colleagues expect Asians to exhibit Western values in the workplace, especially when the Asian professional speaks fluent English and "sounds" American but may still be operating in Asian culture mode in the corporate boardroom.

Outgoing, extroverted Asians who are accustomed to forcefully stating their opinions outside their home can become compliant and reserved when dealing with their parents, grandparents, older relatives, bosses, and work colleagues. When observing Asians in both academic and corporate settings, it is clear that on a continuum of assertiveness, even the most aggressive and outspoken Asians fall into the "moderately assertive" category when compared to their non-Asian peers.

## YAO MING: ASIAN INFLUENCES ON THE BASKETBALL COURT

The Houston Rockets' Yao Ming is a highly visible example of Asian culture at play in a predominantly Western setting. A 2004 *New York Times* article headlined ROCKETS SEEK TO UNCOVER YAO'S 7 FOOT 6 MEAN STREAK described how Yao's traditional Chinese values influenced the way he plays on American basketball courts. According to the article, Yao's way of playing differs remarkably from the American way of doing things, where you have to constantly outdo and outsmart your competition. In the words of Donnie Nelson, an expert on international basketball: "In a lot of the team sports in China, you don't see the same kind of one-on-one domination. It's more team oriented, whereas over here, it's 'I'm going to torch my guy, then only when the double team collapses will I look to make the pass.' " The Chinese culture, because of heavy Confucian influence, promotes a more collegial, "do it for the good of everyone" style, whereas the American style is very individualistic.

The article says that Yao is still working on developing the "aggression and ferocity" that the game's most powerful play, the slam dunk, has come to symbolize. But it would be ideal if he could discover a way of playing that wouldn't make him feel that he's violating his Chinese self—by perhaps scoring points by using teamwork, bringing out the ferocious side only when things get really heated, then going back to his more collegial style. In fact, because Yao has experienced a different approach to the game, there may be tactics the Rockets can learn from him. Then the team would have more tools for adapting their style of play to their opponents. There is no best way of doing things, but it is important to understand how cultural lenses affect you in different situations.

It is important to recognize that your behaviors may or may not be perceived in a positive light.

## MAKING THE MOST OF YOUR ASIAN ASSETS AT WORK

| Behavior | Perceived Liability | Positive Attributes |
|---|---|---|
| Respect for authority | <ul><li>Perceived as a yes-man</li><li>Does not push back or speak up about issues</li><li>Exploitable</li></ul> | <ul><li>Genuine loyalty to employer</li><li>Has desire to learn from others; is "teachable"</li></ul> |
| Collectivist/Consensus Builder | <ul><li>May not make decisions quickly</li><li>Not considered innovative or out-of-box thinker</li><li>Afraid to stand out from the pack</li></ul> | <ul><li>May avoid conflict to save face with the group</li><li>Collaborative decision maker</li><li>Inclusive leader</li><li>Easy to work with</li></ul> |
| Controlled/emotionally restrained | <ul><li>Unemotional, lacks enthusiasm and drive</li><li>Lacks passion about organization's mission</li><li>Arrogant, not interested in work product</li></ul> | <ul><li>Has internal strength to tolerate crisis situations; does not "lose it"</li><li>Demonstrates a resilience to changes in organizational structure</li></ul> |
| Modest/humble about accomplishments | <ul><li>Work efforts go unrecognized</li><li>May be overlooked during promotion season</li><li>May not get assigned high-visibility projects or to special task forces</li></ul> | <ul><li>Encourages team members to receive credit for their work</li><li>Team player</li></ul> |

*Perception Management: Different Communication Styles*

Your ability to communicate effectively in conference calls, group meetings, and large group presentations is a critical competency for any business setting. Most people focus on the mechanics of how to make this happen well. But it's not *what* you say in most cases, but *how* you say it. You must be able to capture an audience, whether of 1 or 100, and communicate your message well.

---

Marilyn Kim, 30, a Korean American pharmacist, reports that when interviewing potential candidates for her hospital, she saw a tremendous gap between the way Asian women and Caucasian women presented themselves. She says that though many of the Asian women sported stellar backgrounds and résumés, they had difficulty clearly articulating what they wanted to do with their futures and were very vague about their interests at the hospital. When she interviewed the Caucasian students, she saw a remarkable difference; they passionately declared their interest in certain fields of pharmacy. Even if they weren't 100% sure of their interests, their style of delivery was enough to gain the attention of and win credibility from the hiring committee.

---

*Level of Assimilation: The Formative Years Matter*

Diversity is a challenging imperative because it is so multilayered. The problem is exacerbated by socioeconomic factors, such as parents' education, occupation, and income. In *Breaking Through,* authors David Thomas and John Gabarro, two Harvard Business School professors, write that their extensive field research with three high-tech companies showed that minority employees' early life experiences are the foundation on which their careers are built. Hence, family circumstances, including education, time of immigration, socioeconomic background, and early familiarity with racially integrated social circles, aid minorities on the job.

## ACCULTURATION BY NECESSITY

Ronald Tanasugarn, 32, a second-generation Thai and manager of business development for a health care company, grew up in a racially diverse neighborhood as a young child on the West Coast. He was the only Thai kid on his block, but down the street there were two Chinese families, a Latino family, and two Indian families. There were always other Asians in his elementary school, and even some of the teachers were of diverse backgrounds.

Later, when his mother's employer transferred the family across the country, he found himself enrolled in a predominantly Caucasian high school in a New England town. He was in for a rude awakening. "I was the only Asian kid in my class, and they constantly asked me what country I was from, no matter how well I spoke English." After the initial period of awkwardness, he cultivated some very solid friendships, and he learned early on how to thrive in a predominantly Caucasian setting. The rest of his high school years were very busy for Ronald, as he played soccer and was an active member of his school's speech and debate team.

Looking back on his experience, he states confidently: "During my high school years, I gained most of the skills I needed to operate in corporate America. My current work environment mirrors, in many ways, my high school experience! If I had never left my very diverse neighborhood, I would never have been challenged to stand on my own as the only Asian in the group. Though I would have been more comfortable hanging out with other Asians, I would have never gained the kind of hands-on experience that I did during high school." Though this is far from being an endorsement to send your children to nondiverse schools, there is value in learning how to operate where you are the only person of color.

### An Ivy League Degree: Perseverance and Plain Hard Work May Not Cut It

Having a degree from an Ivy League institution can certainly give your résumé immediate credibility and help get you in the door, but it doesn't teach you the intangible navigational tools and the know-how that will get you the salary you deserve or that coveted executive position. And a 4.0 grade point average alone is not going to get you into a top firm. Of course, it doesn't hurt to have such indisputably superior academic credentials. But you will need to gain "softer" skills and prepare properly for your job search to navigate successfully in a corporation. You'll have to know what to do to get in the door at your target company, then figure out a unique, perhaps nonlinear career path.

### Conflict Avoidance

Asian cultures have always avoided conflict because of their emphasis on harmony. Thus, showing expression and emotion is discouraged in many Asian cultures and may even be seen as a sign of weakness. It is especially difficult for those from certain Asian cultures to publicly disagree. For example, during an extremely contentious meeting, an Asian person may refrain from expressing his true sentiments even if he has vehement feelings about the issue under discussion. However, if he is allowed to write down his questions or challenges in a situation where his identity can be concealed, he will be open. Another common observation is that after such a conflict-ridden meeting, an Asian may talk about the issue as she is leaving the meeting, an informal context in which it is safer to discuss the issue at hand and public humiliation is not possible. Recalls Nancy Pyon, about a church experience: "After an especially difficult church board meeting where a number of tough topics were discussed, I realized most of the Asian board members had not contributed much. After the meeting, during coffee hour, I asked one of them what he thought, and out gushed an hour's worth of opinions on the topic. Had he brought up some of these issues at the meeting, the meeting would have taken an entirely different course!" Indeed, in many predominantly Asian group settings, you may find yourself in a similar scenario. Hence, the group facilitator should not assume that the group either is disinterested about the issue or buys into it. Follow-up sessions with smaller groups or a few select one-on-one discussions may be necessary for getting to the bottom of the issue.

### Fear of Failure Can Stem from a Shamed-Based Culture

Fear of failure may be one of the worst possible fears for an Asian American employee whose values are steeped in Confucianism. Shame-based cultures operate on the principle that your failures are not just your disappointments but are also public shame. Your failure reflects on your parents and perhaps even your community as a whole. When you make a mistake, a shame-based culture may make you feel that you are flawed as a human being, not merely the perpetrator of a few minor mistakes that can be easily corrected. In Confucian philosophy, you are part of a community, and you have let that community down with your failure. For many Westerners, it is quite different. They may experience the same failure but see it as something unrelated to who they are as people. They may also bounce back faster, knowing that they can correct the mistake, and move on.

## THE SHAME OF MAKING MISTAKES

When I received a C– in an honors math class as a freshman in high school, I was mortified. So much for the stereotype of the Asian math whiz kid! I hung my head in shame as I prepared to tell my parents about this poor performance. I felt as if I had truly let them down, as well as the entire Asian immigrant community. Sensing my mortification during lunch, a Caucasian classmate said something that I remember to this day: "Hey, lighten up! You have to just learn from your early mistakes, and this is just one test, one test out of the entire semester. Why are you so down about it? It's not like you're a failure as a person. I wouldn't worry about it. Be positive. You'll have the rest of the term to master this stuff!" He shrugged it off for me, whereas I was still trying to come to terms with this failure to achieve something. I felt as if *I* were the failure, and not a person who had simply done a less-than-mediocre job on one math test. He was more forgiving than I was of myself. I had felt the shame of a thousand Asian parents feeling sorry for me. It took me many years to accept the importance of learning from my mistakes and using the awareness of my own shortcomings as an opportunity for personal growth.

# Cultural Images
## Asian          vs.          Western

"The loudest duck gets shot!"

"The squeaky wheel gets the oil."

"The nail that sticks up gets hammered down."

"You have to learn to toot your own horn."

Copyright J. Hyun, Crossroads
Career Coaching, 2004.

### *Quiet Ducks Among Squeaky Wheels*

One famous Asian proverb is "The loudest duck gets shot," and another is "The nail that sticks up gets hammered down." Many Asian Americans report having grown up with this type of thinking, which encourages conformity, community over individual rights, self-effacement, and denial of the self. In a highly individualistic society such as the United States, the saying "The squeaky wheel gets the grease" is in play, especially in the workplace. In fact, the form of reactive crisis management in which priorities are determined by which client shouts the loudest is still practiced by many organizations. Numerous American leadership and management books emphasize the necessity of self-promotion, creativity, and campaigning to move up in the corporate world. Not surprisingly, it may take some time for most Asians to incorporate these skills into their career tool kit. Respondents from the 2003 Catalyst study reported that their Asian cultural values were frequently at odds with the corporate landscape they had to navigate. "The discomfort some Asian women have with self-promotion makes advancement problematic, and their strong work ethic appears to limit networking opportunities," said Katherine Giscombe, Ph.D., senior director of research at Catalyst. "Some Asian women report that they feel pressure to change to fit into their work environments, which makes it more difficult for them to advance."

Indeed, the contrast between the Asian and the Western cultures' approaches to interpersonal relations is significant. For Asians who grew up feeling that they had to be modest even if they performed well, this new requirement in their jobs to sell their accomplishments feels completely out of character. One Filipino professional who works as a systems analyst at an insurance company says, "I know I do a good job. My manager likes me and always tells me that I am really doing a great job of understanding some complex IT [information technology] needs in my division. But what surprised me was that his peers don't see this in me at all. My manager came to my desk the other day and said that I need to get out there and toot my horn a little more to the other divisions, like marketing and operations, in order for our department to become more visible. I thought it was his job to tell others about my work quality, not mine!"

## FIRST IMPRESSIONS ARE COSTLY —

Consider the flip side of the culture coin—the impact of other people's impressions of you on the basis of your culture. In the corporate setting, first impressions count for a lot. Research has shown that nonverbal communication counts for 55% of what is communicated, volume or tone of voice counts for 38%, and verbal statements count for only 7%. In some positions such as sales, marketing, consulting, HR, and customer service, you're making first impressions every minute of the workday. Even when you don't say a word, you're making an impression.

Research indicates that many professionals, in job searches, sales meetings, and other business settings, make hasty judgment calls about people they meet for the first time on the basis of the halo effect. The effect means that when your overall initial impression of a person is positive, you tend to believe that everything else about the person will be positive. And if your impression is initially negative, you tend to believe that everything about the person is negative. If you are unfortunate enough to make a negative first impression, few people will take the time to unearth your positive attributes. Because Asian Americans are visible minorities, it is important that they do make the right first impressions and maintain good rapport afterward.

Let's consider the scenario of a non-Asian manager interviewing an Asian job candidate. The manager may observe that the candidate is rather reserved and doesn't say much about his accomplishments. She may conclude, *He isn't like anyone else on my team* or *He does not seem very knowledgeable or excited about the opportunity, and we need more aggressive people to do this job,* jumping to the conclusion that he wouldn't be an appropriate hire. The difficulty of this dynamic is that it is unspoken and thus not openly addressed. And then, though this negative halo effect may not manifest itself in all interviews with Asians that follow, it may continue to influence the manager.

### *Job Searches and Interviews: Choosing the Right Discipline for You*

Many Asian Americans' careers often begin with conflicts in the home. Because career choice involves family honor and parental influences, deciding on a career can provoke quite a bit of anxiety for Asian Americans. As relatively new immigrants or children of immigrants, many Asian American students may feel a tremendous pressure to pursue certain disciplines to satisfy and honor their parents. Though this is not true for all Asian Americans, almost all my career-changing clients with a grain of Asian heritage report that their vocational choices have disappointed their parents. Even after career changes, some continue to harbor guilt and never completely feel successful, sometimes even feeling shame for not honoring their elders.

Kevin, a Chinese American investment banker who quit his premed studies to pursue finance, recalls sadly: "I was the one they were counting on to become a physician. Being the first in my family to finish college, I always got a lot of pressure from my parents to become a physician. Once I started seriously delving into my premed courses, I realized this was not my calling in life. My family was initially saddened by my decision, and even thought that I would eventually see the light and change my mind after such a rash turnaround. After time passed, they came to accept my current profession as a good one and one that fits my personality well. I have to say, though, even if my parents have accepted my new career and time has mended some of the earlier conflicts, I still feel like I let a lot of people down, and I will have to live with this sense of shame for a long time."

### Getting a Job

In one sense, getting a job is about mastering the art of self-promotion, something that may be culturally challenging for many Asian Americans. The job hunter must create an effective marketing campaign directed at potential employers. (Later chapters discuss practical methods for developing and sustaining your own job search campaign.) But first, you must do some self-assessment. Take a good, long look at the skills you've acquired through your work, as well as through academic and extracurricular experiences. That might entail taking a personality test to determine your temperament, organizational abilities, and relational style. And a thorough self-assessment should include an exploration of your values to determine the intangible aspects that you consider important for selecting a career, such as your religious beliefs, family obligations, and moral values. Very few people do this before they launch their job search campaign, however. If they *do* conduct such an assessment, it's often late in the game, after they've begun a career in a certain field and find that it's not for them, or after they've begun their job search and find themselves hitting a brick wall.

## Interviewing

In any employment market, when companies need to add staff, one of the most powerful and widely used selection tools is the interview. It's not just for external hires, either; interviewing is also used by managers to facilitate internal transfers. Interviewing competence is thus critical to advancing your career, especially when the statistics from the U.S. Department of Labor tell us that the average American could have four to six careers in a lifetime. The sooner you become proficient in the art of interviewing, the sooner you can use it to land your new job.

Certain nonverbal communication cues used by Asian Americans may be misunderstood by recruiters and hiring managers—in particular, lack of consistent eye contact and a not-too-firm handshake. In many Asian countries, too much eye contact is a sign of disrespect and can be considered quite rude. If you have been conditioned to avoid prolonged eye contact with parents and teachers, chances are that you will act the same way with an interviewer. Because this can be completely misunderstood in an interview, do mock interviews and ask your peers to give an honest assessment of how much eye contact you make.

## A HEADS-UP TO HIRING MANAGERS: WATCH FOR A TENDENCY TO HIRE AND PROMOTE THOSE WHO ARE LIKE YOU

Harvard Business School professor Rosabeth Moss Kanter found that managers are likely to promote employees who are most like themselves, a phenomenon she called homosocial reproduction. She wrote: "Homosocial reproduction provides an important form of reassurance in the face of uncertainty about performance measurement in high-reward, high-prestige positions." Managers tend to hire others who look like themselves or remind them of themselves. We think we're pretty competent and do a good job, and we'd hire us again. Because of this unconscious bias, employees from nonmainstream backgrounds are at a disadvantage. This is why if you want diversity in your organization you must be careful about who you select to do your recruiting and internal staffing. You also want every person who interviews potential new recruits to complete a thorough interviewing training program that includes a component of diversity training. Interviewers must be able to ask themselves if they are seriously considering candidates from different backgrounds. But companies don't always put a lot of thought into choosing who handles the candidate selection. The companies that do care about this and invest in the right recruiting resources can save themselves infinite headaches down the road: Selecting the wrong person for a job costs plenty of money— severance costs, recruiting costs, and lost productivity.

*Networking*

When you are trying to break into a new field, there are several ways of getting meetings with hiring managers: You can answer a newspaper or Internet ad, work with a good recruiter at a search firm, write cover letters introducing yourself and send them with your résumé, and network with others who can help you get in the door. That last method tends to baffle people. Oh, most say they've done it a lot, but few do it right. When I suggest networking to Asian Americans, I usually get a reluctant look. They tell me: "I've already talked to everyone I know, and no one seems to know anything about this new industry. I'm stuck." Some are extremely reluctant to cold-call potential targets to broaden their professional network, most likely because of a culture that emphasizes self-sufficiency, hard work, and keeping your personal needs to yourself.

*The First Day of Work*

Day 1 may be one of the most important first impressions you can make. Even though you've made it through the company's rigorous interviewing and selection process, you must now prove yourself worthy of having been hired. This means establishing credibility early with team members, making the necessary connections with the groups in the company that could make or break your daily successes, and investing in these relationships over the long term. If you've grown up with a heavy emphasis on independent study and hard work, you may now feel entitled to just put your head down, do a good job, and wait to be rewarded for your work. However, such assumptions are naïve.

### After-Hours Networking

One of the best ways to get to know people on your team or in your company at large is to join them at social gatherings such as happy hours, lunch, and coffee breaks. Doing so allows you to establish a positive rapport and to get the inside scoop on how things are done in your group. It will also go a long way in demonstrating your desire to succeed and your genuine commitment to the firm.

But attending these social functions doesn't always come very naturally to many Asian Americans. Their culture's emphasis on industriousness may make them view going out after work as a waste of precious time that could be spent doing work. Little do they realize that if all they do is work, without paying attention to the political issues in their department, they may be the last to find out about an upcoming restructuring or downsizing. Some of these social events should be considered nearly as important as office meetings.

### Getting Accolades: Managing Your Performance at Work

To win more clients, obtain senior management recognition, and be selected for interesting projects, you must be constantly looking for ways to get your accomplishments known. This can be done by a variety of methods, including joining high-visibility corporate task forces with senior management oversight. But for the Asian who grew up valuing modesty over accomplishments and is reluctant to boast, this constant need for self-promotion may take an emotional and psychological toll. Sometimes the only way to get valuable feedback is to ask for it.

### Running Meetings on Your Own and Speaking Up in Meetings

The meeting setting can really put the Asian American employee to the test. If you are involved in any type of cross-functional project team or a special corporate task force, you will be working closely with junior and senior members from other groups at your firm. At these meetings, it's especially critical to establishing credibility, but they'll also help you connect with others in the company who can foster your career development.

### Standing Up to Your Seniors Diplomatically but Firmly

If you want to be respected by your manager, you'll have to be upfront about your opinions on matters. If you aren't clear about an objective or if you disagree with your boss, you should always ask questions to clarify your boss's position. To avoid embarrassing a supervisor in a public meeting setting, do it in a one-on-one setting. Aim to become more comfortable asking questions and challenging your seniors in a pleasant yet firm manner. This is the only way that you'll be seen as a force to be reckoned with, one who cares about the direction of the company, and not just the quiet worker bee.

### In Search of Mentors

The need to acquire a mentor cannot be stressed strongly enough. Having mentors is very much linked to having a great network. I have a colleague who has never had to go through recruiters or search ads to find a job. She has such great relationships with her former managers and mentors that whenever they heard that she could be interested in other opportunities, they linked her with job leads.

### Asking for Promotions and Salary Increases

Asking for a pay increase or a promotion isn't an easy task for anyone. But for Asians who grew up viewing conflict and calling attention to oneself as taboo, it may seem an insurmountable challenge. Yet it's naïve to assume that your boss will always be looking out for you. Everyone must look out for himself if he wants to be compensated fairly.

## CULTURE CAN AND DOES PLAY A ROLE IN DEFINING CAREER SUCCESS —

Your success is determined by a combination of external perceptions and your own work performance. Though it is rarely blatant in today's politically correct corporate system, racial prejudice still exists, and you must understand the implications of its presence. Until things come to the point that people can say "John Cho is a great physician/accountant/sales manager/head of research" without regard for race or ethnicity, your Asianness will affect your career.

---

# "Technical but Not Management Material": Dispelling Stereotypes and Inaccurate Perceptions

---

Because so few Asians are in positions of power, most non-Asian corporate managers don't understand what makes Asians tick. And the media have perpetuated some stereotypes, including these:

- *The techie or nerdy science whiz:*
  Asians are seen as good at math and other technical disciplines, but not sales or management.

- *Foreigners who can't speak English:*
  Asian Americans are often considered foreigners.

- *The quiet and submissive Asian:*
  Though things have improved slightly over the years, television and films continue to portray Asians this way.

- *The model minority—diligent, loyal employees who don't raise any flags.*

## THE MODEL-MINORITY MYTH —

Despite the evidence for cultural differences, misunderstandings, and potential for conflict or discrimination, the model-minority myth is still in play. The model-minority myth asserts that Asian Americans have overcome all the barriers to success because of their hard work and high levels of education. This leads people (including some Asian Americans themselves) to believe that Asians are doing just fine and don't require the assistance or special treatment that other minorities may receive. Asian Americans are often excluded from corporate diversity programs, minority task forces, and other assistance programs. Because they're often absent at the diversity table, the Asian American perspective is often an afterthought.

This dangerous stereotype can and has pit Asians against other minority groups, creating conflict and tension. For every Asian who has done well, there is another Asian just struggling to survive. Even in an age of multiculturalism and political correctness, many people still make and believe these statements about Asian Americans. The model-minority myth creates unrealistic pressure and expectations that many Asian Americans simply cannot live up to in work, academic, and social settings, which can damage the psyches of those trying to do so. It ignores the realities of subtle racism and discrimination faced by Asian Americans in the workplace.

As with any minority group, Asian Americans come from all socio-economic backgrounds. A Vietnamese immigrant in urban Chicago may share little in common with the second-generation Taiwanese American who was raised in a Midwestern suburb speaking only English at home.

## HARDLY A MODEL MINORITY

Tom Hoang, a 26-year-old Vietnamese American, has never felt like a model minority. His family has always struggled financially, and even now, he helps support his parents, who speak little English and are too elderly to work. He never went to college—breaking another Asian American stereotype—and currently works as a freelance photographer. "I never lived up to what my non-Asian teachers and friends expected of me," he says. "While I'm pretty happy with my career, as an Asian who hasn't lived up to others' expectations, I often feel alienated."

## HELD BACK BY THE MODEL-MINORITY MYTH

The myth can hurt professionals. Barbara Chan, a Chinese American, has worked in the finance department of a midsize retail chain for 7 years and has been the controller for the last 2. Last year, her new boss started making odd remarks about her work and ethnicity.

"My boss would make comments like 'I can always count on you to get the budget right, because I know Asians are good with numbers,' " Chan says. Though on the surface his comments seemed harmless, other department heads thought of Chan as a finance expert and nothing else. "I was a history major, and when I chose finance as a career, it wasn't because I was a quantitative expert. I knew I had an eye for detail, and I appreciated the foundation finance would provide for a long-term career in business," Chan adds.

After a few incidents, Chan decided to approach her boss over lunch. "At first, it was hard to believe my boss would make such comments in this day and age," she says. "I knew he didn't mean to hurt me, but I didn't want him to continue doing it. I might want to make a switch to operations or marketing, and my boss's comments were cornering me into a finance career within the firm."

After their initial discussion, they agreed to continue to communicate about these slips and to discuss them as they occur.

### Even Positive Stereotypes Can Hurt

The model-minority myth is alive and well in many organizations. At best, the myth allows people to think "favorably" of Asians and can make it easier for Asians to fit into the mainstream. You may think this is not an issue, but it is. Some Asians may even be in denial; they may think that they fit in so well that they overlook the effects of their ethnic identity. At worst, this myth can keep people who don't match the "perfect Asian" stereotype from being included in developmental programs because they are inaccurately perceived as self-sufficient. However, even if incidents of prejudice or bias never affect you, it has affected and will affect your friends, relatives, and colleagues. Hence, it helps to be aware of the impact of Asian stereotypes.

Moreover, Asian Americans may still struggle with many barriers to advancement because of their culturally influenced ways of thinking and operating. And no matter how much Asians have assimilated into American culture they still may be objects of prejudice, preconceived notions ("Are you from our Hong Kong office?"), and subtle biases because of their physical features. Furthermore, the myth may cause tension between Asians and other minority groups, who may overhear comments such as "Why can't they work as hard as the Asians? Look how far they have come because of their long hours of study and hard work!" Finally, the myth also limits Asians' access to minority assistance programs.

## THE MODEL-MINORITY MYTH IN LIVING COLOR

Kristy, a Vietnamese American, attended Yale University and began working for a prestigious management consulting firm. She was the first person in her family to attend college and knew she had to work for many years to pay off her school loans. The daughter of immigrant parents, she grew up with none of the comforts of many of her classmates at Yale. However, with good grades, excellent interpersonal skills, and a sharp business acumen, she was off to a great start as a consultant. During the first few years at the firm, she was a star. However, once she reached the manager level and was dealing more closely with client management, she began to feel discrimination. One of her clients told her: "You are the first Asian person to work on this project. Typically I wouldn't mention it, but you've really done well here in America, haven't you?" Clearly, she was seen as an "outsider."

So what can you do about these stereotypes? You could complain that people who believe them don't know any better and ignore the colleagues who think of you in light of them. But you can and should do something about them. Let people know that such stereotypes are an impediment to your success. Though it will take years before these stereotypes can be completely obliterated—and it's unlikely that they will ever be completely destroyed—you can take control of your own actions and statements to break through some of the stereotypes, demonstrating to non-Asians that you are an individual with unique traits. You can help inform others about the rich, heterogeneous Asian American population with its multitude of languages, traditions, religions, and personalities.

## HOW TO COUNTERACT AND BREAK THROUGH ASIAN STEREOTYPES IN YOUR CAREER —

### Find Your Voice

One thing you can start doing is speaking up wherever you can. Learn to voice your opinion even if you don't think that what you have to say is the most important discovery since the invention of the lightbulb. If you have a strong opinion about an issue, hold your ground. You'll gain respect for it.

For some Asians, English is a second language, so it may take a little extra time for new information to sink in. This may lead to a reluctance to speak up, for fear of using incorrect grammar or vocabulary. If this is true for you, take a little time prior to meetings to do some extra homework. Learn about the backgrounds of the meeting attendees, the topics to be presented, and potential areas of contention.

## Be the First to Speak

The tendency is for Asians to let everyone have their turn first before they take the plunge. Hearing everyone out and waiting is the respectful, honorable thing to do. But don't be afraid to show your excitement by interrupting (within reason) and asking a good question. Given your propensity to want to wait to ask relevant, insightful questions, your initiative might be rewarded with positive feedback from your colleagues who are impressed with your knowledge and insights. You may even find other people in the meeting who are your advocates and agree with your point of view.

In Korea and Japan, business meetings tend to be very cooperative and relatively peaceful. When one person speaks, the group typically allows him to finish his statement before another adds a comment. Then, a second contributor can speak. There are few interruptions, and it is rare to see someone cutting someone else off to make a point. An Asian family's dinner conversation can be similar. At the family dinner, if a member of the family has something to say, it is typically listened to politely before another member has something to add to the conversation. But the American way of communicating is very different. Usually, someone serves as a facilitator. There is usually a sense of decorum in any business setting, and meeting attendees are not always cutting people off. Yet lively meetings aren't unusual, and there may be someone cutting another person off, finishing another's sentence, topping off an idea or challenging another's comment, or creating better solutions from one person's initial idea. No wonder that it's not easy for the Asian professional to navigate in this setting. Yet, the creative energy generated in a spirited discussion can result in innovative business practices.

## A Force to Be Reckoned With: Knowing When to Challenge Authority

You'll need to become skilled at managing your boss and disagreeing with her when it matters. I am not advocating that you become the company rebel. You must pick your battles and exercise caution when you take a stand, and at times, it may be beneficial for you to duck out of ugly political conflicts. But to get ahead, you must be recognized as a force to be reckoned with; your boss must see you as an equal, not merely a dutiful corporate citizen who unquestioningly does everything he's told. You can do this by contributing your opinions in your areas of expertise and suggesting ways that things can be done differently, framing them as a win-win.

If you have trouble with strong personalities, get training. Read Part III ("Getting Ahead on the Job") of this book. Practice with a buddy. Start asserting yourself very close to home, by joining the board of your co-op, condo, or townhouse development. Volunteer to serve on the board of a local nonprofit or charity. Many organizations lack minority board members and so are recruiting them actively. Practice being an active, participating voice in your immediate social circles.

### *Changing Attitudes and Modifying Behaviors Without Compromising Your Identity and Values*

The last time I discussed with a group of management consultants some of the ways that Asians can manage perceptions of themselves, I kept hearing, "Do I have to change who I am in order to be successful?" You certainly do not need to become a different person. But you have to know when and how to turn off and turn on certain aspects of yourself. You want to be able to pump up the volume a little when you need to be more vocal about promoting yourself on the job. However, that doesn't mean that you need to be operating out of your comfort zone on a daily basis.

## EXERCISING CULTURAL FLUENCY — KNOWING WHEN TO BE ASSERTIVE

From interviewing and coaching hundreds of Asians in the past few years, I have learned that in some settings, you should kick your assertiveness level up a notch or two. At first you may find this uncomfortable, but with practice, it will become easier for you. When you must deal with conflict head-on, you have to be flexible enough to put on your "tough negotiator" hat. This does not require you to become a different person.

Kevin Hsu, a naturally introverted, introspective operations manager, decided to try this out. The next time he went into a contentious meeting, he had his points prepared ahead of time. He also practiced stating his opinions prior to the meeting, especially the points that really mattered to him. When one of the meeting attendees challenged him, saying that Kevin's idea wouldn't work, Kevin was able to stand his ground. Furthermore, he provided a very strong argument for why he felt that the business should head in a new direction. A few months earlier, Kevin would have backed off from the conflict and tried to appease his challenger.

To thrive in a corporate culture that values outspokenness, assertiveness, and creativity, Asian Americans must arm themselves with new behaviors that can be used in different work settings. You must cultivate a diplomatic, assertive voice for when you need to disagree with someone. And it's okay to show your emotions a bit. I have found that leaders who stand for something are usually passionate, and their expressiveness is charismatic. Their attitude screams, *I have something important to accomplish, and nothing will stand in my way!*

But know what's appropriate for each situation. Dogged persistence may work better for making sales calls than brash aggressiveness. Research shows that companies buy from salespeople who can deliver, are persistent, and understand the client's needs. And different sales techniques work for different client personalities.

When selling a product, people may automatically assume that a quiet, unassuming person may not be effective in dealing with difficult clients. Hence, many Asians who demonstrate this characteristic in an interview setting get shot down during selection committee discussions as too understated or passive. But when I talk to managers who work with Asians, what I frequently hear is that one technique doesn't work with all clients. A vice president of HR from a large organization says, "Some of the most effective client relationship managers I know are rather reserved in personality! When you take a look at their track records, they are sometimes the star performers in their peer group. First impressions carry you only so far. I want someone who is honest, has good business development skills, and can deliver. I can always find the aggressive ones who can knock on doors, but what I need more of are the people who can maintain the relationships and continuously deliver for our clients."

In certain meeting settings, it is perfectly fine to be the listener and not contribute a lot until the opportune moment. However, when you're the expert and the reason why everyone is gathered around the table, then you must run the meeting, and run it effectively.

# THREE

# THE LATEST TRENDS IN CORPORATE DIVERSITY PRACTICES

*In the long run, the world is going to have the best, and any difference in race, religion, or previous history will not keep the world from what it wants.*

—Booker T. Washington

## HOW CORPORATE DIVERSITY PRACTICES AFFECT INDIVIDUAL CAREER DEVELOPMENT —

The latter portions of this book are about empowering Asian American employees and their managers to manage perceptions and understand the impact of culture on thought patterns, behavior, and performance on the job. After reading these chapters, you may feel ready to implement many of these self-improvement and leadership strategies at your company with the goal of moving up. But you can be the most determined, qualified employee and still get overlooked for a promotion. Without the appropriate support mechanisms and a fertile corporate environment that supports mobility, you may find progress to take longer and be more difficult than you thought. Unless an organization has the proper infrastructure and accountability measures in place to identify your raw talents, recognize your potential, develop your leadership skills, and provide you with high-exposure growth opportunities to get you noticed by the right people in the right places in the organization, you will not succeed.

So how can you determine which companies invest time and senior management muscle to diversity issues? Before you make any rash move to another company, determine whether your company will take you where you want to go. If careful analysis shows that the prospects for career development at your current firm are dismal, you can do one of two things: (1) target other companies in which to invest the rest of your career or (2) play an active role in developing diversity initiatives right where you are. You should pursue the latter option only if you see some potential for improvement or signs of senior management's commitment.

Today, most large companies recognize the need for some type of diversity program that empowers all employees, regardless of gender, race, age, religion, sexual orientation, or disability, to reach their full potential in the workplace. But even if yours has one, is it working? Some companies give the responsibility for diversity management to the HR department. Though HR managers can make some headway in promoting diversity and inclusive leadership and even influence business units to take the issue seriously, real change can happen only if line managers have a stake in the diversity initiative. If the diversity flame does not continue to fan down to all levels of the business, its key objectives may never be in operation where it matters. There has to be a constant dynamic of top-down and bottom-up communication for real change to occur.

Some companies may be convinced that this "diversity thing" is important but not know the right approach to take or not be aware of the available resources or best practices. For example, leaders of one large retail organization felt that merely requiring every employee to attend a "diversity awareness" off-site weekend would suffice. Hence, they were able to say that their company had "done diversity" and checked it off their list. These efforts, though well-intentioned, will rarely produce high-potential minority leaders.

A good proportion of executives in senior management may be completely supportive of any efforts made to advance the cause of diversity and support the growth of minority representation in the corporate world. They will readily support networking groups, champion mentoring programs, and communicate the value of these initiatives throughout the corporation. Others may feel that every employee should receive equal treatment, meaning that the company should not give any "extra advantages" to its minority employees. They believe that the "may the best employee win" concept is the way to go. This would be fine if it were always easy to identify the best people.

Many companies have difficulty identifying the high-potential performers because quite often, work performance is judged by some subjective, intangible, relational component, particularly in the management ranks. Thus, there are few perfect meritocracies. Because of this, managing diversity will always be a difficult challenge.

Fair or not, most of the responsibility rests on you. You'll have to seek out the right work experiences, volunteer to serve on committees, and be more vocal about your career development with your employer.

As you begin to manage your career aggressively in new ways, you can ask your colleagues and managers to team up with you. Once they become aware of the fact that they can support you, they can be your allies. Share with them your cultural values so that senior managers can determine the right criteria and strategies for identifying talent for succession planning discussions. Successful executives don't always come from the same mold.

## OUR WAY OR THE HIGHWAY?
## PAYING LIP SERVICE ISN'T ENOUGH —

Nowadays, you can't view a Fortune 500 Web site without encountering a pop-up screen or a link to the firm's corporate diversity programs. Under pressure from competitors and government agencies to be inclusive in hiring and general management practices, companies are eager to do what they can to increase their bottom line, so they jump on the diversity bandwagon.

But what companies are actually effective at creating and developing minority leaders? How do you recognize a true diversity-friendly company? Probably the best information will come from your friends and colleagues who work there or have worked there recently, if you are fortunate enough to have such contacts. If not, you can learn a lot from what the company *doesn't* tell you. If you type in the word *diversity* in the search engine on the company's Web site and fail to get any results, you'll know that it is not investing time and resources in this important area. Nevertheless, give such a company the benefit of the doubt because it may just be beginning its diversity program. If you are invited to interview with such a company, you may be able to get more information when you meet with its staff.

## IDENTIFYING AN ASIAN-FRIENDLY EMPLOYER —

### *Where to Begin?*

If you could have your pick of companies to work for, you would most certainly benefit by starting out with one that will give you the most opportunities to develop and grow. *Fortune* magazine's Annual 100 Best Companies for Minorities to Work For issue or *Diversity Inc.*'s (www.diversityinc.com) 50 Best Companies for Diversity issue are good starting points. But you'll get the most salient and candid assessments from your friends who work at these companies. They may even know some of the players you may be interfacing with in interviews. Nothing can replace the honesty and insight of a personal testimonial. But even if you already happen to work for one of these diversity-friendly companies, there is no guarantee of that senior management spot.

Corporate diversity programs are not all alike. Each company will develop one or more programs that work for it. Here are some variations:

- Mandatory attendance in a 2-day diversity awareness training program
- Diversity recruiting campaign
- Working with HR to keep an eye on attrition rates of minority employees at all levels and reasons for departure. If they are leaving for reasons of prejudice or subtle discrimination, this could initiate proactive measures to retain those remaining.
- Networking groups and sensitivity/cross-cultural training for all employees, including new recruits
- Formal mentoring programs for high-performing women and professionals of color

# INNOVATIVE MENTORING IDEAS

## GROUP MENTORING

Group mentoring involves 8 to 10 professionals meeting with one mentor for lunch once a month. The group mentor acts as a facilitator for lively career development discussions. The protégés have a chance to get to know a senior management member in an informal lunchtime setting.

## REVERSE MENTORING

In reverse mentoring, the senior manager acts as the protégé and the junior professional acts as the mentor. This has proven to be very effective in helping senior management members come up to speed with what it's like to be new to the firm; at the same time, it allows junior professionals access to senior management, a critical link to potential job opportunities.

When you are looking at a potential employer, take note of the opportunities to get involved at every level and make sure you conduct due diligence with insiders in the field who know the true scoop.

Look for companies that walk the talk. Take a look at the senior management team and the level below it. Learn about the individuals who are on the board of directors, as well as the people who are selected to represent the firm in public venues, such as industry meetings and campus recruiting events. If they are a homogeneous lot, chances are you may face high odds against being promoted into certain positions.

Should you find yourself working at a division at your company that is a hostile place for employees of diverse backgrounds, you may want to consider other options, such as an internal transfer or a role that will give you more exposure. Are line managers being held accountable for managing diversity? Are the pay and promotional practices in the company closely tied to the accomplishments of diversity standards? Do managers include you in informal meetings around the watercooler? Do your senior managers feel comfortable when around you? Or do they seem to be walking on eggshells whenever you're present? If, after reviewing your internal options, you still find the overall climate relatively hostile to minority advancement, it may be time to consider finding a new employer. Such a company will eventually lose its minority employees. If enough people leave, the firm may eventually wake up to the fact that it must do some things differently to retain its minority population. Treating employees right ultimately improves the company's bottom line—and that just makes good business sense.

### Find Out How the Company Handles Recruiting

Recruiting can sometimes be an easy antidote for a company's diversity woes. Having said that, however, let's take a look at how one company manages diversity recruiting.

Do business managers have accountability to senior management or a senior diversity coordinator? At one major international bank, the COO, who has completely bought into the concept that hiring and promoting a qualified diverse workforce brings fresh insights, creativity, and unique viewpoints into his global offices, acts as the enforcer and encourager for diversity initiatives. In conjunction with a diversity director of each business, he makes sure, before every new hire is made, that he examines the list of candidates. No hire is made unless it is approved by the COO. Consequently, if none of the candidates are people from diverse backgrounds (and this includes women, elderly workers, people with disabilities, gays and lesbians, as well as African Americans, Latino Americans, Asian Americans, and Native Indians), he challenges the hiring manager to go back to the drawing board to develop a more diverse candidate pool. Without this kind of senior management oversight, diversity recruiting may not necessarily get the attention that it should.

And though I have downplayed the importance of diversity recruiting as merely the bare-minimum starting point for ensuring diversity, recruiters and hiring managers—those who are often the ultimate gatekeepers—must continuously keep an active lookout for candidates from a wide array of backgrounds. We must have a diverse base of employees to work with before we can strategize about how to keep them in place.

In a perfect meritocracy, there would be no need for a diversity program. In the real world, programs must be in place to ensure that companies learn to recruit, manage, and develop leaders from all backgrounds. And it's imperative that there be constant communication about the importance of these issues, as well as genuine support of employee growth.

### *Determine Whether the Company Reaches Beyond Minority Recruiting Programs*

Promoting inclusive leadership means more than bringing in the right people at the front door. It is about enabling each person to meet his full potential in his unique area of expertise. This may be achieved through training, coaching for skills and development (in both one-and-one and group settings), and incorporating a continuous feedback mechanism from managers, clients, and subordinates. The skills development and training should be designed specifically by and for each employee. Hence, an Asian employee can get the type of skills-based training he needs to overcome some of the cultural barriers he may face, and a female employee may decide to get a different type of training to meet her professional development needs.

### *Helping Asians Overcome Workplace Barriers*

One senior manager of a Fortune 500 company, looking at a spreadsheet with the latest worldwide employee breakout by gender and race, noted with excitement at a diversity task force meeting: "The number of Asian senior VPs looks good!" Another manager responded, "That's because all except two are located in Asia." Indeed, nearly all of the Asian senior managers were local nationals from the small local offices in Asia where the company had a presence. When they looked at numbers for the Americas, which represented the largest portion of revenue, the numbers weren't quite as good.

Company support of a diversity-friendly culture starts with its mission statement, value system, and philosophy. But what's most important is the end result of diversity programs and initiatives. Look carefully at who is sent out to represent the company at recruiting events and conferences, and you'll have an idea of whom the firm values.

## QUESTIONS TO ASK COMPANY REPRESENTATIVES DURING INTERVIEWS AND NETWORKING MEETINGS

Without necessarily coming across as the diversity police, you can gain valuable insights into the company that you are considering working for simply by asking some of these questions:

- In what areas does your company need to grow?
- How would you articulate your company's commitment to diversity?
- What is the company's 5-year plan?
- Are your company's products or service lines domestic or global in nature? How about in the next 5 to 10 years?
- What about the face of the company's client base? All women? Large minority population?
- What is the mechanism for diversity recruiting, at both the entry level and experienced level?
- What colleges does the company recruit at? Where do most of the entry-level trainees come from?
- Does the company do smaller targeted recruiting events at Asian clubs and organizations and meetings on college campuses?

The ethnicities of the following can usually be determined only by talking to people in the firm or those who know about the firm firsthand: the people in management, the members of the board of directors, the people who are in the succession plan, and the people sent out to do recruiting and otherwise represent the company.

## CURRENT DIVERSITY PRACTICES —

From interviews with and questionnaires given to individuals who work in financial services, management consulting, pharmaceuticals industries, and media/entertainment conglomerates, I've gleaned information on some of the current diversity trends that may affect Asian Americans' ability to move up the corporate ladder.

### *Senior Management Representation, Buy-In, and Leadership*

Countless numbers of senior business managers, diversity stakeholders, diversity coordinators, and HR directors I've encountered mentioned senior management buy-in and leadership as the top requirements for advancing diversity management in the workplace. Only when a company has a number of very visible, highly respected senior executives waving the flag for diversity can these cultural and development programs begin to bear fruit. Otherwise, the programs will be popular fodder for watercooler talk for a period of time but likely won't be implemented at the levels where it counts. If they're not working at the grass-roots level, the programs may not survive long enough to be effective. Senior leaders, including the CEO, need to champion this initiative. They must effectively communicate the goals of the programs, both internally and externally.

## UBS'S DIVERSITY PROGRAM: OWNED AND DRIVEN BY THE BUSINESS

In order to be effective, diversity practices need to be embedded into the way of doing business. Mona Lau, managing director and global head of diversity for UBS, talks about the company's diversity philosophy: "We are a truly global organization. Senior management recognizes that this can't be a U.S.-driven initiative; hence, there is a global vision and an international focus on driving diversity throughout the organization."

Senior business leaders, representing the United States, the United Kingdom, Asia Pacific, Switzerland, Germany, and Italy, meet regularly via global video conference to update one another. The HR managers work very closely with the business heads to advise, consult, and facilitate the discussion around diversity for their regions. These updates help keep the managers at the very top accountable to their objectives.

UBS's affinity groups include:

- Women's Network
- Multicultural Network
- Minority Leadership Council (comprised mainly of managing directors)
- African American Council
- Gay/Lesbian Network

At KYZ, a consumer products company, the diversity committee was in shambles. They had some diversity recruiting committees that sent African American, Latino American, and Asian American employees out to campuses to recruit people of color, but the retention rate for minority employees was poor. At the launch of a diversity task force, its committees were composed of lower-level middle managers and junior employees, and minority employees could sense that this was just another stopgap or politically correct corporate initiative, not a serious undertaking. But when the CEO designated one of his well-respected senior business heads to take over, the new leader helped to revive the task force by instituting a mentoring program and meeting with many of the managers to discuss how their individual development plans must include promoting and developing their diverse teams. The task force also decided to diversify the face of the company's senior management selection committee, an elite group of people who spearheaded succession planning, naming the future leaders of the firm. Before this, the extent of the committee's diversity was that 30% of the team came from the West Coast and 10% were women—there were no professionals of color. The overhaul process was a long one and just a start in advancing diversity efforts at the company. Examples of accountability in the program include the following:

- Compensation or other incentives dependent on meeting diversity goals
- Performance evaluation with measurements to monitor the progress of recruiting, retention, and career development
- A person or group formally designated to monitor progress, reporting to senior leadership
- A diverse task force with specific subcommittees
- Monitoring of selection and promotion committees to ensure diverse representation so that those doing the hiring and promoting consider candidates other than just those who look like themselves

A large manufacturing company had a great start to its diversity program. The CEO hired an enthusiastic diversity director with a successful track record from a larger Fortune 500 company. The firm's first priority was to take all of its local office employees through a cursory diversity awareness 2-day workshop. It took over a year for the 500 employees to complete this training, but the training gave them tremendous insights into diversity and helped to raise firmwide awareness.

After about 8 months, though, the firm started to lose many of its minority employees to competitors. Where did it go wrong? I suspect that the burden of diversity never left the diversity director's office. Although the employees felt empowered and challenged during the awareness retreats, the need for ongoing diversity management had not been endorsed by the managers in the trenches. No accountability, monitoring of hiring and promotion programs, mentoring, or monitoring of diversity task forces had been put in place. There was rarely any mention of the program in subsequent business meetings and other communication vehicles. The managers knew that there were distinct cultural issues to be dealt with in their respective departments, yet they didn't know how to begin.

## THE TOKEN-ASIAN SYNDROME

Many Asian professionals report to having been designated as the representative Asian sample in their employee population. This isn't always a negative thing, but it gives them very little room for error. If things go well, non-Asians in the company may say, "Look how effective this Asian manager was." But if things go awry, the employee herself may feel she let her "entire race down," a result of a shame-based Asian culture.

## INNOVATIVE CAREER DEVELOPMENT PRACTICES FOR ASIAN EMPLOYEES

### JPMORGAN CHASE'S CAREER DEVELOPMENT PROGRAM

Focused career development can be a great way to support the careers of minority professionals. At JPMorgan Chase (JPMC), the Career Advancement Program (also known as CAP) has proven to be a useful tool for the career development of its Asian employees. The program, developed by David Rottman of JPMC's inhouse career center, didn't start out as a diversity initiative, but it has had significant participation from women and minority professionals at JPMC. Ken Fong, senior vice president of human resources, states: "David was able to use the existing services of the career center and extended the platform to be used as a career development tool that women and minorities needed."

The CAP program provides career advisors to high-potential employees. Anyone can participate in the program, so long as the business unit agrees to sponsor the employee. The results have been auspicious and immediate. The investment banking division once had an attrition rate of 50% among women and minorities in the analyst/associate population. After only one year since inception, that rate had plummeted to an incredible 7%, representing a savings of $224,000 per analyst hire and $255,000 per associate hire in recruiting and training costs. The CAP program's effectiveness demonstrates the importance of one-on-one interventions in boosting the morale and advancement of minority employees. The program works because it saves the firm money while advancing Asian employees.

Their Asian affinity group is called AsPIRE (Asian Pacific Islanders Reaching for Excellence), a networking organization developed by Asian employees at JPMC. This group facilitates the development of mentoring relationships, while fostering networking opportunities.

## IBM

IBM has consistently been recognized as a leader in diversity practices, and the company has made equally great strides with its Asian employee constituency. Under the leadership of Ted Childs, vice president of global diversity, diversity is not just a program; it is a core business capability. One of the roles that the Asian task force plays is bringing together the Asian employees to help them meet their potential at IBM. It's the company mantra that all employees, regardless of race, sexual orientation, religion, or disability, have the chance to reach their full potential. The Asian diversity task force prepared an "Asian value proposition" for senior management that clearly articulated Asian employees' value to the firm. Karen Fukuma, one of the four Asian diversity task force cochairs, says, "What started out as an advocacy group for the Asian constituency has evolved into an effective communications and networking vehicle."

"What sets us apart," says Wes Hom, another task force cochair, is that the firm has "an enlightened management team who believes in the benefits of a diverse workforce." Not only does IBM have task forces for its diversity constituencies, it also assigns one of the top 50 IBM executives to work with each task force on a global level. The four Asian task force cochairs meet with Steve Mills and Jon Iwata, senior vice presidents, every 6 months to report on their task force's progress and plans.

*A Strong Commitment to Training and Leadership Development*

To date, IBM has sent over 600 people to LEAP's (Leadership Education for Asian Pacifics) Leadership Development Program. About every 18 months, IBM hosts the Asian Executive Leadership Conference, where over 150 Asian executives (director level and above), as well as high-potential leaders-in-training, get together for an intense 3-day leadership conference to exchange ideas, form networks and alliances, and develop strategies for developing the careers of their Asian employees.

A diverse team of cochairs leads the Asian task force. They include Karen Fukuma, Wes Hom, Satish Gupta, and Vijay Lund. The four cochairs act as advisors to the Asian constituency at IBM, and all hold vice president positions in various IBM business units. It was clear that they take their responsibility seriously.

A number of the large professional services organizations such as Deloitte and PricewaterhouseCoopers (PwC) have also developed proactive ways to promote the career development of their Asian American employees.

Deloitte has made great strides in implementing diversity recruiting and networking initiatives. Deloitte's Tri-State Asian American Alliance in New York sponsored a financial services networking event with the Asian Corporate Leadership Network. The alliance also invited panelists and participants from Asian diversity networks of other firms to participate. Together with Deloitte's South Asian American Group, these organizations have also provided leadership training and soft-skills coaching to Deloitte's employees. Partner Caroline King, sponsor for the Asian American Alliance, also sits on the Northeast Diversity Council. Deloitte's Career Connections program, which is a career counseling center similar to that found in an MBA program, helps employees identify other job opportunities within the firm. With the cost of turnover being so high (as much as three to five times a consultant's salary), the program has paid for itself.

The value of retaining the Asian American workforce in light of the growth of the global economy was articulated in a statement from Jim Wall, head of global human resources at Deloitte: "There is an unprecedented opportunity for Asians to reach their potential here, and we absolutely need them to stay at Deloitte and help us maintain our competitive edge. There are not enough of them here, and we cannot afford to lose the ones we have."

PwC calls diversity networking groups "networking circles." The women's circles are for the manager level and above across all business lines. These circles serve the purpose of providing role models and networking opportunities for high-potential women in the company. Leadership courses, information-sharing Web casts, and training seminars are offered by the women's circles. Multicultural circles are offered to employees at all levels in the organization.

PwC encourages the growth of new "circles" as well. Kimberlee Washington Barr, director of diversity recruiting at PwC, explains: "When a new circle crops up in one of the local offices, it involves buy-in from the local practice managing partner. Someone in the office usually takes the initiative to launch the group and coordinates with us to develop a strategy." PwC executives have also discussed launching virtual circles, particularly to include practice offices in smaller cities with very little minority representation. And of course, diversity events are open to all employees, not just the diversity constituency that sponsored it.

Large Fortune 500 companies are not the only ones focusing on the development of their high-potential Asian leaders. Paul Tokunaga, coordinator of Asian American ministries at InterVarsity Christian Fellowship, a campus organization, developed the proposal for the Daniel Project, a leadership program designed to mentor and develop high-potential Asian American staff to take on management positions. The Daniel Project took Asian staff workers to a 5-day leadership training conference to provide training and allow access to a range of career possibilities. During the conference, the participants had access to consultations with senior Asian American staff. In addition, they were each given a personal mentor—a senior Asian American staff leader. The program provided Asian staff a prime opportunity to receive focused one-on-one career mentoring and opened up the possibilities of future opportunities in the organization.

# PART II

# CAREER CHOICES
## AND GETTING IN
## THE DOOR

– FOUR –

# DOCTOR? LAWYER? OR INNER-CITY TEACHER? HOW CULTURAL INFLUENCES IMPACT YOUR CAREER CHOICES

*This is America. You can do anything here.*

—Ted Turner

*Afoot and lighthearted I take to the open road,*
*Healthy, free, the world before me,*
*The long brown path before me leading wherever I choose.*

—Walt Whitman, "Song of the Open Road"

*Eventually, I found the inner resources to pursue the career I had dreamed about. I studied for a master's degree in counseling and, several years ago, got my license. But I did so with the knowledge that not only would I disappoint my mother, I would also be entering a profession that Asians generally regard with suspicion. My parents had passed down a cultural imperative that strongly discouraged exposing personal or family matters to public scrutiny. . . . Children are to make choices that bring honor to the family, not that fulfill individual dreams. The culture is family-centered, not child-centered.*

—Claire S. Chow, *Leaving Deep Water*

## PARENTAL EXPECTATIONS OFTEN CLASH WITH
## CAREER GOALS AND DEFINITIONS OF SUCCESS —

"You can be anything that you want to be—follow your dreams!" Most Americans hear that statement throughout their lives from family, teachers, and popular media. But what if you've been raised with the notion that you can dream—but only about a few select professions? Or that pursuing alternative professions means that you'll alienate yourself from the parents you love and respect? Many Asians growing up in America hear a different variation on the "Be all that you can be" theme: "Be anything that you want to be, as long as it is a stable, honorable profession that provides long-term financial security and status." As a result, writes Audrey Kim, psychologist at University of California, Santa Cruz, in *Counseling American Minorities,* "many Asian immigrants think in terms of family unit rather than individuals, and Asian parents are often willing to make extreme sacrifices for their children, with the expectation that the children will reciprocate by achieving academic and career 'success' and taking care of their parents later on. Thus, Asian American parents may expect to have a say in their children's choice of a college major, occupation, and even marriage partner."

I recently asked a group of 100 young Asian professionals in the legal and consulting professions who graduated since 1999 this question: "How many of you are in careers that you are happy with?" Only a dozen or so raised their hands. I followed up with another probe—"How many of you are in the same careers because of early parental pressures?"—and nearly 90 hands shot up. It was astounding that very few were in fields that they absolutely loved. And of the few who were in their dream jobs, many of them had overcome tremendous odds to get to their desired state. When I met them individually after the speech was over and asked them what they planned to do with their careers, at least 20 of them were already exploring career directions outside of their current area of expertise.

## EDUCATION AND ACHIEVEMENT —

The Asian American's struggle for the right career begins long before the first day on the job—even as far back as childhood. Many Asian Americans grow up understanding that a good education yields only one of these options: a professional job in medicine, law, or engineering, or additional degrees. Business professions, which include finance and accounting, are often considered secondary alternatives only if the top three alternatives aren't viable.

John Kim, Korean American, born to immigrant parents, a physician and a physicist, lives in a suburb of Indiana. He grew up thinking that he had only four career options: doctor, lawyer, engineer, or garbage collector—and that if he couldn't be one of those first three professions, he might as well skip college. Many of his high school friends—non-Asians— went on to pursue any one of a diverse array of disciplines, such as acting, journalism, architecture, and retail management. His parents often said, "Those professions are fine and good for your friends, but you have an Asian face, so you need to find a profession where you can find security in your own field of expertise, something no one can take away from you. A good education from a well-known school and a technical profession— those things no one can take away from you! Business careers or artistic fields are too risky for a lifelong profession."

John majored in biomedical engineering as an undergraduate. But rather than become an engineer in the research and development department of a high-tech company, he wanted to do management consulting. His parents, one a medical doctor and the other a physicist, came to the United States in 1971, after the passage of the Immigration Act of 1965, which allowed professionals in scientific disciplines, including engineering and medicine, to immigrate here because of a U.S. shortage of health care workers. John's parents, like many Asian immigrants, are from a society in which education is the most important vehicle for upward mobility and status. In China and Korea, even a poor country peasant could achieve wealth and status for himself and his family by passing difficult university and government entrance exams. That strong emphasis on academics leads many Asian immigrants to seek entry into only the top U.S. universities. The pressure to attend a prescribed list of prestigious schools and to pursue only a limited number of job functions makes it difficult for Asian Americans like John to break free from parental expectations and create their own career path.

## ASIAN IMMIGRATION PERSPECTIVES

It is very important for employers to understand how and why an Asian professional's family came to the United States, because that background affects all aspects of how the professional functions on the job. As can be expected, the fully acculturated third-generation Chinese American dot-com entrepreneur in suburban Chicago who grew up speaking only English at home and is not very culturally Chinese shares little in common with a Cambodian immigrant in upstate New York who still adheres to many of his Asian cultural traditions and is experiencing cross-cultural differences.

Danielle, a third-generation Japanese American and a corporate recruiter, says, "My parents raised me as if I were no different from my white friends. I never spoke Japanese in the home. We were actually discouraged from being 'too Japanese.' " Many Japanese Americans, because of their longer history in the United States than other Asian groups, and perhaps in part because of the trauma of Japanese internment in America after World War II, tend to be more acculturated than other Asian American groups. It was not until the 1960s that Americans of diverse Asian ancestries began to recognize commonalities in their histories and experiences.

After the late 1970s, Southeast Asians came to the United States in large numbers, from Vietnam, Cambodia, and Laos. They had not originally intended to emigrate. They were war refugees.

Some of the more recent Asian immigrants do not necessarily come from such educated backgrounds. Nevertheless, many of them expect their children to pursue higher education as a major step toward assimilation into American culture. No wonder these parents, many of whom experienced difficulties and discrimination because of the language barrier, hold technical licensed professions in America in high regard. That's why it's not surprising that even today, young adult Asian Americans who mention the possibility of entering such occupations as social services, fine arts, nonprofit services, or writing to their immigrant parents may earn looks of genuine concern.

## FILIAL PIETY AND RESPECT FOR AUTHORITY —

Because group welfare—the family's well-being—is valued over individual rights in Asian societies, parents often play a significant role in their children's choice of college, major, occupation, and even marriage partner. During an informal portion of a campus recruiting trip, one Asian candidate told me, when asked why he wanted to work in investment banking, "Well, I knew premed was out because I never enjoyed the sciences, and the attorney route did not make me happy, and there was really nothing else left except for banking. It was the third and only option left for me to try within the acceptable career paths."

An Ivy League–educated executive in a large Fortune 100 company recalls, "After I finished law school and two years in a law firm, I decided that the partnership track at a prestigious law firm was not going to be my lifelong career objective. I decided to work for a high-tech company in a strategic marketing role. But for many years, whenever I would meet my parents' friends at social gatherings, they would say, 'What's the matter? Why is he not practicing law? Did he not pass the bar?' as if following the traditional path at a law firm was the only possible ticket to success!" They could not imagine why an Ivy League law school graduate would "resort" to working in the business world when he could have practiced law, something they saw as being worthy of more respect.

These sentiments strongly resonate with Jinny, an American Born Chinese (ABC), who recalls her mother telling her, "You must try to get into a top university." When she decided to enroll at a small liberal arts college, she felt as though she had disappointed both her mother and her broader Chinese community. Later, when she thought about changing careers—leaving a very lucrative career at a prestigious, well-known international law firm—to pursue her dream of writing short stories and fiction, she had to do a lot of convincing to help her mother understand that she could actually make money as a writer. However, at an important crossroad in her career, when she found herself being considered for a promotion at her law firm, she seriously reassessed her future. Clearly, she enjoyed working with people rather than documents and transactions; she was beginning to resent the significant amount of time she spent stuck inside an office reviewing documentation. After completing some self-assessment exercises, she realized that she possessed extremely good interpersonal skills and could sell or negotiate her way into anything. Her uncanny ability to influence and energize others led her to consider a new career as a corporate trainer. Her presentation skills, coupled with her ability to master new information quickly, helped make her a skilled trainer with a consulting firm. Even though she didn't become a full-time writer, her new profession better uses her affinities than the law career did. She still dabbles in writing from time to time and plans to take writing courses at night. And her legal training didn't go to waste; today, when Jinny isn't traveling to another client site, she does pro bono legal advisory work for an important charity she believes in.

Mark Ly is a dot-com entrepreneur who is still trying to convince his parents that he is in a serious profession. His parents, who emigrated from China, not only think business is not a sufficiently honorable profession, but they also believe that people go into business management only because they can't hack it in medicine, law, or engineering. Says Mark: "My parents went to good schools, but they struggled here because of their English. I have a command of the English language and am respected in my field, but they still ask me when I might come to my senses and go to med school." Most of his peers—children of his parents' friends—followed the traditional career paths, and even they couldn't understand why Mark decided to go into business. It's no wonder, then, that young Asian Americans struggle so vehemently with their career choices.

One's profession plays a very significant role in U.S. society, where individual achievements and awards are important. Additionally, Americans place a high emphasis on personal fulfillment. In the Asian culture, which celebrates higher education, knowledge, and "honorable" professions, there are some occupations that just do not seem to fit into those paradigms. Numerous Asians have revealed to me, in focus groups and informal coaching sessions, that they feel unusually burdened by such parental influence. They say: "I know it's the right thing to do—to follow my dreams—but why is that so difficult to accept?"

Serena, a Vietnamese American, reports: "I never felt that I had much choice in my career direction. When I decided to be a social worker for this nonprofit organization, my parents practically disowned me. I was discouraged from doing anything that wasn't technical or licensed, so working in a human service profession with very little security did not make them feel secure." When Steve, a Chinese American, left his cushy, prestigious job as a medical doctor to become a low-paid staff member of a religious organization, his father used negative reinforcement, saying that he'd return to Asia because he could never face the local Asian American community again.

At this point, you may be saying, "So what's so bad about becoming a doctor, lawyer, or engineer? There's good money and security in those professions, and you can get your parents off your back!" The problem isn't those professions per se; it's the *reasons* for entering them. Most people (Asian and non-Asian alike), when faced with the need to seek other career opportunities, look immediately for job postings or other obvious, quick-fix methods of seeking employment, often bypassing a careful analysis of their experiences, skills, personality, and work style.

But, as we know, it is not about finding another job. And, much too often, when Asians feel pressured to enter certain professions, it may be at the expense of completely ignoring their skills, aptitudes, personalities, and, most of all, their passions. It's dangerous to make a career decision as an act of blind obedience to others, because job dissatisfaction can be life-sapping. And making a career switch requires a job search, which includes an honest self-assessment, a well-crafted pitch, and a solid grasp of the new job target. Psychologists have reported that when people work in professions that go against their natural abilities and personalities, they are under stress and can burn out quickly. Inevitably, many change careers after 5 to 10 years, or spend protracted lengths of time in these highly respectable professions with very little job satisfaction. When you are not happy in your job, you are going to be less effective with your clients, patients, and coworkers. Sooner or later, it will affect your morale on the job.

## AN IVY LEAGUE EDUCATION, STRAIGHT A'S—DING LETTERS

During her senior year in college, Laura Shin started to worry. It was the winter of 1990, a very difficult employment year for graduating seniors. The recession had started to hit many of the investment banks, consulting firms, and other large companies that had routinely recruited at her prestigious, large university on the East Coast. Laura had always been a straight-A student. She also sang in an a cappella group and was active in student government.

When it was finally campus recruiting season, she didn't progress in her job interviews. She'd studied economics and international relations in college, and her parents wondered what she would do with her degree. To them, if she wasn't bound for an M.D., J.D., Ph.D., or M.Eng., her future looked blurry. Though she'd started out as a premed major, Laura did some intense soul-searching in her second year of college and changed her major. She felt more drawn to business than to medicine or research. It was a good decision. As soon as she started taking courses in her new major, she was breezing through classes, actually enjoying them.

She got a lot of first-round interviews but was called back by only one of the companies. By April of her senior year, she had received rejection letters (so affectionately termed "ding letters" by her peers) from every one of her potential employers. To Laura, this was the failure of a lifetime, and a public failure at that. She felt that she'd let her family down.

But everything did work out well for her, thanks to her perseverance. After graduation, she continued to pound the pavement in search of the perfect job. After only a summer of active interviewing, she responded to an ad in the *Wall Street Journal* and was offered a position at a midsize market research company. She got great training and worked with some excellent managers who also served as her mentors. The company wasn't one of the high-profile banks or consulting firms that had gone to her campus to recruit, but the position gave her the experience she needed to move up in her field and achieve greater success.

## MAKING MUSIC

Paul Lee is a jazz musician with about 12 years of experience. He's well known in the entertainment community, but when he goes home to visit his parents, his mom continues to ask, "How are you doing? Do you need help with living expenses?" In her eyes, he hasn't truly made it because he didn't become a lawyer. Paul no longer takes her comments too seriously, but it used to be quite painful for him to acknowledge that his music career dishonored his parents.

## CHOOSING A CAREER TO FULFILL YOUR DREAMS, NOT YOUR PARENTS'

### A Top-Flight Banker Goes Dot-com Start-up

Tom Nam, now 30, had never been very academically inclined. A fun-loving, gregarious extrovert, he loved popular culture and good food and music, and he enjoyed life to the fullest. He always felt that having fun was important—sometimes more important than work. He did well in school, but he never liked studying and preferred

82 BREAKING the BAMBOO Ceiling

being out in the field, doing a team project in his management class, instead of reading a 500-page textbook or doing homework. Also, having grown up in the inner city of Chicago, he had developed a heart for giving back to the community. He saw his parents work 14-hour days, 6 days a week, at a self-service laundry, with no vacations, for 20 years. Though his parents spoke little English, they were very supportive of Tom's education and music lessons and never hesitated to send him to extra summer enrichment classes to get him into the right college.

After college, he started working for a commercial bank doing financial analysis. He liked the novelty of working in a highly elite professional environment, and he was always well liked, but he was never great with accounting principles and he was never as detail oriented as his role required him to be. Still, working in the bank was a respectable job, and because he assumed that he would be going for an MBA, he pressed on, working as hard as possible. After 4 years, he completed an Ivy League MBA program and landed a job with an investment banking firm, helping to execute corporate mergers and acquisitions.

Tom was fairly proficient as a first-year investment banking associate, but he knew that he didn't have the necessary killer drive. In the first few years of such jobs, analysts are expected to put together pitch books, conduct valuations of companies, review financial statements, and crunch numbers. Though he liked the idea of client contact and negotiating deals, his first year at the firm turned out to be 80% number crunching and quantitative analytical work supporting the senior bankers. He made deadlines and enjoyed great in-office camaraderie, but he never made the extra effort to network effectively with the senior people in his firm. He always felt that he'd been born to do something else for a living.

After his first year, his firm underwent a major downsizing— an across-the-board cut of 75% of employees. His job was one of those eliminated. As Tom searched his soul and assessed his skill set, he couldn't find the nerve to search for a new job in an industry for which he had no passion. He received numerous calls from recruiters who knew of other opportunities in similar fields. Friends offered to forward his résumé to their employers, but he couldn't go through the motions of doing work that was mediocre and not great. He wanted to change careers, but he faced a monumental conflict—his parents.

Tom's parents had initially wanted him to become a lawyer. They had always thought his verbal skills were outstanding and assumed that if he became a lawyer, he'd be set for life. They did not want him to struggle with the same issues that they struggled with as immigrants. Both his parents had been professionals in Asia: His mom was a pharmacist and his dad was a senior administrator for a hospital. When they arrived in the United States, however, it was difficult to find employment without having to go through the U.S. accreditation process and at the same time develop a full command of the English language. With two young children in tow (Tom was 5; his sister, 2), they had to produce income right away to survive. His parents' words echoed in his head: "We had to deal with too much discrimination and difficult times because we could not speak English well. You are great at speaking and you will never have to deal with the issues that we've had to encounter. You should do everything that your abilities allow you to do and make sure you are in a good, secure company. Being an attorney would fit you well." Though they fully supported his decision to pursue an MBA, Tom always sensed that they thought being in business was risky. But an MBA was an MBA, which made them happy for him.

After Tom completed some of the assessment exercises, one of them revealed unused abilities. As he filled out the Seven Stories Exercise (see pages 93–102), an assessment tool designed to uncover motivated skills, he realized that he had a special knack for working with young people. As we reviewed the results from the exercise, his previous stories repeatedly pointed to the situations when he had worked with youth. As a college student, he'd wanted to become a high school teacher of economics or history, possibly doing part-time soccer coaching, too. He thought that after 9 years of a secure, well-paying job, it was time that he follow his own career aspirations. During his years in banking, he always volunteered with his church and got involved with the Big Brothers Big Sisters program in Chicago. But now that he had to seriously consider changing careers, he could no longer deny his desire to work full time on his dream. At 30, he was ready to take steps toward his long-term goals.

He started taking courses to obtain his teaching certificate. Meanwhile, he became a substitute teacher for the local public high school. When he finally spoke to his parents about his intentions to change careers, they were surprisingly very excited for him. Recalls Tom: "I was so worried about what they would say. For years, I felt a subconscious pressure (though they never forced me to do anything) to become an attorney, a physician, an accountant (a CPA license counted for something, didn't it?)—as long as it was something that mattered in their eyes. I guess most of the pressure originated from me and my desire to please and honor my parents. I wanted to have them see that their hard work in a new country was worthwhile, so that they could feel a sense of satisfaction." But he realizes now that he was seeing his success through outdated Korean lenses.

His father says: "We were a little surprised that Tom decided to change careers. We knew he enjoyed working with kids and youth, but I always thought he would pursue it as a hobby or an extracurricular thing, not as a full-time job. We were concerned when he went into the business world, because it can be a volatile place. Having managed our own business, we know that it's not easy to make a living in this country. We faced a lot of prejudice and people not respecting us because of our bad English. It's always better for us as Asians to do something more stable, more secure.

"But Tom seemed to do well and thought he enjoyed it. When he got laid off, we were shocked. How could they let go of such a smart guy? We didn't know that you could lay off such a young person. Had he done something wrong? Had he stolen something? In Korea, you tend to have a job for a long time if you're hired from a top university into an elite training program. It's not common to see massive layoffs. We were not sure how he would recover from it.

But now we understand him more. Of course we want him to be happy. Now if we can only find a nice girl for him!"

Will some of the cross-cultural/cross-generational issues disappear after two or three new generations of Asian Americans enter the workforce? Perhaps. But I would venture to guess that they will be a concern for several more generations, owing to the deeply ingrained nature of cultural values passed from one generation to the next and to the continued influx of new Asian immigrants. Here is some anecdotal evidence: In almost every Asian Pacific American professional group that I address, I ask the participants how much they identify with their Asian background. Most of the participants—sometimes all—still identify quite strongly with their Asian culture. In one corporate seminar I facilitated where 75% of the participants were second-generation Asian Americans who speak only English, I asked these 15 participants to rate, on a scale of 1 to 10, how Asian they felt. The responses were astounding: All but one participant reported a number between 7 and 10. Furthermore, they shared that although they were quite assimilated, having grown up in homes where English was spoken, and they had many non-Asian friends, the majority of them still felt that their parents had raised them to follow many of the deeply rooted Asian traditions.

Moreover, newer Asian immigrants from a range of countries other than China, Japan, Korea, the Philippines, and India are now entering the United States in large numbers and are comprising a larger percentage of the U.S. Asian population. Projections from the 2000 census were that Asian Americans will make up approximately 8% of the U.S. population by 2040. Many grow up in Asian homes where they read Asian-language newspapers and speak an Asian language.

## OPENING THE DOORS TO FAMILY COMMUNICATION

You *can* engage parents in your career decisions and avoid potential conflicts:

- Include your parents in your career selection process as early as possible. If you don't know exactly where you are headed, you can plant the seeds to indicate your interest in varied paths, then later, when you fully develop your career targets, revisit the topic with them.
- Take the time to complete self-assessment exercises, including skills inventories, personality profiles, and values/affinities exercises. Then show your parents your results, relating the results to the profession you've selected. Solicit feedback from your parents.
- Involve your parents in your decision-making process by giving them examples of success stories for the career targets you have chosen, and be honest with them about your enthusiasm for the field.

### TAKING SELF-ASSESSMENT SERIOUSLY —

Vocation is one of the most important determinants of satisfaction in American society, which is highly focused on goal attainment, self-fulfillment, and individualism. When you can't pursue the role that you were born to play in society, you're not going to be productive.

Before you can decide on your career direction, step back and get acquainted with yourself. Self-awareness is critical for measuring emotional intelligence, according to Dan Goleman, author of *Working with Emotional Intelligence*. He cited a study by Boyatzis that found that accurate self-assessment is a hallmark of superior performance. Without an adequate, honest assessment of who you are, your values, and what you have to offer the world, you will find it virtually impossible to target the right career.

## MOVING INTO A FIELD IN WHICH ACADEMIC CREDENTIALS ARE LESS IMPORTANT

Susan Choi, a Korean American, is another career innovator. After earning master's degrees from Ivy League universities, she decided to work in advertising and public relations (PR), a field in which her degrees were not required. When first confronted with this transition, her parents were surprised that she wanted to leave academia for PR, a field that they knew nothing about. Susan had been pursuing a Ph.D., following her grandmother's career path, when she decided to change course. She got creative about convincing her parents that PR was an acceptable choice. "Instead of quitting my Ph.D. program outright, I took a one-year leave of absence to try my hand in a new career direction. Once my parents were able to see my progress in my new field, they became very supportive." She adds, "I looked at my personal skills and interests and determined what I felt I truly enjoyed doing—and it was writing, event planning, looking at creative ways to manage projects, coordinating promotional events. PR seemed like the perfect fit."

If you take the steps described here, the chances are great that you'll remain in your chosen career. If you're still trying to figure out what you want to do, go immediately to Chapter 5 ("To Thine Own Self Be True: Understanding Yourself, Your Vision, and How to Break Your Bamboo Ceiling") to do some self-assessment exercises. If you dread getting up on weekday mornings and the Sunday-night blues are getting unbearable, try a personality assessment with a career coach to determine your relating style. Get a step closer to achieving more fulfillment in your career. If you are completely thrilled with your career choices and have no interest in making a change, you may want to complete the Career Mobility Checklist (see page 134) to determine if you are someone your company will promote or someone who is not highly regarded. After all, you should never be complacent about your position. As you discover yourself and where you would like to take your career, don't neglect repeated self-assessment; it may be the most important action that you take.

## KEY LESSONS

■ *Take a long, honest look at your career.*
Are you satisfied with what you're doing? If not, determine why not. Come up with a plan.

■ *Be self-aware.*
If you do not know what to pursue or how to go about changing your career, use the assessment tools in the next chapter—they may change your life.

■ *Involve your parents as soon as possible in the career decision-making process.*
This could also include a decision to change careers. Don't alienate them, even if you do not agree with their line of thinking. Explain to them the reasons for your career decisions. The more they are brought into the process, even if they are not 100% on board, the better off you will be in the long run. I can't guarantee that all parents will become supportive of their adult children's career goals overnight, but it is possible to change careers without alienating parents.

■ *Do an accurate self-assessment with a career coach to determine your skills, interests, and competencies.*
Once in a while, it's helpful to have an objective party help you assess your skills, develop a plan, and keep you on course. Some people decide to do a career checkup once a year to keep their career on course over the long term.

■ *Don't pigeonhole yourself into one or two acceptable careers.*
Expand the range of possibilities and investigate careers that interest you during this exploration phase. Explore career disciplines that are differ-

ent from what you consider acceptable for an Asian American. The important thing here is to try out things risk free in different, safe environments first, before jumping into a major career change. For example, if you have always wanted to try marketing and you have the right drive and skill set, try getting involved in marketing the youth organization where you volunteer once a month. Set up the group's marketing program or help revamp marketing efforts. Then, when you feel confident about making the leap, you can speak with authority on some of these matters.

## A CHALLENGE TO CAREER COUNSELORS, COACHES, AND MANAGERS

If you are a career counselor or coach, you need to remember that Asian students and professionals may have difficulty deciding on a vocation. Even when all of the assessment exercises, personality tests, and skills inventories clearly point to certain career paths, these clients may struggle with internal conflicts. Therefore you may want to use these techniques:

- Encourage clients to explore career choices with their family, bringing up potential issues with them as early as possible.
- If you suspect that your client's family could be causing career indecision or refusal to leave a career your client is unhappy with, ask the client what his or her family thinks of the client's occupation and then review the responses carefully.
- Encourage your Asian client to try out his new career interest or vocation risk free, by volunteering for an industry association, taking on a project within his company (if the function exists within the company), or even joining the board of a nonprofit group whose mission he believes in. This will allow him to demonstrate that he can indeed be

competent in the new industry or job function, without risking financial stability or job security. He will also gain confidence.

## Envisioning Your Career Future —

The road to discovering your natural gifts, affinities, and dislikes can be a wonderful journey, one you can enjoy for many years to come. If you find yourself in a career that isn't satisfying, it's never too late to make a change. Gone are the days of lifetime employment, when a person could retire after 30 years at the same company and expect a pension, a gold watch, and life-long health care benefits. Most managers today won't penalize you because you've changed companies or taken an entirely different direction. But you do need to clearly articulate to your potential employers *why* you are making the change. Your risk taking will be rewarded in the long term. Nowadays, if you stay in a job for too long, you may be considered outdated and your skills may not be as marketable.

If you're making a career change and aren't getting the encouragement from your parents, you may need to seek other sources of support. Develop a new network of friends, mentors, and fellow job hunters.

As you manage your career, keep an eye out for industries of the future that are poised for aggressive growth. You must always be aware of market conditions both inside and outside of the company you currently work for and often reassess what you have to offer. As you continue to move up and refine your expertise, always ask yourself what new skills you need to develop.

# FIVE

# To Thine Own Self Be True: Understanding Yourself, Your Vision, and How to Break Your Bamboo Ceiling

*This above all: to thine own self be true,*
*And it must follow, as the night the day,*
*Thou canst not then be false to any man.*

—William Shakespeare, *Hamlet,* act I, scene iii

In order to break through your bamboo ceiling, you must first take the time to fully understand yourself—your skills, motivators, cultural assets, and limits—as well as your vision of your ideal life goals. Self-assessment is one of the most important tools that can help you achieve this understanding as you get your first job, change career direction, attempt to manage work relationships, or relate to your clients. Given that the average American today may have four to five careers in his or her lifetime, it's best to know yourself as soon as possible. Whether you are undergoing a major career change or trying to figure out how to best work with your new boss, you should critically analyze what assets you have to offer before you take action. This hands-on chapter introduces you to a wide array of assessment tools for your career development. Such tools give you the freedom to explore your options without restrictions and allow you to have some fun. Others, like the Seven Stories Exercise, are very practical, grounded in your personal experience, and allow you to use your previous life experiences to identify skills that can be used in your future jobs. I highly recommend that you complete, at a minimum, the Seven Stories Exercise (pages 93–102), the Forty-Year Vision (pages 117–31), and Identifying Your Bamboo Ceiling (pages 132–34).

Assessment is the most commonly ignored step by job hunters, yet it is the true foundation for (1) a productive job search closely aligned with long-term personal and professional goals and (2) the development of a realistic strategy for career advancement.

Unfortunately, very few clients take self-assessment seriously, and many undergraduate schools don't require that students complete in-depth assessment exercises to be eligible for their on-campus recruiting programs. Most get some résumé coaching from a career counselor and then proceed to look for a job through Internet searches or with the help of headhunters. Some people looking for another job often find themselves in such a hurry to keep money coming in that they never do what it takes to find out what would really make them happy. There is nothing worse than being in a job that you hate because you're not cut out for it. If you're in a financially rewarding profession, you may find it increasingly difficult to leave it behind to pursue your true aspirations. However, since declining morale almost always leads to burnout, depression, and poor job performance, you are doing your employer and, most important, yourself a disservice by remaining where you are unhappy.

During one small group career coaching session at a charity organization, a young woman joined our workshop, which was well under way, and demanded that I refer her to some top headhunters in her field of retail management. When I suggested that she introduce herself to the group so that we could understand her job search targets better, she said, "The targets and assessment stuff would be all fine and good if I had the luxury of time, but I am the sole breadwinner of my family, and I need to find employment ASAP. Let's just jump to the search part and focus on fixing up my résumé so I can fax it to the executive recruiter." When I told her that we needed to first understand her top two or three job targets, she left the meeting in a huff and I did not hear from her again for 4 months. Through a mutual contact, I learned that she had found a job shortly after her visit to the workshop but within 2 months had lost her job because of a merger with a larger retail firm; her position had become redundant. Moreover, she had received a meager severance package because of her lack of tenure. About a week later, she called me to inquire about personality assessment and skills inventories. She wanted to learn how to do the job search properly. Three months after I helped her complete them, she found a senior management position at one of her primary target companies.

## Understanding Yourself

TOOL # 1

### THE SEVEN STORIES EXERCISE®: DISCOVERING YOUR MOTIVATED SKILLS

When deciding on the right vocation to enter, it is important that you have a strong understanding of your skills and the environment and manner in which you like to work. Whatever you do, *do not* skip the Seven Stories Exercise. Most career coaches conduct some type of skills assessment with their clients, and many of them resemble the Seven Stories Exercise. A skills assessment tool developed by Kate Wendleton at the Five O'Clock Club, it aims to determine your motivated skills. Motivated skills are those that you are adept at and enjoy doing. Hence, knowing your motivated skills should help you know what will make you happy in your career.

*(continued)*

If you are really skilled in accounting and finance but don't enjoy it, then accounting is not one of your motivated skills.

Although many report that they add to their inventory of motivated skills as they grow older, the majority of motivated skills remain constant, and therefore, the Seven Stories Exercise can be a reliable tool that allows you to identify the common threads throughout your life experiences. This type of skills exercise is based on your real-life experiences and therefore is hard proof that you have used these skills before. Analyzing these results together with other assessments can help you develop your targets.

In addition, as you discover your motivated skills, you will be better able to identify jobs, positions, and projects that allow you to use your motivated skills. Most people who aren't using these skills on the job already find ways to use them in other aspects of their lives. If you could integrate them into your job, your entire day would be much more enjoyable.

To get started, reflect on your past. Think through the moments in your life where you felt that what you were doing was what you were created to do. You were good at the tasks required to accomplish the project. Even if it takes you two or three sittings to complete the exercise, take the time to do so. It will be well worth your effort. Analyze each story with a fine-toothed comb, paying special attention to why you enjoyed performing the task.

## THE SEVEN STORIES EXERCISE —

Write down examples of 15 to 20 different experiences that met the following criteria:

- You were good at it.
- You enjoyed the experience.
- You obtained a sense of accomplishment from it.

Feel free to draw on a variety of past experiences; but make sure to *include at least two or three examples from work-related situations.* Try to pick a variety of experiences from every stage of your life (elementary school years, high school years, college years, early working years, most recent employer, volunteer experiences).

Be specific: You were able to sell your boss on a great marketing idea; in high school you were a vital part of the debating team's efforts to win the district championship; at work you received accolades because you skillfully managed the data review project for the system conversion.

1. _____
2. _____
3. _____
4. _____
5. _____
6. _____
7. _____

*(continued)*

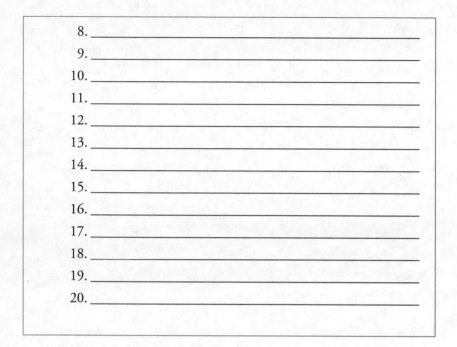

Next, select seven of the experiences that were the most important to you. Prioritize them from 1 to 7. For each, write down a short synopsis of the experience, following the guidelines below.

---

STORY 1 ANALYSIS

1. What role did you play in the story?

   _____

   _____

2. What type of environment were you in (corporate, academic, etc.)?

   _____

   _____

3. Who were the others involved in the story? Did you do it alone or with others?

   _____

   _____

4. What made you good at what you did? What skills did you use in your story?

   _____

   _____

---

Complete a similar analysis of the next six stories on extra sheets of paper, then, using the Seven Stories Exercise Skills Matrix, check off the applicable skills found in each story.

# THE SEVEN STORIES EXERCISE SKILLS MATRIX

| STORY # | 1 | 2 | 3 | 4 | 5 | 6 | 7 | TOTAL |
|---|---|---|---|---|---|---|---|---|
| Administration | | | | | | | | |
| Advising/consulting | | | | | | | | |
| Analytical skills—qualitative data | | | | | | | | |
| Analytical skills—quantitative data | | | | | | | | |
| Artistic ability | | | | | | | | |
| Budgetary skills | | | | | | | | |
| Client relations | | | | | | | | |
| Coaching skills | | | | | | | | |
| Communication | | | | | | | | |
| Community relations | | | | | | | | |
| Computer/technical skills | | | | | | | | |
| Conflict resolution | | | | | | | | |
| Contract negotiation | | | | | | | | |
| Control | | | | | | | | |
| Coordination of projects/tasks | | | | | | | | |
| Counseling skills | | | | | | | | |
| Creativity | | | | | | | | |
| Crisis management | | | | | | | | |
| Decisiveness | | | | | | | | |

| STORY # | 1 | 2 | 3 | 4 | 5 | 6 | 7 | TOTAL |
|---|---|---|---|---|---|---|---|---|
| Design | | | | | | | | |
| Detail orientation | | | | | | | | |
| Discipline | | | | | | | | |
| Facilitation skills | | | | | | | | |
| Financial skills | | | | | | | | |
| Flexibility | | | | | | | | |
| Focus | | | | | | | | |
| Foresight | | | | | | | | |
| Frugality | | | | | | | | |
| Fund-raising | | | | | | | | |
| Human relations | | | | | | | | |
| Imagination | | | | | | | | |
| Individualism | | | | | | | | |
| Influence skills | | | | | | | | |
| Information/systems management | | | | | | | | |
| Initiative | | | | | | | | |
| Inventiveness | | | | | | | | |
| Leadership | | | | | | | | |
| Liaison skills | | | | | | | | |

*(continued)*

# THE SEVEN STORIES EXERCISE SKILLS MATRIX
## (CONTINUED)

| STORY # | 1 | 2 | 3 | 4 | 5 | 6 | 7 | TOTAL |
|---|---|---|---|---|---|---|---|---|
| Logic | | | | | | | | |
| Management | | | | | | | | |
| Marketing | | | | | | | | |
| Mathematical skills | | | | | | | | |
| Mechanical skills/dexterity | | | | | | | | |
| Mentoring | | | | | | | | |
| Motivational skills | | | | | | | | |
| Negotiating skills | | | | | | | | |
| Observation | | | | | | | | |
| Operations management | | | | | | | | |
| Organization | | | | | | | | |
| Organizational design/development | | | | | | | | |
| Ownership | | | | | | | | |
| Perceptiveness | | | | | | | | |
| Perseverance | | | | | | | | |
| Persuasiveness | | | | | | | | |
| Planning | | | | | | | | |
| Policy making | | | | | | | | |
| Practicality | | | | | | | | |

| STORY # | 1 | 2 | 3 | 4 | 5 | 6 | 7 | TOTAL |
|---|---|---|---|---|---|---|---|---|
| Presentation skills | | | | | | | | |
| Problem solving | | | | | | | | |
| Procedural design | | | | | | | | |
| Program concept | | | | | | | | |
| Program design | | | | | | | | |
| Project management | | | | | | | | |
| Promotion | | | | | | | | |
| Public relations | | | | | | | | |
| Public speaking | | | | | | | | |
| Quality assessment | | | | | | | | |
| Research | | | | | | | | |
| Resourcefulness | | | | | | | | |
| Sales ability | | | | | | | | |
| Showmanship | | | | | | | | |
| Speaking/talking skills | | | | | | | | |
| Staff development/ people management | | | | | | | | |
| Strategic planning | | | | | | | | |
| Stress tolerance | | | | | | | | |
| Teaching/training | | | | | | | | |

*(continued)*

# THE SEVEN STORIES EXERCISE SKILLS MATRIX
## (CONTINUED)

| STORY # | 1 | 2 | 3 | 4 | 5 | 6 | 7 | TOTAL |
|---|---|---|---|---|---|---|---|---|
| Teamwork | | | | | | | | |
| Tenacity | | | | | | | | |
| Travel | | | | | | | | |
| Troubleshooting | | | | | | | | |
| Writing | | | | | | | | |
| Other skill: _____ | | | | | | | | |
| Other skill: _____ | | | | | | | | |
| Other skill: _____ | | | | | | | | |

**TOP SIX OR SEVEN SPECIALIZED SKILLS ACCORDING TO WHICH HAD THE MOST CHECK MARKS:**

1. _____
2. _____
3. _____
4. _____
5. _____
6. _____
7. _____

# Understanding Your Asian Identity

TOOL #2

## ASIAN IDENTITY EXERCISE:
## HOW ASSIMILATED/ACCULTURATED ARE YOU?

Your family upbringing and early childhood experiences can play a significant role in how you think, behave, and perceive others in the workplace. You could be an immigrant who feels very comfortable operating in Western culture because of the way that you were raised. Or you could be a second- or third-generation Asian American whose identity is primarily Asian, whose most intimate friends and most people in a personal network are Asian. Aside from understanding your skills, work-related motivators, and long-term goals, how Asian do you feel? To make the process easier, use the list of descriptions that follow to help you gauge your identification with the Asian culture. Far from being a precise measure, it is another tool to assist you in understanding yourself better and can provide a basis for some insightful dialogue with your family, friends, and work colleagues.

Below the questions you will find the four quadrants of assimilation, originally developed by psychologists Harry Kitano and Roger Daniels and adapted by Jeannette Yep of InterVarsity Christian Fellowship/USA. Used by psychologists to identify challenges faced by immigrant Asian clients, it can help you understand how assimilated you are to the mainstream American culture.

As you read the descriptors found in the four quadrants, you may find that you identify with more than one quadrant. The fact is that you may have moved through the different quadrants during the course of your life. If you immigrated to the United States at a young age, you might have once been in cell D (low assimilation, high ethnic identity) but during high school moved into cell A (high assimilation, low ethnic identity) and eventually into cell B (high assimilation, high ethnic identity) as a working professional.

Can you identify with the behaviors listed below? Select *Agree,*
*Somewhat agree,* or *Disagree* for each statement. This exercise is not a
true psychological assessment tool designed to measure how Asian
you are, but it will help you understand how you may or may not
demonstrate culturally Asian behaviors in your work and personal
life. After you answer the questions, you should ask a work colleague
to answer on your behalf the questions found in the "Work Life" section and a trusted friend to answer on your behalf the questions
found in the "General" section.

GENERAL

I have a strong affinity for my cultural heritage and hold
strongly to Asian values.

        Agree      Somewhat agree      Disagree

I speak a language other than English at home.

        Agree      Somewhat agree      Disagree

I read Asian newspapers, books, or magazines.

        Agree      Somewhat agree      Disagree

I celebrate Asian holidays (Lunar New Year, Diwali, and so on)
in addition to mainstream holidays such as the Fourth of July,
Christmas, and Thanksgiving.

        Agree      Somewhat agree      Disagree

I feel more comfortable with Asians.

        Agree      Somewhat agree      Disagree

My parents play a strong role in my career decisions.

        Agree      Somewhat agree      Disagree

I prefer to socialize with other Asians during nonwork hours.

        Agree      Somewhat agree      Disagree

*(continued)*

## WORK LIFE

I have a hard time standing up to my boss or others in higher positions when I have too much work on my plate or challenging her on an issue because of her position of authority.

Agree        Somewhat agree        Disagree

When I need to make a decision, I tend to check for agreement/consensus with my team/group before making the final call.        Agree        Somewhat agree        Disagree

I am very open about my cultural heritage with my boss, clients, and coworkers.

Agree        Somewhat agree        Disagree

I feel comfortable being myself in the workplace.

Agree        Somewhat agree        Disagree

In large town hall meeting settings, I hesitate to ask a question or state a different opinion, as a gesture of respect for the keynote speaker.

Agree        Somewhat agree        Disagree

## SOCIAL LIFE

I dislike conflict and work hard to make things harmonious.

Agree        Somewhat agree        Disagree

I am more formal when meeting new people/approaching new social situations.

Agree        Somewhat agree        Disagree

It takes me a long time to feel comfortable opening up about my personal life.

Agree        Somewhat agree        Disagree

I have a strong sense of respect for people who are older than me.        Agree        Somewhat agree        Disagree

## ASIAN-AMERICAN IDENTITY

Used with permission from Roger Daniels, University of Cincinnati, co-author with Harry Kitano of *Asian Americans: Emerging Minorities,* Third Edition, and Jeannette Yep, vice president of Multiethnic Ministries at InterVarsity Christian Fellowship/ USA.

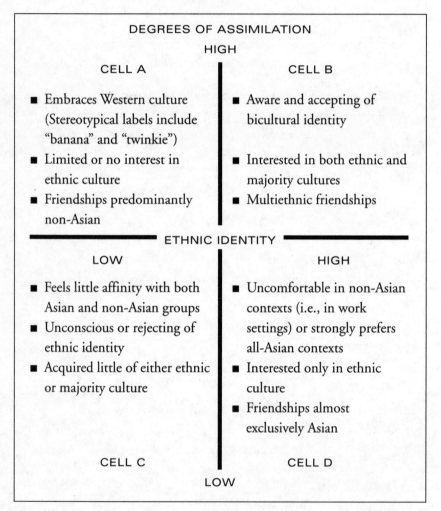

DEGREES OF ASSIMILATION

HIGH

| CELL A | CELL B |
|---|---|
| ■ Embraces Western culture (Stereotypical labels include "banana" and "twinkie")<br>■ Limited or no interest in ethnic culture<br>■ Friendships predominantly non-Asian | ■ Aware and accepting of bicultural identity<br>■ Interested in both ethnic and majority cultures<br>■ Multiethnic friendships |

ETHNIC IDENTITY

| LOW | HIGH |
|---|---|
| ■ Feels little affinity with both Asian and non-Asian groups<br>■ Unconscious or rejecting of ethnic identity<br>■ Acquired little of either ethnic or majority culture | ■ Uncomfortable in non-Asian contexts (i.e., in work settings) or strongly prefers all-Asian contexts<br>■ Interested only in ethnic culture<br>■ Friendships almost exclusively Asian |
| CELL C | CELL D |

LOW

TOOL #3

# WORK-RELATED VALUES AND MOTIVATORS EXERCISE

## VALUES AND PERSONAL INTERESTS

1 = Not at all important in choice of job    3 = Reasonably important

2 = Not very but somewhat important    4 = Very important

\_\_\_\_ Opportunity for promotion

\_\_\_\_ Personal growth

\_\_\_\_ Inclusive work environment

\_\_\_\_ Working on cutting edge of knowledge/technology

\_\_\_\_ Having authority/responsibility

\_\_\_\_ Being an expert

\_\_\_\_ Competition

\_\_\_\_ Helping others

\_\_\_\_ Helping society

\_\_\_\_ Recognition (from loved ones, clients, peers, superiors, etc.)

\_\_\_\_ Enjoyable colleagues

\_\_\_\_ Enjoyable work tasks

\_\_\_\_ Ease (no worries)

\_\_\_\_ The satisfaction of doing a good job

\_\_\_\_ Self-actualization

\_\_\_\_ Amount of money earned

\_\_\_\_ Having time for personal life

\_\_\_\_ Power/influence

\_\_\_\_ Risk taking/adventure

\_\_\_\_ Recognition from superiors/peers

\_\_\_\_ Security/stability

\_\_\_\_ Artistic/other creativity

\_\_\_\_ Autonomy

\_\_\_\_ Contributing to a winning team

What are your top three work-related motivators?

_____    _____    _____

## THE TRUSTED ADVISOR ASSESSMENT

If you want to advance in your field, it is important that you understand how others perceive you. It may be a little painful if you are not used to getting constructive feedback from others, but obtaining constant feedback from those who know your work, your relating style, and your blind spots is absolutely essential for you to be effective in today's multicultural workplace. Dan Goleman notes in *Working with Emotional Intelligence* that true constructive feedback about how we are doing is among the more difficult kinds of information to get in organizational life: "Coworkers, subordinates, and bosses have an easier time complaining to each other out of earshot of a person than having an honest and open talk with that person about what's wrong." Furthermore, if the employee is a professional of color, the manager may be more likely to hesitate before approaching him about performance. One HR director at a consumer goods company says, "One of our business managers, who happens to be white, has two Asian employees and one African American employee on his team. He told me that he feels overly concerned about offending his employees about their backgrounds. He didn't want to bring up sensitive issues that might cause conflict or dissension in the group. But by not doing so, he was unable to give his professionals of color an opportunity to honestly assess their blind spots as they performed their work. He walked on eggshells around them. If he could have only learned how to bring up these issues during the course of natural conversation! Meanwhile, his subordinates sensed his discomfort and translated it as animosity or lack of interest."

Given people's natural propensity to shy away from giving honest feedback, it would be helpful for you to get in the habit of soliciting it from others especially after important transactions, deals, and projects are completed. In politically charged or otherwise sensitive circumstances, your HR department may provide you with an internal career advisor or an executive coach to interview your colleagues from a third perspective. But it's always most beneficial for all parties if you can get direct feedback.

To complete the Trusted Advisor Assessment, select one or two people at your company, perhaps a level or two above you, who know your work intimately and know you relatively well on a personal level. Ask them to answer the following questions about you and then ask them for informal, ad hoc feedback throughout the year. They can also be mentors who know your work very well and can give honest feedback. You may also want to include in your list other Asian professionals who understand how your culture may affect your behavior (parents, friends, relatives, siblings, Asian mentors). Here is a sample script that you can use:

> Dear [insert colleague's name here] _____:
> I am interested in obtaining feedback from you about my professional behavior and skills. I am using this tool to [select one that matches your objective] (1) understand my strengths and weaknesses as a manager; (2) assess how I am perceived by others who work closely with me; (3) determine what careers might be appropriate for my skills, personality, and experience; (4) create a practical development plan for my current role at my company. Please be as candid as you feel comfortable with being. You can rest assured that your responses will be held in the strictest of confidence. Thank you in advance for participating in this important exercise.
>
> Best regards,<br>_____ [your name]

Soliciting such honest feedback may be more difficult for Asian Americans, but obtaining external feedback is critical to measuring one's performance, and it should not be neglected.

Note: It is strongly encouraged that you have a face-to-face meeting with your trusted advisor(s) shortly after the completion of the assessment.

**QUESTIONS**

1. Technical/product/systems skills:

_____

_____

_____

2. Interpersonal skills (assertiveness, articulation, oral/written communication, conflict management, personal style, flexibility, and ability to deal with ambiguity):

_____

_____

_____

3. Area(s) of development (leadership, functional skills):

_____

_____

_____

4. Area of specialty—"trademark value":

What do others remember most about me? If I were to ask you what value I bring to your team, what would that trademark value be? My greatest contribution? What two adjectives would you use to describe me?

_____

_____

_____

5. Personal strengths and areas of development that may be linked to cultural traits (be specific):

_____

_____

_____

6. Organizational/project management skills/ability to get things done:

_____

_____

_____

7. Suggestions for development, skills required, etc.:

_____

_____

_____

8. Summary statement (describe me using two or three adjectives, and please identify one specific area that would help me become more effective in my professional life; please be as specific as possible):

_____

_____

_____

9. Required technical skills for my job/product knowledge:

_____

_____

_____

*(continued)*

10. Interpersonal skills (please give details):

Strong ability to assess situation and work with ambiguity:

_____

_____


People management skills/interpersonal acumen (please rank each
from 1 [demonstrates very little of this skill] to 5 [this is one of my
strongest abilities], and elaborate with an example of each):

_____ Can advise others/lead and influence others: _____

_____ Can resolve conflicts easily: _____

_____ Knows how to deal with different personalities:_____

_____ Influences and motivates others: _____

_____ Good at networking:_____

Strong communication skills (please rank each from 1 to 5, and elaborate with an example of each):

_____ Large group presentations: _____

_____ Gifted storyteller and conversationalist:_____

_____ Good meeting facilitator: _____

_____ Conflict resolution skills: _____

_____ Strong writing skills that clearly deliver intended message:

_____

## THE MYERS-BRIGGS TYPE INDICATOR AND
## USING IT IN CAREER PLANNING —

The Myers-Briggs Type Indicator (MBTI) is the most well researched and widely known personality style indicator. For more than 50 years, the MBTI inventory has been used throughout the world to help individuals gain a deeper understanding of themselves and how they relate with others. With this knowledge, you can use the tool to improve relationships with people at work, decide on your career direction, and maximize your understanding of yourself. Once you have determined your personality type, you can determine if your cultural lenses make certain aspects of your personality demonstrate themselves in different ways. The MBTI tool helps you determine what you are like in your most natural state; it also allows you to understand how you are energized, how you interact with the world, how you make decisions, and how you gather information. It is important for people to assess these skills to know that it is an indicator of preferences, not skill, mental health, or intelligence. Hence, people from all personality types can have satisfying careers in all disciplines. For further information about the 16 MBTI types and to take the exercise, you can go to the Crossroads Web site (www.breakingthebambooceiling.com) or contact the Association for Psychological Type (www.aptinternational.org) to find a certified MBTI coach near you.

"When I used to work in a large company, I really valued the money I earned and the title that I held. After I had two kids, it was less about how much income I brought in and more about doing enjoyable tasks and having time to spend with my family," says Sue Chang, 34. Some people must work with people they respect. Others must make a certain level of income before they can find a job satisfying. Others make innovation and being on the cutting edge of knowledge a top priority when making their career decisions. Still others must be in a field that allows for working alone. It is common for work-related motivators to change over time, especially as your personal priorities shift throughout the seasons of your life.

What are the things that are important to you in *your* work?

TOOL #5

# AUTHORITY AND HIERARCHY EXERCISE: A VIEW OF YOUR RELATIONSHIPS WITH BOSSES, PEERS, AND SUBORDINATES

## BOSSES

1. Make a list of all the bosses you have ever had in work situations. Include supervisors, project managers, internship managers, professors, mentors, or any others who were in positions of authority. Clearly state names and roles.

NAME                                        POSITION/ROLE

_____          _____

_____          _____

_____          _____

_____          _____

_____          _____

_____          _____

_____          _____

2. Now divide the names from above into three lists: those with whom you had no problems in the working relationship, those with whom you had some problems, and those with whom you had severe problems.

NO PROBLEMS          SOME PROBLEMS          SEVERE PROBLEMS

_____          _____          _____

_____          _____          _____

_____          _____          _____

_____          _____          _____

3. Finally, think about the bosses with whom you had some
   or severe problems. As you think about why you may have
   had problems with them, consider things such as age,
   gender, prejudice, their title/position in the organization,
   and personality.

- Do you see patterns regarding the type of people? Regarding
  the structure of the relationship?
- Do you find it difficult to establish good working relationships with people who are in positions of authority?
- What is it like to work with bosses who are significantly
  older than you?
- Do you see patterns regarding the context? Size of the
  project? Company size?

## PEERS AND SUBORDINATES

1. Make a list of all the peers and subordinates you have ever
   had in work situations. Include subordinates, protégés, and
   team members who worked with you. Clearly state names
   and roles.

NAME

POSITION/ROLE

_____      _____

_____      _____

_____      _____

_____      _____

_____      _____

_____      _____

_____      _____

*(continued)*

2. Now divide the names from above into three lists: those
   with whom you had no problems in the working relationship, those with whom you had some problems, and those
   with whom you had severe problems.

NO PROBLEMS                SOME PROBLEMS              SEVERE PROBLEMS

_____            _____           _____

_____            _____           _____

_____            _____           _____

_____            _____           _____

3. Finally, think about the peers and subordinates with whom
   you had some or severe problems. As you think about why
   you may have had problems with them, consider things
   such as age, gender, prejudice, their title/position in the
   organization, and personality.

■ Do you see patterns regarding the type of people? Regarding
  the structure of the relationship?
■ Do you find it difficult to establish good working relationships with certain people?
■ Do you find it easier or more difficult to work with subordinates, protégés, or team members who are younger than you?
■ Do you see patterns regarding the context? Size of the
  project? Company size?

## Understanding Your Vision

It is difficult to plan your future when you can't even see beyond your next
paycheck! Yet if you don't have a deliberate, thoughtfully crafted life and
career plan, you may move from company to company, ultimately making
career decisions that may take you off your career path. You may find your-

self in 15 years wondering how you stayed in your company so long! Stephen Lee, 35, a Chinese American CPA who works in a large accounting firm, recounts, "There was a time in my early years at my company when I knew that it would be a good strategic move for me to go to a smaller company to get more breadth of management experience. Yet I was getting salary increases every year, and a few years ago, we had our first daughter, and my wife decided to stay home. This meant that I needed more stability, and I had trouble making the move when I could have. If I had done the Forty-Year Vision exercise earlier in my career, I would have known that I should have made the move at that time, to put me in position to take on a different role this year."

## TOOL #6

# THE FORTY-YEAR VISION®

This exercise has been reprinted with the permission of Kate Wendleton, the Five O'Clock Club, Inc. All rights reserved.

*Where there is no vision, the people perish.*

—**Proverbs 29:18a (Bible, King James Version)**

The Forty-Year Vision, a future-oriented life-planning exercise, provides a simplified way to help you cast a long-term vision for yourself in manageable 5-year increments. If you have a hard time envisioning the future, try doing the exercise on vacation, when you can more easily reflect on what you would like to accomplish in life. Once you have completed the Forty-Year Vision exercise and the Seven Stories Exercise, a career coach can help you fit your career strategy into your life plan. An external perspective is extremely important in helping you obtain an objective view of yourself. Moreover, an effective coach can help you through the critical junctures of your job search process and identify any roadblocks to your mobility.

Now that you have assessed your motivated skills, it's time to focus on your career future!

Think about how your life could be 5 years from now. Would you have different friends and/or colleagues? Different hobbies and interests? Children? How about in 10 years? In 15 years? You may be in business for yourself, or in a senior management position at a different company, or in a completely different occupation. Life looks very different, right? The best way to get started on planning for your next job is to think about where you see yourself going. Take 5 years at a time, and if you find that you are really struggling with the 40-year concept, attempt to envision at least 20 years from now. Many things can happen to you over the next few decades, and lots of them are up to you. Enjoy the journey!

1. THE YEAR IS _____ (CURRENT YEAR). YOU ARE _____ YEARS OLD NOW.

What is your life like now?

_____
_____
_____

Who are your friends? Name your closest friends.

_____
_____
_____

What do these friends do for a living?

_____
_____
_____

Are you married? ____ Single? ____ Children? ____ List the ages of your children.

_____

Where are you living?

_____

What are your hobbies and interests?

_____

What languages do you speak?

_____

What do you do for exercise?

_____

How is your health?

_____

How do you take care of your spiritual needs?

_____

What kind of work are you doing? What level (entry level, middle management, senior executive, CEO)? Are you self-employed?

_____

_____

_____

Don't worry if you don't like everything in your life right now. The point of this exercise is to determine what you want to change about your life in the years to come. Please continue.

*(continued)*

**2. THE YEAR IS _____ (CURRENT YEAR + 5). YOU ARE _____ YEARS OLD NOW.**

What is your life like now?

_____

_____

_____

Who are your friends? Name your closest friends.

_____

_____

_____

What do these friends do for a living?

_____

_____

_____

Are you married? \_\_\_ Single? \_\_\_ Children? \_\_\_ List the ages of your children. _____

Where are you living?

_____

What are your hobbies and interests?

_____

What languages do you speak?

_____

What do you do for exercise?

_____

How is your health?

_____

How do you take care of your spiritual needs?

_____

What kind of work are you doing? What level (entry level, middle management, senior executive, CEO)? Are you self-employed?

_____
_____
_____

3. THE YEAR IS _____ (CURRENT YEAR + 10). YOU ARE _____ YEARS OLD NOW.

What is your life like now?

_____
_____
_____

Who are your friends? Name your closest friends.

_____
_____
_____

What do these friends do for a living?

_____
_____
_____

*(continued)*

Are you married? ___ Single? ___ Children? ___ List the ages of your children. _____

Where are you living?

_____

What are your hobbies and interests?

_____

What languages do you speak?

_____

What do you do for exercise?

_____

How is your health?

_____

How do you take care of your spiritual needs?

_____

What kind of work are you doing? What level (entry level, middle management, senior executive, CEO)? Are you self-employed?

_____

_____

_____

4. THE YEAR IS _____ (CURRENT YEAR + 15). YOU ARE
_____ YEARS OLD NOW.

What is your life like now?

_____

_____

_____

Who are your friends? Name your closest friends.

_____

_____

_____

What do these friends do for a living?

_____

_____

_____

Are you married? ___ Single? ___ Children? ___ List the ages of your
children. _____

Where are you living?

_____

What are your hobbies and interests?

_____

What languages do you speak?

_____

*(continued)*

What do you do for exercise?

_____

How is your health?

_____

How do you take care of your spiritual needs?

_____

What kind of work are you doing? What level (entry level, middle management, senior executive, CEO)? Are you self-employed?

_____

_____

_____

5. THE YEAR IS _____ (CURRENT YEAR + 20). YOU ARE _____ YEARS OLD NOW.

What is your life like now?

_____

_____

_____

Who are your friends? Name your closest friends.

_____

_____

_____

What do these friends do for a living?

_____

_____

_____

Are you married? ___ Single? ___ Children? ___ List the ages of your children. _____

Where are you living?

_____

What are your hobbies and interests?

_____

What languages do you speak?

_____

What do you do for exercise?

_____

How is your health?

_____

How do you take care of your spiritual needs?

_____

What kind of work are you doing? What level (entry level, middle management, senior executive, CEO)? Are you self-employed?

_____

_____

_____

*(continued)*

6. THE YEAR IS _____ (CURRENT YEAR + 25). YOU ARE
_____ YEARS OLD NOW.

What is your life like now?

_____

_____

_____

Who are your friends? Name your closest friends.

_____

_____

_____

What do these friends do for a living?

_____

_____

_____

Are you married? ____ Single? ____ Children? ____ List the ages of your
children. _____

Where are you living?

_____

What are your hobbies and interests?

_____

What languages do you speak?

_____

What do you do for exercise?

_____

How is your health?

_____

How do you take care of your spiritual needs?

_____

What kind of work are you doing? What level (entry level, middle management, senior executive, CEO)? Are you self-employed?

_____

_____

_____

7. THE YEAR IS _____ (CURRENT YEAR + 30). YOU ARE _____ YEARS OLD NOW.

What is your life like now?

_____

_____

_____

Who are your friends? Name your closest friends.

_____

_____

_____

*(continued)*

What do these friends do for a living?

_____

_____

_____

Are you married? ____ Single? ____ Children? ____ List the ages of your children. _____

Where are you living?

_____

What are your hobbies and interests?

_____

What languages do you speak?

_____

What do you do for exercise?

_____

How is your health?

_____

How do you take care of your spiritual needs?

_____

What kind of work are you doing? What level (entry level, middle management, senior executive, CEO)? Are you self-employed?

_____

_____

_____

8. THE YEAR IS _____ (CURRENT YEAR + 35). YOU ARE
_____ YEARS OLD NOW.

What is your life like now?

_____
_____
_____

Who are your friends? Name your closest friends.

_____
_____
_____

What do these friends do for a living?

_____
_____
_____

Are you married? \_\_\_ Single? \_\_\_ Children? \_\_\_ List the ages of your
children. _____

Where are you living?

_____

What are your hobbies and interests?

_____

What languages do you speak?

_____

What do you do for exercise?

_____

*(continued)*

How is your health?

_____

How do you take care of your spiritual needs?

_____

What kind of work are you doing? What level (entry level, middle management, senior executive, CEO)? Are you self-employed?

_____

_____

_____

9. THE YEAR IS _____ (CURRENT YEAR + 40). YOU ARE _____ YEARS OLD NOW.

What is your life like now?

_____

_____

_____

Who are your friends? Name your closest friends.

_____

_____

_____

What do these friends do for a living?

_____

_____

_____

Are you married? ___ Single? ___ Children? ___ List the ages of your children. _____

Where are you living?

_____

What are your hobbies and interests?

_____

What languages do you speak?

_____

What do you do for exercise?

_____

How is your health?

_____

How do you take care of your spiritual needs?

_____

What kind of work are you doing? What level (entry level, middle management, senior executive, CEO)? Are you self-employed?

_____

_____

_____

# Understanding How to Break Your Bamboo Ceiling<sup>SM</sup>

Before you can implement the focused strategies found within this book, you need to consider very carefully what may be holding you back from moving forward in your career—your personal bamboo ceiling. Few of us are exempt from having fears. Find out what yours are before you launch into a risky new venture or try out a stretch opportunity.

TOOL #7

## IDENTIFYING YOUR BAMBOO CEILING™

Note which barriers are applicable to your situation, and understand the potential barriers to personal and organizational effectiveness.

ORGANIZATIONAL BARRIERS

_____ Lack of understanding of Asians and their diversity/ethnic distinctions; employer either does not care or does not know what to do to motivate and appropriately develop Asian employees

_____ Organization does not practice inclusive leadership; workplace does not promote an open, inclusive environment; workplace is exclusive and cliquish to the point of hurting qualified people of color

_____ Company does not have women or professionals of color in senior leadership or on its board of directors

_____ Company is not open to alternative viewpoints and perspectives, tends to be insular or closed-minded, is slow to move with the times—may take a long time to innovate

\_\_\_\_ Company lacks training resources and accountability measures for promoting Asian professionals and other professionals of color. Recruiting, selection committees, and other programs lack focus on diversity representation and development.

PERSONAL BARRIERS

\_\_\_\_ Cultural values/traditions that may hinder you from demonstrating the right behaviors in the workplace

\_\_\_\_ Inner impediments and barriers

\_\_\_\_ Fear of conflict/offending others

\_\_\_\_ Fear of failure resulting from fear of public shame/career derailment

\_\_\_\_ Fear of success ("I've made it—now what?")

\_\_\_\_ Fear of imperfection

\_\_\_\_ Fear of not meeting people's expectations/disappointing others (for example, letting your manager or your company down)

\_\_\_\_ Indecision/hesitation/thinking too much

\_\_\_\_ Procrastination

\_\_\_\_ Lack of self-awareness or lack of clarity about what you can offer

\_\_\_\_ Shame-based cultural background: Failure is a public thing and may keep you from taking risks and learning new skills

\_\_\_\_ Lack of understanding about external perceptions; no knowledge of how others perceive your day-to-day actions (for example, not speaking up in meetings gets translated into ignorance, arrogance, or lack of interest in the business)

*(continued)*

---

**BREAKING THE BAMBOO CEILING ACTION STEPS**

Skills and competencies required to overcome the personal barriers:

_____     _____     _____

_____     _____     _____

_____     _____     _____

---

TOOL #8

---

# THE CAREER MOBILITY CHECKLIST

**Are you on the way up or on the way out?**

\_\_\_\_\_ Are you asked to participate in recruiting events and other public forums where you represent the firm?

\_\_\_\_\_ Are you asked to serve as a member of special project teams inside your company?

\_\_\_\_\_ Do senior managers ask for your input when making important decisions?

\_\_\_\_\_ Are you respected and liked by your peers and subordinates? By others in different business units?

\_\_\_\_\_ Do people give you information about future plans for your company?

---

## IDENTIFYING THE RIGHT JOB TARGETS —

After you've done your self-assessment but before you can create a customized branding statement, you'll have to create a set of articulated job targets (if you're looking for a new job) or career mobility goals (if you're looking to advance in your current job). Then you can develop a list of companies that fit those targets and your career objectives. After that, you can create a pitch tailored for the target(s). A target must have a job title/function and specify an industry. Try also to define the types of things you want to do. But how do you know what you want if you don't even know what your target jobs entail?

Do some research and talk to people in your network. If you don't know anyone who works in your field of interest, then broaden your network by going to industry meetings, association committees, alumni events, educational conferences, and other networking venues. My friend Dean took a finance course at night at a local state college when he was changing careers. Through that one class, Dean developed a network of contacts. The professor teaching the class, who was also a practitioner in the field, was so impressed with Dean's drive and motivation that he introduced my friend to his colleagues. This helped Dean as he transitioned from accounting to financial planning. As you think about your targets, consider what type of environment you thrive in. Do hypercompetitive, large corporate environments inspire you? Do you do well in small start-up companies where you can have a tremendous amount of autonomy to run the business? Or do you prefer midsize companies where you can wear many hats?

A client of mine came back to me with the results of her self-assessment and reported that she wanted to get into sales. That was not a clear enough career target. What types of industries interested her? Did she want to sell equities and fixed-income securities, work at a pharmaceutical company selling drugs, be a sales manager for a computer company, or sell office furniture to corporate clients? Each of those sales positions offers different clienteles, different work environments, and different work cultures.

Ask yourself how your skills can be used in the corporate environment. What companies are hiring someone with your skills? What are these positions called? Clearly, it's not enough to know what you want to do. You must find out what the profession is called in the specific industry, then use that term in your marketing pitch. Job titles differ from firm to firm. Take the HR discipline, for example. There was a time when people used to refer to the head HR person as head of personnel and records. The title has evolved to director of human resources, and in some firms, it is director of human capital. Corporate recruiters are now often called talent acquisition specialists. With the availability of information on the Internet, there's no excuse for walking into a meeting without knowing some pertinent facts about the industry, the company, and its management. Make sure you know your interviewers' job titles. People will think that you're at the top of your game, on the inside track, and not another faceless job seeker.

### How to Create a Target

If you are looking for a job, you need to identify your job target first. A target consists of a job function and industry, as well as the type of work environment you would thrive in (small family-owned business or large international Fortune 500 company with over 100,000 employees). Be very specific about your targets if you think you may be interested in looking for other opportunities. Here are some examples:

- Research analyst/equity research analyst for a sell-side broker-dealer, New York and San Francisco
- Marketing manager, midsize pharmaceuticals or consumer products company, metro New York and New Jersey
- Comptroller or assistant comptroller, small or midsize retail company, New York
- Financial analyst, working as a right hand to the CFO on various projects, major nonprofit or foundation
- Editorial assistant, publishing company, Boston–New England area

## PUTTING IT ALL TOGETHER —

After you have completed some of the above assessments, you can develop a
career plan that summarizes the results of these exercises.

### Assessment Results Summary

1. What I need in my relationship with my bosses:

   _____

   _____

   _____

2. Top three work-related values (from the Work-Related Values and
   Motivators Exercise, page 107):

   _____, _____, _____

3. The threads running through the Seven Stories Exercise (pages
   93–102):
   a. Main accomplishments:

   _____

   b. Key motivators:

   _____

   c. Enjoyed most, did best:

   _____

   d. My role:

   _____

   e. The environment:

   _____

   f. The subject matter:

   _____

4. Top six or seven specialized skills:

   _____

   _____

_____
_____
_____
_____
_____

5. From the Forty-Year Vision (pages 117–31):
   a. Where I see myself in the long run:

   _____

   b. What I need to get there:

   _____

6. My personality and the corporate cultures that work best for me:

   _____
   _____
   _____

7. Skills to develop:

   _____
   _____
   _____

*Action Steps*

1. Job targets that fit my background:

   _____
   _____
   _____

2. New competencies and skills I need to develop:

   _____
   _____
   _____

## ON WORKING WITH A COACH —

There may come a time where it is appropriate for you to work with a professional coach to take stock of where you are. When you are working in a stressful work situation, it may be difficult to think objectively about your marketability without some external feedback from trusted colleagues or friends. Periodically, an objective external perspective may help give your career a boost or move a derailed career back on track. Particularly when you are completing the Trusted Advisor Assessment (pages 108–12), it may be beneficial for you to ask an executive coach or a career counselor to interview your third-party evaluators on your behalf.

Enjoy the self-exploration process. Treat it as a personalized journey to self-awareness with the end goal of achieving your personal and professional objectives. With adequate self-assessment, you will have the know-how to survive the most turbulent employment markets. When you are faced with an unexpected layoff or personal crisis, it will be difficult, but you will be ready. Invest in your personal development now; it will pay dividends later.

## KEY LESSONS LEARNED —

■ *No matter where you are in your career, it is never too early or too late for self-assessment.*

■ *Get external feedback from mentors, bosses, or coworkers by taking the Trusted Advisor Assessment (pages 108–12). Incorporate the feedback into your development plan.*

■ *Review your career plan every year or at key career milestones with a career coach. These career checkups may be the objective external feedback that you need to keep your career on track.*

■ *Before making external changes, look internally first: Take an honest look at how your work-related values, motivations, and upbringing have impacted your behavior in the workplace.*

■     *Get organized. Create an assessment folder for yourself. Include the results of all exercises in it, and refer to it as you develop your pitch, create your résumé, prepare answers to difficult interview questions, and establish your job search campaign.*

■     *Take assessment seriously! If properly done, it can impact every area of your personal and career life. Let it empower you to take charge of your own career future.*

# PERFECT FOR THE PART: MASTERING THE FACE-TO-FACE JOB INTERVIEW

## A PERSONAL RETROSPECTIVE

As I visited some of the most prestigious college campuses across the country to recruit the best and the brightest, I became acutely aware of cultural influences that affected Asian students' behavior and communications styles at corporate presentations, networking receptions, and interview rooms.

At first I ignored the differences, dismissing them as individual variations in temperament or personality. Perhaps the Asians I met on campus happened to be the reserved, modest Asians, not the outspoken, assertive ones? But as I went from campus to campus, encountering only reserved Asians, and later encountered the same qualities in experienced professionals, it was apparent that even second- and third-generation Asians were under the same cultural influences.

During interviews and corporate presentations, the non-Asian candidates were very aggressive, to the point of effusively bragging, and quite persistent about getting "air time" with me about their experiences. On the other hand, the Asian candidates who were equally or sometimes more qualified than their non-Asian counterparts, took an understated, almost self-effacing approach to selling themselves. At times I had to use techniques that bordered on interrogation and excessive follow-up questions to extract information about their job accomplishments and experiences. They were so unused to tooting their own horn. Clearly there was a need for a self-awareness program. Now don't get me wrong—we recruiters can spot bragging and insincerity from a mile away and don't expect applicants to resort to extreme brownnosing techniques to get a job offer. During a job search, however, it is paramount that the candidate know how to properly express his interest in the company and verbalize his enthusiasm. No recruiter can be expected to read minds.

## FREQUENTLY HEARD STATEMENTS ABOUT THE JOB INTERVIEW

- The job candidate who is unaware of how others perceive him: "I thought I did a great job at my second round of interviews; I hit it off with the director of operations and everyone else who I met. Everything seemed to be going well, so why the rejection letter?"
- On lack of eye contact, respect, and nonverbal communication: "The HR person told me after I met with the hiring manager for the final round of interviews that I didn't give him enough eye contact. I grew up in a family where showing deference to my elders means not looking anyone in the eye. It makes me very uncomfortable."
- On lack of preparation: "One of the worst things about the interview process is not knowing what to expect."
- When modesty doesn't pay off: "I tend to be a pretty modest person when I talk about my accomplishments. Do I have to

fundamentally change who I am in order to make a good impression in an interview?"

■ On underselling oneself: "I am a known leader in my field. In fact, I'm one of an elite group of fifteen in the country who has this specific industry expertise, but when it comes to selling myself in an interview, I sell myself short, or worse yet, downplay my wins to the point of sounding pretty mediocre. I know my colleagues have been selected for certain positions over me, even when I know I am more qualified for some of those roles."

■ On being overly polite at the expense of being passed over: "The group interview at the company was just awful! There was this one guy who completely dominated the group with his rude, overpowering style. In the end, he wasn't offered a position at the firm, either, but somehow I let his strong personality get the best of me and I wasn't able to put my best foot forward during the group meeting, and this was one of my top job target companies! How do I deal with these situations in the future with more finesse?"

## INTERVIEWS ARE USED EVERYWHERE —

The ubiquitous job interview—it is the only way to get in the door in almost every industry. Medical students have to interview with potential residency placements for fit and qualifications. Business schools require interviews for entry into their 2-year MBA programs. Even high school students who want a part-time position at the local clothing store have to undergo a 30-minute interview with the store manager. But interviews aren't just for getting in the door for the first time, either. Even if you are looking to transfer to a different business unit or functional group at your company, the new department will still be interested in interviewing you informally to assess your skills and determine your fit with the new group. Even if you have your own business, you will need to meet with clients who will interview you to determine their comfort level with you as a service provider.

No matter how you feel about interviewing, it is a nonnegotiable skill that you must master if you want to move either vertically or horizontally in your career. The sooner you learn it, the sooner you'll be more comfortable when you're put to the test.

## WHERE INTERVIEWING FITS IN —

If you pick up this book and this chapter is the first one you read, I'm going to assume that you have already completed a basic self-assessment workup and identified some clear job targets. If you haven't, you should at the very least do the Seven Stories Exercise (pages 93–102) to determine what you want to do and why you want to do it.

Hiring managers and recruiting directors can use many types of interviews to determine a candidate's skill set and fit for the organization. What technique they use can be based on your industry, job requirements, and even personal whimsy.

### *Behavioral Interviews*

To create the behavioral interview model, human resources professionals and business managers develop a list of critical skills and corporate values by interviewing a sampling of high performers in the same functions. They translate these competencies into tangible skills that they would like to see in their new hires and then generate interview questions that determine which candidates have demonstrated these behaviors in their previous jobs or have the potential to do so. The behavioral interview is very popular in many companies.

### *Case Study Interviews*

The case study interview is widely used by professionals in management consulting and product management, though it has certainly been used by managers in other disciplines. As the name suggests, the case interview method is used by firms to decipher how a candidate thinks through some typical problems that he or she might encounter on the job. If you are preparing for a case interview, you should prepare as many questions as you can that will help you understand the depth of the problem you are asked to solve. Be careful not to speak too quickly; make sure that you understand the question and its direct and indirect implications. When you respond, you should clearly articulate what you did to arrive at your solution. You may also want to show that you can analyze such problems from different perspectives: from a pure bottom-line/profit-and-loss standpoint, from a people management standpoint, from an operational standpoint, from a technology standpoint, from a strategic long-term business plan standpoint, and so on.

### Chronological Interviews

Some companies may decide to use the straightforward chronological interview, going through each of your work experiences and attempting to unpack the key skills and competencies you have acquired by reviewing the details of your previous work experiences. The chronological interview follows your academic and employment history from the earliest date and moves to the present. To prepare for this type of interview, make sure that you keep notes on what you did at each of your prior jobs.

### Screening Interviews

Companies may also choose to contact a handful of candidates by phone for a screening discussion with a recruiter or hiring manager to make a general assessment for communication skills and general qualities. The strongest candidates from the phone screening process would be invited in for a round of face-to-face interviews. Don't take such phone screens lightly. Treat them as seriously as you would a job interview.

## FROM THE JOB HUNTER'S PERSPECTIVE: ACING THE INVESTIGATIVE METHOD OF INTERVIEWING —

Interviewing is sometimes about knowing the right questions to ask rather than about having all the right answers. Outside of questions that address basic factual data, such as where you worked, who your top clients were, what your major responsibilities were, and who you reported to, there is a lot of elbow room for what you can present during the interview.

Moreover, a face-to-face interview is a ripe setting for you to ask the kind of questions that will help you determine if the company is the right one for you. In turn, the level of sophistication of your questions and follow-up comments will give your potential employer an easy way to assess how you would operate in a business setting or client meeting. It may give you a chance to showcase a level of depth and insight into the company that other candidates lack.

Any good consultant knows that it is important to get as much information about the client before she develops recommendations and solutions to the client's problems—that it is critical to understand the client's motivations and fears. A good consultant won't necessarily find all the answers right away but will uncover the problem just enough for the client to see the solution on his own, or will identify the root of the issues and help the client solve it. A good consultant is not necessarily a know-it-all. If you adopt this model, you'll be ready for an investigative interview. You will also move from sounding like a "John the Job Seeker" to sounding like a credible hire.

### The Steps in the Process

In the exploratory phase of a job search, the job hunter is meeting people at all levels, at all different types of companies, just to get information, especially about her new targets. She should be asking many fact-finding questions—of anyone who will meet with her. As she moves into the credibility phase of a job search, she should be meeting more of the people who can help her identify real job opportunities—people who could be in a position to hire at some point. In the active interviewing phase, she will be talking to her contacts about actual job opportunities, not hypothetical ones. The classic job interview is part of this final phase.

> Exploratory phase → credibility phase → active interviewing phase

### Ways to Get in the Door

There are many ways to get interviews and meetings. You can respond to Internet job postings through popular online job sites, answer newspaper ads, get a colleague's introduction, send a cover letter and résumé to a company, follow up on a good job fair interaction, contact a headhunter, or follow up with someone you meet at a professional networking event.

### Informational Meetings Are as Important as the Job Interview

Informational meetings can often lead to job interviews and therefore are just as important as face-to-face job interviews. You should aim to include as many informational meetings as possible, especially in the earlier stages of your search. You should also recognize that informational meetings are just that; don't assume that the person you are networking with will automatically send your résumé to the department that is hiring. If you become aware of a potential opportunity at the company, ask your contact if you could connect with the hiring manager directly.

## WHICH ONE OF THESE IS NOT LIKE THE OTHER?

In a recruiting committee meeting I once facilitated, a group of six business managers were arguing about David Takata, the Japanese American candidate they had just interviewed. They were divided about whether to extend him a job offer. Three of them felt strongly about David and wanted to hire him right away. The other three thought he had great experience but wouldn't be a good fit for the group. When I pressed further, one of them said that David didn't come across as someone who would enjoy hanging out with them after hours; he seemed very formal and polite during the interview. Yet they had no proof that he was antisocial; I sensed that the problem was merely personality and style differences at play. No one in the room could identify a concrete statement he had made that alluded to a lack of interest in connecting with the group socially.

One of the three naysayers pulled me aside after the meeting to say, "You know what? He may be a great addition to our group. Fact is, he just really came across formally, and we didn't feel comfortable with that."

I asked, "Why don't we bring him in again to meet with us over a recruiting lunch? I will let him know that we are still interested and that we want to get to know him better." I remembered his mentioning to me during an informal conversation that he came to the United States at the age of 10 and was raised in a pretty traditional home, which tends to be more structured and more formal with people in positions of authority. If going out for drinks was the only factor holding my clients back from hiring him, might he not add some diversity to the team and contribute new perspectives that five men who grew up in the business by following in their fathers' footsteps may not have? My suggestion was a risky move because these men were my internal clients and I was their new HR director.

After the recruiting lunch, we regrouped again to discuss David's potential for the department. I continued to hold my ground and urged them to give David a try. Finally, one of the three piped in: "She's right. Dave seems like he could be molded. His product knowledge and ability to bring in clients is the most important thing to this group right now. He was fine at the lunch, and it is obvious he has been successful in his own right. We have to make sure that we don't pass up a great candidate because we feel like he wouldn't want to go drinking with the rest of us." We extended him an offer the next day—a good thing, too, because David already had two

other offers from our competitors. We had to work hard to get him.
I asked two of the interviewers to make "influence" calls to David to
reiterate our interest in him and the efforts paid off. He joined our
firm 2 weeks later and has been a superior performer there for the
past 5 years.

It's human nature to want to hire someone who is familiar,
with whom we feel comfortable. All things being equal, people are
more likely to hire a candidate who seems to have habits, values,
and behaviors similar to their own. If hiring managers and HR
professionals want to be serious about recruiting diverse candidates,
they need to be extra careful about this natural tendency.

### We Tend to Hire and Promote People Like Us

Managers tend to bring in new hires who are most like them, in a
phenomenon called homosocial reproduction. A senior manager may hire a
junior CPA simply because he reminds him of himself when he was just
starting out. The head of sales may hire the woman who happens to be
from the same sorority at her alma mater. This phenomenon was noted first
by Rosabeth Moss Kanter, a renowned leadership expert and author of
*Women and Men in the Corporation.* Such a tendency may hurt the professional of color who is being interviewed, especially if there are very few professionals of color in the organization. Many companies look for a good fit,
but if the candidate with good technical skills doesn't fit into the group itself, she won't necessarily be selected. HR managers and hiring managers
should be careful to interview a diverse array of candidates and make decisions on who to hire from a range of candidates. As part of their recruiting
strategy, they should first define what "fit" actually means to them.

### Redefining Good Fit: When You Don't Resemble the
### Rest of the Company

Good technical skills, strong interpersonal abilities, *and* a good
long-term potential fit for the firm—those are the criteria used by hiring
managers looking to select the perfect candidate. A person's academic

credentials or work experience alone rarely gets him in the door at the top companies. Instead, it is a combination of qualities, both tangible and intangible, that inspires the hiring manager to say with strong certainty, "She's the perfect person for the job. I have no doubts that she would do a phenomenal job of handling our projects." Usually, the concerns I hear have to do with some interpersonal quality that causes a manager to doubt the wisdom of hiring a particular person.

A face-to-face interview provides a telling snapshot of the way you relate to others, the way you articulate your thoughts, and the way you influence others. Hence, when an interviewer isn't confident about you during the interview, he will be unsure about your presentation style, your confidence level, and your ability to convincingly help his clients overcome their objections. Because the interviewer has only 30 minutes to see you in action, you must have your personal pitch perfected so that you can incorporate it into the interview.

Interviewing is an important form of presenting yourself, and you should treat it as such. Approach a job interview as you would any serious meeting, by coming prepared with your pitch ready and your mind clear about what you have to offer. Take a consultative sales approach to the interviewing process so that you seem confident and knowledgeable.

### People Want to Hire Competent People Who Are Fun to Work With

Some of the Asian clients I coach say that they have a hard time relaxing or being themselves in interview settings, especially given the authority figure that the hiring manager or interviewer represents. Yet many employers say that being comfortable in one's own skin is a quality that they look for in job candidates. U.S. managers want to hire intelligent, capable people who are competent in their fields and are also fun to work with. What employer would be short-sighted enough to hire a person who will upset the balance of their team because of their bad attitude or negative disposition? As one hiring manager told me, "He's great. He's totally focused and intense and has a great deal of raw intelligence. What makes it so great is that I also *like* him. He is the kind of guy who would never get flustered under pressure. He exudes confidence and a positive good humor that my overworked team really needs right now. With me traveling and out of the office fifty percent of the year, I need a hands-on manager who can also produce. He is the perfect fit for the job. Let's hire him." This hiring manager's statement is indicative of the informal nature of the American work culture. He valued a candidate who could get along with everyone in his group.

### Who Would You Select?

Put yourself in the hiring manager's shoes for a moment. If you had the choice between two candidates for a sales position:

1. Good technical skills (but lacks deep understanding of the product and industry) + excellent ability to communicate ideas succinctly and clearly + strong reputation in the industry + confidence

Or

2. Excellent technical skills + below-average communicator + did not project confidence and positive energy

Who would you select? Because most of the communication done in an interview is done through nonverbal cues, the hiring managers may sometimes make a judgment call based on how confident they feel about a candidate after he walks away. Are you projecting a positive, can-do attitude to your potential employer or a tentative, nervous image?

There are a lot of smooth talkers who do not know what they're doing, even if they can talk up a storm. If you already have the technical skills, you are already standing on good ground because you know what you are talking about. Remember, no one wants to hire someone who is not qualified with the right technical skills! If you feel uncomfortable with your interpersonal skills, you need to develop the presentation skills necessary to be a more prepared candidate.

Here is a great example of how the "techie" Asian stereotype backfired for a hiring manager at a hedge fund. A business colleague of mine re-counted this tale to illustrate how the Asian stereotype of the math whiz is still pervasive inside corporate walls.

## WHEN A "GOOD" STEREOTYPE BACKFIRES

TYR Investment Company, a hedge fund, was looking for a financial analyst with a few years' experience and superb quantitative modeling and valuation skills. After working with external recruiters to find candidates, the head of research decided to hire Ken Wu as an analyst to support the fund managers. After the first 2 months, however, people were starting to complain that Ken's analyses were inaccurate and that he actually didn't know the basics of analyzing financial statements. A colleague said, "I thought it was strange that Ken received an offer after only one round of interviews. Later, when I talked to the guy who fired Ken, he confessed, 'I should have tested Ken more on his quantitative skills, his ability to create complex Excel models. I assumed he was good at math because I have yet to meet an Asian person around here who is not good with technical analysis.' " Ken performed so poorly at quant work that the company eventually had to let him go, after only 3 months' service. Had the company taken the time to assess his quantitative skills as they did with all the other candidates they interviewed, it could have avoided this hiring mistake.

### *Your Asian Cultural Upbringing May Affect You During Interviews*

Related to some of the issues of collective thinking in Asian cultures, some Asian professionals may find it difficult to promote their accomplishments in the interview setting. Compare two possible responses to the question "What was your greatest accomplishment this year?"

**Response 1:**

"Well, I just conducted the client meeting with my team. I oversaw the analysis that they completed, but my analysts did most of the work. I just had to check it over and make sure that it was approved by the senior managers. It was really a team effort."

The manager comes across as being mostly passive in this client engagement process, almost unemotional about the whole thing. Consequently, the hiring manager is likely to assume that this candidate didn't really contribute a lot to the project; the hiring manager wasn't there to see how the interviewee dealt with obstacles or the way he motivated people during a very challenging time.

**Response 2:**

"What a great project opportunity that was for me! From beginning to end, I took the ball and ran with it. When assigned to calculate the profitability of this potentially belly-up business group, I asked my lead analyst to do a comparison study year over year, and then with my other analyst, I prepared some detailed cost models that showed some similar businesses and their profit margins over a five-year period. We were given two weeks to complete the analysis, but we were able to do it within a week. I recommended that we give the business line one more year, as they were just about to introduce a new product in the summer that would potentially be a huge seller. Our VP gave all of us glowing feedback about the project, and my entire group got quite a bit of exposure. This project propelled us onto the fast track."

Both responses discussed the same project, but the latter approach gave the candidate a lot more credibility and expressed more spark and interest. As the hiring manager later reported, "The latter response sounds a lot more convincing, like she really knew what it took for them to accomplish this. It also showed a lot of initiative, drive, and good judgment when a difficult decision had to be made."

PREPPING FOR YOUR PRESENTATION —

*"How Am I Doing?" Getting Feedback About*
*Your Interviewing Skills*

The directions for navigating the road to success start like this: Self-awareness → action plan → mock interview → feedback → more interviews → additional feedback → refining pitch → ongoing practice and feedback. Notice the repeated component? Yes, it's feedback.

Get an assessment of your interview skills. Practice with a career coach or a friend and ask how you come across. Are you stiff? Do you project confidence? Are you maintaining eye contact? Though you don't want to stare your interviewer down, you should make sure that you give her adequate eye contact. One hiring manager who interviewed a Japanese woman remarked, "Sue had a strong résumé and good qualifications, but she did not give me sufficient eye contact during our interview. In fact, when I would ask her the tough questions, she would look away. Those actions projected little confidence. As she continued to lower her gaze when asked challenging questions, she almost seemed deceitful at times. Once she worked on these nonverbal cues, her interviewing skills improved dramatically."

## MISUNDERSTOOD NONVERBAL CUES

Michael Lee, a Korean American who came to the United States at age 10, speaks English fluently. He went to a small liberal arts college and had been looking for a job as a retail buyer for a department store for more than 6 months without success when I started working with him. Though he responded well to most interview questions, he had a tendency to avoid eye contact during his responses.

During a mock interview, my colleagues and I noticed that he was doing it at almost every interview question that he was asked.

When we played the videotape of the interview back for him, he said: "You know, I catch myself looking away when I am placed in a job interview setting. There is something in the structure of that interaction that is very hierarchical: The hiring manager is a person in authority. And I was always raised for many years to respect authority, to give heed to the person in charge, the one who has the upper hand. Almost automatically, my gaze is lowered out of respect for his authority."

I told him that his constant looking away and his sense of formality during the interaction may make the hiring managers feel that he is not passionate, is not interested, and is unsure about his responses. In essence, lowering his eyes and keeping his distance signaled the very opposite of what Michael intended. What Michael wanted to communicate (a sense of respect for the person in power) was mistaken for a lack of self-awareness and indifference.

Said Michael, after receiving the feedback, "I didn't realize that my nonverbal communication was signaling lack of interest and lack of respect!" Armed with this knowledge and some mock sessions in which he practiced making focused eye contact for a few seconds, then for longer periods, he went back to his job search to practice his newly acquired interview skills.

Michael landed a new position within 2 months.

---

### Your Hiring Manager Is Not a Mind Reader

Having a good attitude is just as important as your responses to interview questions. A smile, positive demeanor, and a sense of humor are all important ingredients that impact how others perceive you. It's not necessarily what you say but how your words and behavior make the hiring manager and the rest of the people you meet in the interview process feel. In an interview setting, you often have to be quite assertive about telling someone that you want the job. Unless the hiring manager is a mind reader, he will never be able to guess that you are interested merely because of your presence in the job market. This is especially true when there are fewer candidates for the job opening. The hiring manager may assume that you are interested in other companies if you don't express your interest in his company explicitly. Don't leave it up to interpretation. Be blatant about your preferences.

### It's All in the Attitude

While working in a recruiting function, I was responsible for filling a variety of job openings, but there were very few appropriate candidates. It got to the point where I needed to recruit candidates who weren't even looking, because the candidates weren't coming to us. One candidate, Rebecca Chan, came through the recruiting process with an absolutely phenomenal résumé. She had the perfect experience for the job we were looking to fill, as she had worked for one of our competitors and had completed an MBA from a prestigious program. On meeting her, however, I found it difficult to determine where she stood. During our meeting, she said not one positive word about our company and whether we were high on her list of potential employers. The other interviewers who met with her that day also couldn't figure out where she stood. We extended her an offer, but if we had seen another candidate who was more openly enthusiastic about his or her interest in our company and the position, we would have selected that person over her.

One of my first clients when I started my coaching practice was Larry, a man who came in with an unhappy disposition and a surly attitude. He was called in for numerous first-round meetings, but he never got called back for follow-up interviews. It was obvious that his poor first impression was putting a damper on his job search. After just one coaching session in which I told him how his negative body language and unhappy expression were affecting how he was being perceived, he became aware of his negative demeanor for the first time. He was able to turn it around within days. As early as our second meeting, it was amazing to see how that one piece of feedback had changed his disposition. Self-awareness made the difference. Larry and I explored the possible reasons behind his negative attitude, and we figured out that he was so discouraged over not having an offer on graduation from an MBA program that his entire face was showing the weight of his burden. His parents, who came to the United States just 15 years earlier, helped put him through school, and he felt that he was letting them down by not finding employment right away. Once he recognized this about himself, his entire persona became lighter, and we practiced a few mock interview questions, opening up his body language and helping him to smile more during the interview. Within 3 weeks, Larry had landed a job offer.

### Get Ready to Handle Difficult Questions

Some of the most difficult questions to answer in an interview are open-ended ones. It's easy to answer questions such as "What did you do at your job?" and "Tell me about your project management skills." But when the interviewer says "Tell me about yourself," it's hard to know what to say. You can give a myriad of details about yourself, but as you are already aware, that is not the point of such a request. If you don't like talking about yourself, such a request is even more difficult.

For one job hunter, it was really tough: "I was ready with my answers, and I had thought through almost every type of behavioral and technical question that could be asked, and then they end up throwing me for a loop! I was completely unprepared to answer this question. I ended up giving a boring rundown of my work experience, starting from my first employer and moving to the present. The hiring manager, I could tell, was not unhappy, but he wasn't overly impressed, either."

When you go into the interview process, you need to be prepared to talk about yourself in a free-form way. The best way to do this is to prepare your marketing statement. Have both a shorter version and a longer version ready to go, because you never know the kind of situation you'll be called into. In crafting your job interview pitch, think about the top one or two things that you want the hiring manager to know about you.

Another common question you will be asked is "Why did you leave your employer?" Make sure you know the answer. When I used to hire people for administrative clerical positions early in my career, I would use this question in conjunction with the chronological interview (working from past to present) to identify the people with large gaps in their employment history. The chronological format is valuable: Later, I was to discover that one candidate with a long gap between his employers spent 3 months in prison for grand larceny. If I had simply asked the candidate to mention some of the highlights of his background, he'd have omitted those months, and my company would have made a hiring decision based on incomplete information.

### Handling Phone Interviews and Screens

Phone interviews, or phone screens, are a tool that helps recruiters and hiring managers determine if you are a candidate worth pursuing. They may get hundreds of applications—solicited and unsolicited—every day; it is in their best interest to make a face-to-face interview worth their time. So never take a phone conversation lightly; the phone interview is a very important skill for you to master. If you are in a position that requires you to be on the phone quite a bit, so much the better for refining your phone skills. Salespeople know very well that it takes more than one or two phone calls to gain direct access to a very important client. Your approach should be no less rigorous. I'm not advocating pestering your job contacts by phone, but you do have to be persistent about contacting busy professionals.

If you are seriously interested in a company, you must make it your personal mission to determine the optimal way for getting in the door. As a hiring manager of a large national insurance company said, "If you are pleasantly, professionally persistent in trying to get through to me, I will usually give you that five minutes on the phone. If you are rude, demanding, and inconsiderate in your request, I will never give you the time of day." The way you come across in voice mails and messages and even the way you treat administrative assistants can significantly impact how you are perceived by the organization. A person's phone manner can give the hiring manager a glimpse of how the job candidate will interact in a tough situation with clients and colleagues.

Phone interactions also allow the hiring manager to hear how effective you are as a communicator. When I was trying to reach a potential client, I played phone tag with the director of diversity for more than six rounds. It got to a point that we were leaving friendly voice messages for each other. When I finally got through to her, she told me the reason why she persisted in calling me back: "Though I knew I couldn't meet you for a couple of months because of my travel schedule, I knew you would be someone whom we would want to work with our employees. I had a sense about you since your very first voice mail to me—your comfortable conversational style, pleasant demeanor, and ease of approach were immediate attractions."

### Passionate but Pleasant Persistence

Research has shown that it may take as many as six to eight phone calls to reach a person. You should expect to do no less in a job search. Senior executives are busy people with hectic client loads and travel schedules. When you call a senior executive, you will often have to coordinate with his or her administrative assistant. If so, befriend the assistant. If the senior executive calls you back and misses you, that gives you a reason for calling him again: "Mr. Kildare called me yesterday; I'm returning his phone call. Is he in the office? If not, when might you expect him back? I would be more than happy to give him another call tomorrow."

A phone conversation is another opportunity to exercise your personal marketing pitch. Make sure your statements are eloquent, succinct, and courteous. Using good manners never hurt anyone. Your first impression on the phone must be as good as that in any face-to-face meeting. Make sure that your home answering machine and cell phone voice mail messages show your professionalism and enthusiasm as well. A senior executive recalls trying to track down the VP of programming of a research organization. His answering machine tape said, "I'm not around, so give a shout if you want a call back." If a senior management professional will be calling you on your home phone, you should make your message more courteous and professional.

## *Selling Yourself in an Interview*

An interview is an excellent opportunity for you to shine. But this can often be a problem for some Asians. Here are the remarkably different responses that one Chinese American client gave—before and after coaching—when an interviewer said, "So, tell me how you won this new client engagement."

**Before:**

"Yes, that was a good engagement. I worked with my manager and my team to find out what issues they were grappling with. My analysts helped put together the numbers, and my manager was the one who guided me in the process of developing the pitch story at the meeting. I couldn't have done it without them!"

While the woman's answer was acceptable, it didn't appropriately showcase her skills. The hiring manager was interested in hearing about *her* accomplishments, not how she worked with the group. It would have been helpful if she had described how she drove the project as the project manager. She developed a better response after some thoughtful analysis.

**After:**

"That deal with XYZ Company was one of the best transactions I closed this year. My boss had handed the lead to me and told me to run with it, so I did. I started out by doing the financials, then led my team in extensive research on what makes the business units tick. Through a series of meetings, I found out that the CFO was losing a lot of sleep thinking about how to implement some cost-cutting measures. Over a series of four follow-up meetings, I was able to convince him that our software application would save him over half a million dollars, without his having to downsize his staff. I was impressed with how our group really came together to close this client deal. Researching the company's needs and actually coming through with a viable solution really went a long way."

*Your Mind-set for the Face-to-Face Interview: Playing the Part*

When people complain to me of their dislike of the job search process, they're usually thinking about their reluctance to go on so many informational meetings and job interviews. Interviewing isn't necessarily everyone's favorite activity, but it helps to have the right mind-set about it. As a professional in a rapidly changing business world, you may need to be flexible in your style to accommodate different work situations. And that might mean that sometimes you'll have to be a bit of a chameleon, not unlike playing a role in a drama. In elementary school, I had to play the part of one of Santa's elves in one scene, then quickly take on the role of one of the children in the Christmas Eve scene. When the time was right, I simply took off (literally, in this case) my elf hat and donned my "child hat," while remembering my lines for this new scene. The role I played determined how I acted. You definitely have to be in the interview mind-set to sell yourself. Even if you are not naturally very vocal about your achievements, you'll have to step out of your comfort zone to ace a job interview.

# PROMOTING YOURSELF WHEN YOU HAVE BEEN CONDITIONED TO BE MODEST: GOING OUT OF YOUR COMFORT ZONE

If you've been conditioned to be modest—to not take all the credit for your work—you'll face some challenges during the interview process. When I was being interviewed for a campus tour guide job in college, I recall going through rigorous interviewing by a panel of peer and faculty. And I was pitted against six other equally qualified, well-spoken candidates who could answer every question that was thrown at them. During the first three questions, I was taken with how my cohorts would immediately pipe up with an answer, whereas I would politely wait for an open spot to speak.

Fortunately, I realized that my turn might never come in this very competitive atmosphere. When the fourth question was asked,

I mustered enough nerve to answer immediately, convincing the judges that I could think on my feet. I realized that what was being tested was not necessarily my knowledge of how to handle difficult questions but my ability to be assertive and quick on my feet. It wasn't enough to know what to say in this case; I needed to make my voice heard. There is a happy ending to this story—I got the job. Though I rarely had to interrupt anyone again, I was pleased to know that I could do it if I had to.

## BEYOND TECHNICAL ABILITIES

Donald Song was a management consultant who wanted to move into marketing. Because his background was in consulting, it was difficult to convince the marketing executives that he had what it took to do the job. Moreover, because he was slightly reserved, unlike the other 10 people in marketing who appeared to be cut from the same mold (gregarious, loud, and self-promoting), the head of marketing had some doubts about Donald's ability to effectively sell services to clients. After all, because he had an entirely different style, he didn't seem to be a good fit for the group.

Luckily, however, because of glowing references from Donald's clients and his ability to connect with clients learned from his consulting days, the marketing executive decided to take a chance and hire Donald. In addition, during the interview, Donald implemented some strategies to help the executive see how effective he was. Here are some excerpts from the interview:

**Donald:** Do you have any reservations or concerns about my background and how I might be a fit in your marketing group? I am really excited about the possibility of moving into your group and working directly for you, as I have always felt that understanding how to satisfy our clients in the way we sell and market our services was the heart of our business.

**Marketing executive:** That's a good question, and I have to be completely honest with you. I know you come highly recommended, and all the partners you've worked for have given me the thumbs-up. But how comfortable are you getting in front of some of the highest level of clients and engaging them with who we are and answering their tough questions? I know you have been good technically, but I haven't seen you in action with a client.

**Donald:** How funny that you bring that up, because I'd like to share an example. At ABC Client, I came in at a time where we had a very precarious role with them—the client was close to taking their business elsewhere because of our inability to solve their most difficult problem. So I met with the people in all the different functional areas, not just the ones responsible for managing the consultant relationship, to get the full story. I got to know each of them personally. I invested long hours to understand their concerns over a period of two intense weeks. It turned out that we were neglecting them as clients—they felt that we were not giving them the time of day. The senior people would come in for these update meetings, do these extraordinary status presentations, and then disappear, leaving the junior consultants to deal with the problem on a day-to-day basis. The juniors were often clueless about what to do! So the questions I asked them helped them to establish this level of trust with me. To this day, they come to me with their issues and rarely interact with the partner in charge.

---

### *Expressing Your Emotions and Enthusiasm*

If there is ever a time to show your enthusiasm about something, a job interview is it. Companies want to know who really wants to work for them because sometimes candidates have many choices of companies. Some Asian cultures reinforce emotional reserve, discouraging outward displays of emotion. But do your career a favor: Show excitement in a job interview. This is not the time to be modest or laid back about your accomplishments.

## Investigative Interviewing

Using the investigative interviewing style gives you an advantage in a job interview. As Kate Wendleton points out in *Job Search Secrets That Have Helped Thousands of Members (the Five O'Clock Club),* "Pretend for a minute that you own a small consulting company. When you first meet a prospective client, you want to probe to better understand the problems this person is facing. If the client has no problems, or if you cannot solve them for him, there is no place for you." Once you understand the client's problem and have determined that you have the right skills to help solve his problems, then you can go into high gear and seek to get as much information as possible about the problems so that you can begin to help solve them in subsequent meetings. You want to do a great deal of research and figure out your selling points *before* you go into the meeting.

## INVESTIGATIVE QUESTIONS TO ASK DURING JOB INTERVIEWS

Ask yourself this: *If they were to offer me a job that starts a week from Monday, what is the gap between what I know now and what I need to know to get started there?* Then be prepared to ask questions and make statements like these during the interview:

- "I'd like to talk to the head of operations so that I can get an idea of what the department does."
- "What is the most important task that you want to have accomplished by year's end? Of those priorities, what are the most important things that you would like to take off your to-do list right now?"
- "I'd like to talk to some of my prospective peers before I take this offer so I can figure out exactly how I would interface with them."
- "I need to give this some thought, come up with a few ideas, and then meet with you again. I'd like to propose

meeting next week to discuss some specific ways to solve some of the issues you and your group have been working on." (You can do your homework about the issue as quickly as you can before the next meeting.)

■ "What are some of the problems that keep you up at night?"

By asking these questions and making these statements, you will help the hiring manager and others in the interview process seriously consider the most important issues to them, giving you an opening to help them create solutions. It's a win-win for everyone involved. What manager wouldn't want to hire someone who is already getting things done—before the first day of work?

## INTERVIEWING ASIAN CANDIDATES WITH SENSITIVITY: A NOTE TO RECRUITERS AND HIRING MANAGERS

When interviewing Asians for potential positions, you as a recruiter or manager must keep in mind certain aspects of Asian cultures. Asians' modest descriptions of their accomplishments and self-effacing answers to your questions may mask leadership qualities. If you suspect that this may be the case, ask a third-party question. That is, pick someone from the candidate's current or most recent employer (client, boss, colleague) who knows the candidate's work intimately and ask, "If I were to call this person for a two- or three-word description of you, what would he or she say?" Asians may be more open to sharing what others say about them. Remember that the degree of acculturation can vary from one Asian candidate to the next. Make sure that you ask them questions that help them promote themselves. You may also need to probe more if you get answers that don't really showcase their skills. If you have trouble getting responses with your initial inquiries, try rephrasing the questions:

Helpful probes:

- "If I were to call your biggest client tomorrow, what would your client say was your greatest contribution to the project?"
- "What would your team members say about your leadership on this deal?"
- "If I were to ask the internal client to describe your work style to me in three words, what would she say about you?"
- "What specifically was your role in turning the company around?"
- "What would your coworker(s) say about your accomplishment?"

Be wary of who comes to mind when you think of who would be an appropriate fit. At times, you may need to pick someone who looks quite different from or sounds unlike the rest of the team to get a fresh perspective on solving client problems. A diverse group of views may take a little more effort to manage initially, but it will result in some great synergies that will be beneficial for everyone involved.

## INTERVIEWING IS A TWO-WAY CONVERSATION, NOT AN INQUISITION —

When you're interviewing for a job, you're being checked out by the company, but you're also taking a look at the company to see whether you would be happy there. It's important for you to get away from viewing the interviewer as a formidable authority figure. Yes, in such a situation, he is the buyer and you are the seller. Yet you have just as much authority as he does to steer the interview to one issue or another. Moreover, hiring decisions are rarely made by one person, so you must also profoundly affect the opinions of the interviewer who influences the hiring manager's decision. It's your responsibility to ask the right investigative questions so that you can determine whether you want to be associated with a particular company, boss, or department and whether the position fits into your long-term career goals.

## Frequently Asked Questions About Interviewing —

**Q:** *How do I sell myself to people when they ask open-ended questions such as "Why should I hire you?" I usually come prepared to answer the toughest questions about my qualifications, but when they hit me with that, I freeze up!*

**A:** You should always be prepared to answer such a question. Though such an open-ended question can leave you a lot of room for hanging yourself, you can easily avoid that by preparing in advance a 2- or 3-minute marketing pitch that quickly summarizes who you are and what you've accomplished. You should add in a sentence or two that explicitly makes the link between your qualifications and the reason you would be good for the position. In other words, don't leave it up to the hiring manager to determine why you would be such a great fit. It is so important to expressly state in your response why you want to work for that particular company. You won't get anywhere by being self-effacing. Ending your pitch with a statement like this can really put some power into your interview: "After speaking with you and your operations manager, I learned about your company's plans for expansion to the West Coast, and that confirmed it for me. Your five-year plan fits in exactly with my interest in helping to grow a business beyond the Northeast. I would be very excited about the possibility of working with you during this important growth period."

**Q:** *How do I respond when the hiring manager asks a blatantly racist question or makes an insensitive comment such as "Oh, I had no idea that you were Oriental on the phone. You sounded so American since I could not detect an accent"?*

**A:** As an Asian American candidate, you are part of a minority group protected by U.S. laws and EEOC guidelines, which prohibit companies from discriminating against you. Although the hiring manager should not have been discussing your Asianness in such a manner, you should respond to him in a positive way that does not alienate him and put him on the spot. He may even have been trying to pay you a compliment! Because it's difficult to tell whether the hiring manager was in fact making a racist comment, or is just making such statements out of ignorance, the best thing to do is to respond to it quickly, then move on to the real reason why you are there, which is to let the person get to know your professional qualifications and personal qualities. Here is an example of how you might proceed:

"You're right—I am Asian American. I'm glad to finally meet you in person. I have a few questions for you about this position, and I am curious to hear how recent changes in management have brought about the new project initiatives for this department." This is probably not the ideal time to bring up the fact that the word *Oriental* is used to describe cultural artifacts (such as an Oriental rug or vase), not a group of people. You can bring it up later, if you do decide to pursue the job. In the back of your mind, however, you can note that the hiring manager wasn't very sensitive to the different Asian cultures. Some candidates may be completely turned off by the hiring manager and decide to pursue opportunities elsewhere. You need to decide which battles you choose to fight.

**Q:** *How do I answer this series of questions? "Have you ever been in sales before? How do I know that you can do this job if you don't have a proven track record? I just met three other candidates who have proven sales experience, with a strong record of bringing in new revenues for their employers. What would make me select you over them?"*

**A:** First off, this is not the time to be modest. These are exactly the types of questions that you need to be prepared to answer, and with confidence and conviction. If you are likely to downplay your accomplishments or be casual about your abilities because of your cultural tendency to be modest and self-effacing, you need to practice kicking things up a few notches with a trusted friend or colleague. This is when you need to learn contextual fluency—that is, the ability to be flexible in your relating style on the basis of the situation at hand.

Once you have gotten used to the idea that you might be out of your element during an interview, draft an answer to such a challenge in your own language and then practice. Don't respond with "You're right.

I've never done this before . . . but I think that I have the skills to learn whatever I need to succeed in sales." Instead, craft your answer so that you show a track record of sales support or your contribution to new revenue generation:

"All of my jobs for the past five years have involved some sort of sales experience. In my last role, as a strategic marketing manager, I came up with a creative plan to increase our exposure to Asian American homeowners, an untapped market in our campaign. Using my contacts at local community organizations, I gave ten presentations that incorporated our new product strategy, and I was the one who closed the largest deals. Though I never held the title of salesman, I was the sole person who brought in that new revenue. If I were to stay at my current firm, I would easily segue into a sales role. But after seven years in this industry, I'm ready to take my career in a new direction. Your firm seems to be growing rapidly. I can see tremendous synergy for us working together!"

**Q:** *How do I move from a back-office to a front-office position? I work in operations for a mutual fund company, but I'm eager to make the move to an analyst position. Do I need an MBA? And how do I impress the hiring managers during the interview process to convince them that I can do this job?*

**A:** Whenever you are making a transition from a support function to a line position, you must cross organizational barriers. First of all, you should understand what skills the entry-level analyst roles require. The hiring manager in the front office may be used to hiring a certain type of candidate, so you must make her comfortable with the fact that you are not a traditional candidate. Also, make sure you do a lot of research, both at your company as well as in the industry, so that you know how she might perceive your background. Some companies are better about internal transfers than others. Not all jobs require MBAs, so find out the specific job requirements before you invest time and money into getting new credentials. If you're interested in an equity analyst role, a CFA (chartered financial analyst) designation may be sufficient.

**Q:** *How do I respond to this? "How do I know that you can hit the ground running in equity research? You've been an assistant controller for* *a large investment banking organization, but you don't have any valuation experience."*

**A:** You must assure the hiring manager that you can handle the technical requirements of company valuation, a skill that is obviously very important to moving into equity research. It's not enough to say it; you may want to also show her a few of the Excel models or charts you have created to follow some of your favorite companies.

Here's an example of a good response: "I've been following the market for quite some time now in addition to doing some great coursework in stock analysis and fundamental analysis in my executive MBA program. I'm very serious about making a career change from accounting to equity research. Though I've worked in accounting for six years, my true passion has always been stocks, and you can tell that by some of the financial models I've created to help me follow my favorite companies. I've focused many of my models on the biotech and semiconductor industries, but of course, I am completely open to any industry for experience and exposure. I would be willing to do basic spreadsheet analysis or maintain conference call lists—basically anything that would expose me to this exciting field and help out an analyst with the day-to-day work."

**Q:** *I am in the middle of a career change; I just finished conducting at least a dozen or so informational interviews with some contacts in the pharmaceutical industry. However, I haven't been as good about turning those meetings into potential leads for jobs. How do I do this effectively without putting my contacts on the spot?*

**A:** A great question, and one that I get quite often. When you are conducting informational meetings, you need to prepare just as you would for a job interview—perhaps even more so, because you've asked for the meeting and so must set the agenda. Set the tone early by saying something like this at the beginning of the meeting: "Thanks so much for agreeing to meet with me. George told me that you would be the best person to connect with in the biotech field. I'm considering opportunities, and biotech is one of the fields I'm very interested in exploring further. I don't expect you to find me a job here, but I have a few specific questions about the industry and your role." That will make the networking contact feel good for two reasons: (1) he'll be happy that you took him off the hook by not pressuring him to get you an interview, and (2) though you have stated clearly that you don't expect him to help you, he knows that you'd accept his help if he offered it.

**Q:** *Interviewing and selling myself seems so unnatural! Is this the only way to get a job?*

**A:** Until companies come up with a revolutionary way to assess candidate's capabilities, you'll have to deal with face-to-face job interviews. If job interviews make you clam up, then you should mentally prepare yourself. Remember, actors and performers do it all the time—they always warm up and rehearse before a big production. But for some reason, many job seekers try to wing it. As a result, they are rarely very confident or dynamic in their responses to the tough questions. Before any job interview, prepare a list of "potentially dangerous" questions that you may be asked. Then spend time preparing your answers. But preparation isn't just about knowing your lines. Research the interviewing companies ahead of time so that you know what you're talking about. With the availability of the Internet research databases and search engines, there is absolutely no excuse for not knowing the basic facts about a company.

# Moving Past the Hors d'Oeuvres Table: Finessing the Art of Networking

*You gain strength, courage, and confidence by every experience in which you really stop to look fear in the face.*

—Eleanor Roosevelt

*Those who know do not speak. Those who speak do not know.*

—Lao-tzu, Chinese philosopher

## Using Networking in Your Job Search —

Networking is touted by business books and magazine articles as a critical element of any job search. It is an important skill to learn, especially in a competitive job market where your raw intellect and past track record don't always guarantee you a job offer or move you to the top. From the job hunter's perspective, the benefits of having a strong professional network are obvious. Companies also like the idea of hiring candidates who have been recommended by an employee in the firm. Recently, an HR director

who works at a technology consulting firm confided, "Last year, we hired no less than seventy-five percent of our new hires through employee referrals. Not only did it make my job easier but the CEO was impressed at how that drastically cut our headhunter fees, and we never had to place an ad in the paper! Our referral program is so widely used now." She was especially proud of the fact that the new hires who were referred by the internal employee network tended to stay longer, because those who referred them knew the skills (both technical and soft skills) required to excel in the jobs in question. Moreover, their employee referral program greatly improved their attrition rates.

In many companies whose most precious assets are employees' expertise and intellectual capital, hiring applicants who come strongly recommended by high-performing employees is especially valuable and reliable. Without the right people in the right job functions, managers at these firms would be unable to run their businesses effectively. So if you're ready to get a new job or move up to a new position, you ought to carefully plan your job search campaign around networking.

Employee referrals are a good way to find potential candidates, but they should not necessarily be the only source of new recruits. If your company is seeking a more diverse employee population, use other sources as well.

## HIERARCHY IN INTERPERSONAL RELATIONS: A PRODUCT OF OUR CULTURAL ROOTS —

Though some Asian Americans are expert communicators adept at building and using their network of contacts to find jobs or develop professionally, many others still struggle with the idea. Less acculturated Asians might find that their family upbringing impacts their comfort level with networking. What do you do if you're part of the latter group? Wanla Cheng, president of Asia Link Consulting, a market research firm with expertise in the Asian American market, says, "The American concept of networking is entirely foreign to Asians. Many wouldn't dare to ask a stranger for help."

# CULTURAL BARRIERS POSE PROBLEMS IN A NETWORKING CAMPAIGN

## KATE'S PROBLEM

Kate Chang, 29, a Chinese American management consultant, tells her story:

> I am very good at what I do, and I get great feedback from my managers and clients. But last year, when I had to network with new people to facilitate an internal transfer, I hit some major roadblocks. I had the hardest time calling up senior people in different business units to get more information about their group and their hiring needs. I knew they would help me because lots of influential people in the firm had recommended me highly to them, but when I finally met them face to face, my sense of respect for them took over and I couldn't get past the basic social pleasantries. It was difficult to ask them for help. I watch my peers, and many of them are *fluent* at shifting quickly from talking about details of their personal lives to discussing client needs and work with senior executives. I always feel a need to keep a certain level of distance from senior management. How can I become more comfortable being myself around them?

## KATE'S SOLUTION—LEARNING HOW TO RUN HER MEETING

Kate learned how to run a networking meeting just as she would any serious business meeting for her work projects. When I told her that she was the one who was in charge of these meetings, I could almost see the lightbulb go on over her head. Because she was the one asking for assistance, she had to be prepared to open up, direct, and take the lead in running a meeting with her contact. She had to prepare the right opener:

> Thanks so much for this meeting. I had been looking forward to opportunities such as this to connect with a management team member in your business group, and I'm thrilled to have you as a resource. I have a keen interest in learning more about your group. Here are some of the questions I have been wanting to ask you.

> Moreover, she prepared a list of questions. She has used this strategy in other meetings as well, and though she admits that it's still not easy for her, she's getting used to it.

---

A Chinese American friend and colleague who works in benefits consulting meets hundreds of Asian professionals at conferences and panels in the course of her travels, and invariably, some of them ask her to be a mentor or ask for her counsel on political issues at work. But they rarely follow up. I've had similar experiences with many Asians I've met at public events. If these people had approached me with a good enough case and pursued me despite my busy schedule, I would have happily carved out a little time for them.

It's not only Asians who dread networking with new people. I've spoken with dozens of non-Asians with reserved personalities who prefer doing things one on one or in small groups. As Susan RoAne, former teacher and best-selling author of *How to Work a Room: The Ultimate Guide to Savvy Socializing in Person and Online,* said to me, "It's not just Asians who feel this reluctance; we all fear being rejected. At the next business event you go to where open mingling takes place, take a look around, and you will see a lot of uncomfortable people—even CEOs and CIOs. White people, blacks, Hispanics, Asians, older people, younger people, and others are just as scared as anyone else. It's not just Asians. It is a universal problem." If you're reserved, your natural behaviors don't necessarily have to dictate your networking potential. You can manage your predisposition to being reserved with careful preparation.

## WHY NETWORK? —

You may think that you can get away without networking in your career. Certainly, people have found jobs and landed new clients due to other means, such as having a proven track record or benefiting from the brand-name reputation of one's school or employer. Yet, the effective use of your personal and professional networks can be one of the best ways to obtain interviews and new job leads. If you plan to stay in the same line of work for the foreseeable future, you may be able to get away with maintaining a small network in your industry. However, if you are planning a job change or a major career overhaul, you are not likely to know many people in your new line of work. For many of you, a career change, minor or major in scope, is inevitable in the course of your career lifetime.

While Internet postings, ads, and recruiters work in certain situations, these are relatively passive ways to search for a job, since you, as a job hunter, are waiting quietly for a job to be posted in order that you can respond. The problem is that you will never hear about the slots that never get posted, because those jobs will typically be filled either by external candidates who get referred in by current employees at the company or by internal transfers and proactive job seekers who contact the company directly to create jobs for themselves that didn't exist in the firm before.

## CREATIVE WAYS TO FIND
## NEW NETWORKING CONTACTS —

Almost anyone in your everyday life can be part of your network, including relatives, local merchants, neighbors, and fellow alumni. Most of us have these resources, but it doesn't occur to us to use them. My colleague Adrienne had been in the job market for 6 months before she remembered that her second cousin worked for Microsoft, one of her major targets. Once she realized that her cousin might be able to provide information about Microsoft and help her determine what functional group she might be a fit for, she wasted no time in contacting him. He had no idea that Adrienne was looking for a job, but he was happy to oblige and made the appropriate introductions.

When you're networking, don't underestimate the level of help you might get. Senior-level contacts might certainly help you get in the door faster because of their access to job openings, but don't neglect administrative assistants and contacts at your level. You never know who your networking contact might know. Jennifer, a researcher at a biotechnology company, recalls meeting someone at a cocktail party who had expressed an interest in making a career change to advertising or marketing. But Jennifer noticed that as soon as the woman realized that Jennifer worked for a biotech company, the woman lost interest and abruptly moved on to the next person. Little did the woman know that Jennifer's best friend was a senior person at marketing giant Young & Rubicam. Had she continued to build rapport, Jennifer might have shared her friend's contact info with her. The lesson here is this: Treat networking contacts with the kind of respect that you would want to be given, no matter where you meet them.

## NETWORKING IS A RECIPROCAL RELATIONSHIP —

I can't say enough about the importance of maintaining your network. If you want to be someone to whom people give assistance, you have to give in a networking relationship. When someone offers you a personal contact, it's part of networking etiquette to let him know the outcome of your meeting with that contact. Whether or not the meeting outcome is favorable, send a thank-you note to your initial contact. If you weren't able to reach the referral contact, you should still maintain contact with your initial contact. You might send him an e-mail that says, "Hi there! I really appreciated the time you spent with me in March to discuss your position at XYZ Company and wanted to keep you in the loop about the progress of my job search. I called John Doe a few times in the course of the last 2 weeks but was unable to track him down because of his busy travel schedule. Should I continue to pursue him, or do you think I should go a different route?" Such a note might prompt him to make a call on your behalf to John Doe, increasing the chances that John would take your next call. Be someone whom others won't hesitate to endorse—always hold up your end of net-working relationships. You never know—your contact may end up being one of your competitors, coworkers, bosses, or clients one day.

Create an organized system for keeping track of your contacts. This can be in the form of an e-mail distribution list, a newsletter mailing list, or a spreadsheet that tracks all of your contacts and the latest action taken for each. Then send e-mails, newsletters, or cards periodically.

## CHANGING CAREERS WHEN YOU HAVE NO CONTACTS IN YOUR NEW FIELD

Monica Sonido, 29, a Filipino American, was ready for a career change. After having worked in pharmaceutical sales for just over a year, she realized that her skills and personality traits seemed to be pointing her to a different job and perhaps an entirely new industry. The results of her Seven Stories Exercise, various other assessment exercises, and one-on-one sessions with me appeared to indicate that she should go into journalism, but she had no contacts at all at any of the local newspapers or TV stations. None of the search firms that used to call her to offer her opportunities at other pharmaceutical companies seemed to have any large media clients, and Monica didn't have a journalism degree. Determined to make the career change within 1 or 2 years, she got involved with a local charity organization that happened to have a handful of assistant producers from the local TV station as members. While planning their annual benefit dinner, she was able to get an introduction to some of the top media executives in the industry. Her experience with the organization put her front and center in the view of many media execs at the TV station. Though there was no immediate opening, within 11 months she'd created a job for herself as a production assistant to one of the new producers of a weekly news show. This position would have been impossible to land without the creative use of her network.

## Making the Most of Your Personal Marketing Pitch —

One of the easiest ways to practice and improve your personal marketing pitch is to use it in networking. Many people also have a 30-second version ready to go because they never know whom they might meet and they always want to be ready to introduce themselves. The shorter version will help you introduce yourself in internal group meetings and establish your credibility quickly.

### CREATING YOUR PERSONAL MARKETING PITCH

1. Know your audience.

   Whom are you addressing? What is his or her level? Make sure your marketing pitch is appropriate for your functional/industry expertise.

2. Determine what you have to offer.

   Select one or two key accomplishments from your assessment exercises that are relevant to the people you will be meeting.

3. Do research about the company/industry.

   - With the widespread availability of the Internet and online information sources, there is absolutely no excuse for not knowing current information about the company and the person you are meeting, be it an informational meeting, job interview, social party, or casual networking meeting.

   - Understand the fundamentals of how the industry operates. How does the business run/what makes it tick? How does the economy or other current events affect the day-to-day operations? Learn recent news about the company, get a copy of its annual report, and make sure to read the company's press releases.

4. State your career objectives explicitly.

   Do not leave it to your listener to question why it is that you have called this meeting.

   - Identify your top three selling points and incorporate them into your marketing pitch. How does your background link to the company's business objectives?

- If you just give a play-by-play of your biographical history, you may bore the listener with unnecessary details. Make it crisp, direct, and focused. If you're not sure what you want to communicate, your listener won't get it, either!

5. Practice your pitch with a friend or colleague.

   Your pitch is a work in progress. Practice it in the mirror, and continue to refine and perfect it until it sounds natural and unrehearsed.

If you have already completed your self-assessment, you should be able to easily draft this marketing pitch for yourself. You should *always* have a pitch ready to go, no matter what your employment situation. Having a great pitch in your back pocket can be useful in any social or professional setting. If you plan to use your pitch as a tool for a job search, consider developing a different pitch for each job target. Start with a foundational pitch for your top job functions/industries, then tailor the others accordingly.

Here are a few sample pitches:

I am the global project lead for the e-commerce division. I manage the development, implementation, and ongoing maintenance of our corporate e-commerce initiatives. In addition, I have a dotted line to our corporate technology group and align myself closely with some of their special projects.

I am a senior marketing and communications director with experience in the advertising and publishing industries. Early in my career, I worked as an account executive for an ad agency, then segued into marketing communications for an entertainment company. During that time, I worked with the executive team in the due diligence process as it prepared for an acquisition, after which I started working with my current employer. I especially enjoy helping to package and launch new products and working with the broader corporate strategy to help make the company reach its financial targets. I'm really excited about the prospect of helping my next employer achieve similar goals.

I have been the financial analyst supporting one of the consumer goods units of my company. I serve as the profit and loss expert for the business unit director in charge of consumer products, and this year, I am working on a cross-functional project team that is evaluating a new general ledger system with external consultants.

My role as a compensation analyst is quite broad. Not only do I get involved with the annual salary surveys with competitor firms, but I am also the president of the California chapter of the Compensation Association. My latest project examines how our unit could provide additional support to the human resources generalists in the business groups that we support. My special interest lately has been in the area of 401(k) programs and creative ways to work with employee pay packages.

I am currently an assistant director at a foundation. I have experience in reviewing grants, policy making, and developing programs. I can bring to your company's community relations group a depth of knowledge and practical know-how from my hands-on experience with most of the educational nonprofit organizations in our local geographic region. My boss has always said that I have an eye for identifying great innovative programs.

## ADDITIONAL TIPS FOR USING YOUR MARKETING PITCH TO TELL YOUR STORY —

### *Remember the Three S's*

- *Be succinct.*
  A marketing pitch should be concise and to the point. Don't spend a lot of time repeating your résumé. Identify one or two accomplishments that are relevant to the networking contact and make your objectives clear.

- *Be sincere.*
  People can spot insincerity from a mile away. Don't ask people to meet you for an informational interview and then expect them to recom-

mend you for a job. Going in planning to fish for a recommendation is deceptive and in poor taste. If you were referred to the networking contact by a friend, you could end up burning bridges with both the contact and your friend by such manipulation.

■   *Be specific.*
    Tell your networking contact why you are interested in speaking with her, and state your job targets right up front.

## NETWORKING FOR THE LONG HAUL —

A professional network is useful to the extent that you invest the time in cultivating relationships prior to your need to land a job. A few years ago, a new client of mine was eager to start a job search after being affected by a corporate downsizing. His strategy of working with search firms and answering ads in the paper resulted in two interviews at companies that weren't exactly his targets, and eventually, those leads petered out. When I said, "I think it's time that you reached out to your professional network to obtain new contacts," he was initially very resistant. I gave him specific instructions on who to contact and gave him follow-up homework. It wasn't that he didn't want to call his contacts; apparently, he didn't even have a contact to call. He'd been too busy working in his job for the previous 3 years and hadn't bothered to keep up with contacts from his prior jobs or build relationships with others in his industry at other firms. It took him several months to rebuild his network. The earlier in your career you begin to build these relationships, the better it will be for you as you make various transitions. But you must maintain them so that you don't end up in my client's position.

## FAVORITE QUESTIONS FOR INFORMATIONAL INTERVIEWS —

When you are preparing questions for your networking meetings, start with the easy ones. Then move on to probing questions that get more sophisticated and industry-specific. If, after networking with a dozen or so people, your networking questions are still very basic and elementary, something isn't right. Make sure that you understand your new job targets and what they expect you to know.

- "If you had unlimited resources to accomplish your objectives for the year, what would be the first thing you would implement?"
- "What are some of the key priorities for your division as a result of the new acquisition?"
- "How would you describe the ideal candidate for your group? Could the person be molded, or are you looking for a certain personality?"
- "What has been the trademark contribution of your group this year?"
- "If the budget doesn't get approved, what would happen to the e-commerce project (or international expansion plans or growth plans or training opportunities)? How could this affect day-to-day operations?"

## KEY LESSONS LEARNED —

- *Take the time to build and maintain an active professional network.*
  Once you meet new people, take the time to nurture those relationships. Aim to have five people in your network at any given time who can vouch for the caliber of your work. Choose from previous bosses, co-workers, clients, mentors, and subordinates.

- *Think of networking as an investment in your career.*
  As you progress in your career, you will find that your deep and broad network will be useful both when you're looking for a new job and when others need your help.

■ *Networking is a reciprocal relationship.*

Make sure you follow up with your contacts, and if your contacts ask you for assistance, make sure that you return the favor.

■ *Develop your own marketing pitch.*

Use the three S's as guidelines: Your personal pitch should be succinct, sincere, and specific. Practice it, know it, and use it often when you meet new people. It is a work in progress; continue to make it better as you move upward in your career.

■ *Determine what method you will use to keep in contact with your network: E-mail, periodic mailings, newsletters, holiday cards, or phone calls.*

Create a system to track communication with your contacts.

■ *Remember that during networking meetings or informational interviews, you are responsible for sustaining the conversation. Prepare as many questions as possible for such meetings.*

# PART III

# GETTING AHEAD ON THE

# - JOB -

## – EIGHT –

# ON-THE-JOB MOBILITY STRATEGIES

---

## Learning to Toot Your Own Horn: Navigating in Corporate America

---

*"Zi," my high school teacher said, then corrected herself. "I mean Zia, how come you never told me how to say your name after all these years?"*

*I didn't know how to answer. It had never occurred to me to correct my teacher. In the Confucian order of the world, teachers were right up there with parents in commanding respect and obedience. I simply had no voice to raise to my teacher.*

—Helen Zia, *Asian American Dreams: The Emergence of an American People*

*I am the greatest.*

—Muhammad Ali

## MAKING YOUR MARK ON A BLANK SLATE —

Everyone starts off on the same level on the first day of work. Your prior jobs, honors, college grades, and extracurricular activities may have gotten you into the corporation, but the burden is now on you to begin carving out your own niche. This is a concern shared by all new recruits regardless of race or ethnicity, but unique cultural influences take it to a new dimension for Asian professionals. As Paul Tokunaga writes in *Invitation to Lead: Guidance for Emerging Asian American Leaders,*

> No matter how fluent our English is, how hip and American we dress, how easily we seem to hang with non-Asian Americans, we live in a liminal world. . . . We (Asian Americans) are always in between, with a foot in this world, a foot in that world.

## NETWORKING HORIZONTALLY, VERTICALLY, AND DIAGONALLY —

Your first few weeks on the job is when the hard labor in managing work relationships takes place. First, be deliberate about forging strong working relationships with your boss, clients, and colleagues who are immediately impacted by your job responsibilities. You also need to be managing up, taking the time to get to know managers who are at your boss's level and people who are a few levels above your boss. But networking with senior managers should never be pursued at the expense of losing the pulse of your peer network in the firm.

Often an effective informal network of professionals at your own level in a different part of the organization can help you obtain critical inside scoop and unwritten rules particular to your company, as well as give you insights into who is good to work for and how to best approach this person about a project. Says Jonathon, a second-generation Asian Indian, 26, who works in a consulting organization:

I am still very close to the group of people with whom I started out in the same training program. While we have all moved on to different business units, our relationships have remained strong. When I was looking to leave my group to go into the emerging businesses unit, my trainee friend who had once had a project in the emerging businesses group introduced me to her former boss, who later ended up hiring me into her group. It was so great to not have to deal with the normal transfer process, which could have taken me a while to figure out. It was great for them, too. My new manager was relieved to not have to interview the dozens of candidates who would apply through internal job postings.

Clearly, his peer network was valuable to his career mobility.

Many companies consider peer and subordinate feedback about how you work with others to be critical to an overall assessment of your work, so it is important to continue to manage positive rapport with your peers, subordinates, and clients. The popular 360-degree feedback coaching tools provide this type of performance feedback from everyone who affects your position at your company, not just your boss, and can help you achieve optimal performance on the job. (A search of the term *360-degree feedback* on any Internet search engine will yield plenty of background information on these tools.)

## Tweaking Your Style Without Fundamentally Compromising Your Values —

Once you land a position, it is important that you understand how your job function fits into the grand scheme of things. It's not enough to buckle down to work. You need to map out a plan for promoting yourself so that your accomplishments will be known throughout the firm, not just to your boss during an annual review! But how do you accomplish this without feeling as though you're compromising your Asian cultural values and ideals? Becoming a leader in corporate America doesn't mean that you need to undergo an entire cultural makeover or even compromise your cultural values at all. Aside from mastering both spoken and written English and working with your company's corporate culture, there are simple, straightforward techniques that you can use immediately, no matter what your personality or cultural background, to help you manage the attitudes and behavioral habits that might otherwise hold you back.

One Chinese American managing director from a large global investment banking firm agrees wholeheartedly: "There are a couple of skills you need to have if you want to move up the ranks around here. And while some of these practices may not be natural for many, they are, nevertheless, skills you absolutely need to have in your tool kit if you want to advance beyond the analyst level: (1) public speaking skills, (2) self-promotion/internal marketing ability, and (3) openness to stretch assignments, including overseas assignments."

## STARTING OUT ON THE RIGHT FOOT —

# AN OVERACHIEVER WITH A PERFORMANCE CRISIS

### BACKGROUND

Bob Lee is what people would call a "well-assimilated" Asian American. Always popular in Asian circles on campus, he also socialized frequently with non-Asian classmates. He graduated from one of the top five Ivy League universities and always achieved beyond everyone's expectations. The summer after graduation, with a liberal arts degree in hand, Bob completed an investment bank's systems training program so that he could help analyze, build, and support the firm's sophisticated trading technology.

### PROBLEM: THE PERFORMANCE REVIEW SHOCK

The challenges began once Bob started on his first project for the bank. Three months flew by as he worked long hours, often skipping dinner, trying to meet every deadline. He never socialized during work hours. At his 6-month review, however, his manager gave him a rating of 3 on a scale of 1 to 5, with 5 being the highest score. In the performance discussion, Bob, a Korean American born in the United States to immigrant Korean parents, was told that despite his productivity and strong work ethic, he did not communicate adequately with his manager or coworkers. The team failed to meet the systems conversion deadline because Bob neglected to inform his manager that the deadline couldn't be met. Imagine the frustration Bob felt after working until midnight for over 2 weeks! Being the best and brightest wasn't enough to get him a high performance rating in this scenario.

## RESULT

Bob left the performance discussion feeling downright miserable. He had never received any grade lower than a B+ in college and certainly had never been rated average at anything. A 3 out of a possible 5! It was unthinkable. His confidence was shot, and he felt completely alienated from his work team. What would his parents think, especially his mom, who had often winced in disappointment when he brought home anything less than an A–? Bob had hit a low point.

## CULTURAL ISSUES

*Beneath the Surface*

It might seem that Bob had only a minor communication issue, that he was simply unaware of the value of constant communication with his peers, internal clients, and manager. Throughout your academic career, you were graded on individualized criteria: You took tests on your own and wrote papers based on your knowledge of a given subject. In a corporate environment, your performance is intimately linked to your coworkers' contributions. When Bob and I spoke about this during a coaching session, it was evident that there were other factors contributing to his behavior at work.

*One Life at Home, Another Life at Work:*
*A Case of Cultural Schizophrenia?*

Bob was raised to put his head down and do his work, expecting that his efforts would be rewarded. It is considered impolite in many Asian cultures to give bad news or attract negative attention to yourself, as Bob would have had to do had he spoken up about the project deadline. In his culture, the less fuss you make, the better, because that means that you are diligent and hardworking. As a result, when Bob realized that some of the tasks might not be 100% completed, he thought it was more important to just do as much as he possibly could and avoid raising a red flag to his boss. Also, he truly believed that with enough effort on his part, he would be able to complete the project on time. He didn't realize that some things would be out of his control. As Bob recounts: "I thought that as long as I put in the time with the project and did as much as I could by the deadline, I should still receive a good performance rating. My intention going into the project was to finish everything as planned. I was unaware that what I should have done was let my manager know the instant I felt that the deadline was not going to be sufficient to get everything done."

*The Concept of Teamwork*

In his new job, Bob was quite suddenly thrust into a corporate culture with an extremely strong teamwork orientation, where his success was closely linked with others' success. But he was still operating in "individual success" mode, so it didn't occur to him to give updates to his manager or meet with his coworkers for lunch occasionally to see how they could work together more effectively. Bob didn't realize that even if he did his part, *he* hadn't succeeded unless the group succeeded in meeting the project deadline. Also, his attempts to compensate by working later and by himself made him seem very insular and not inclusive.

## Action Steps

*Putting His Head Up*

Bob took a lot of the feedback from his review to heart. After spending some time in thought, he came up with a tangible, measurable action plan with his manager to work on his communication and teamwork skills. He scheduled weekly status meetings with his manager to inform him of his progress. Nowadays, he doesn't hesitate to go into his manager's office to let him know what he's up to or to just hang out. Bob pushes himself to speak to his manager at least twice a day, even if simply to shoot the breeze and enhance their working relationship. Bob made his manager aware of his natural cultural tendency to "put his head down" to get the work done and to not really concern himself with other people while working. Now that some of Bob's issues had been identified, his manager is thrilled to have such a dedicated guy on the team. He's now committed to helping Bob succeed.

*Getting His Manager Involved*

After this incident, Bob asked his manager to keep him accountable when notable issues arise, favorable or not. His supportive manager appreciated Bob's openness and encouraged Bob to approach him at any time. In addition, when the firm started a department-wide diversity awareness campaign, the manager attended the seminars to learn more about Asian cultural influences on his employees. He made attendance at the seminars mandatory for everyone in his reporting structure. After all, his internal client managing director is Chinese, and he often has oversight over employees in Singapore and Hong Kong.

KEY LESSONS LEARNED —

- Your success is not about your productivity alone. Your individual performance rating is not determined by your diligence and the quantity of work you produce; it is a collection of factors, including communicating with the team and working effectively with others to contribute to the larger project.
- Be proactive about understanding and managing your ingrained behaviors.

### Practical On-the-Job Tool

So how do you start off on the right foot in a new job? Once you are settled in, find a reliable buddy who can help you ferret out the little things that make the company run, such as the best time to ask for vacation, how to solicit performance feedback, and where you can submit your medical reimbursement forms. Find a peer in a different business group or even an administrative professional to act as your buddy. Senior managers are often too busy to help with the little questions.

Ask for a comprehensive organizational chart of your group, other business units, and any internal infrastructure groups from which you can benefit. If face-to-face meetings with your peers, subordinates, and internal clients haven't been set up for you yet, then set up a 15-minute one-on-one with each person in your group as well as each person in your client group or finance/information technology/administration group. Go in with an open mind and a lot of good, insightful questions (see the list on pages 195–96) that will help you get to know the person better. For openers, share some information about yourself, your former employer, and your previous jobs and allow the person to feel comfortable with you. Here's one good opener.

I didn't have a chance to meet with you during the interview process, and I really wanted to meet everyone with whom I would come in contact early on in my tenure here. I honestly don't believe I can do this large-scale project on my own. I know I'll need all the help I can get! I wanted to speak with you for 15 or 20 minutes to ask how we can work together and to get to know you better.

## TIPS FOR STARTING A NEW JOB ON THE RIGHT FOOT

Here are some useful follow-up questions to ask your colleagues if you're new to your job. If you intend to use some of these questions, make sure that your delivery style is casual and conversational—and your own. Take special care not to be annoying or overly intrusive. In American business culture, it's acceptable to be assertive and up front about what you want on the job, but you want to be likeable, too. Don't worry too much about not being able to ask all of the questions at once. Just choose the ones that are appropriate for each situation and work them into conversations.

- How can I work well/better with your group in the newly established organizational structure?
- Let's explore some of the functions that you and I will be participating in together. More specifically, I have some questions about ___. (Be sensitive whenever you ask questions that deal with job descriptions or boundaries. Some people are reluctant to release too much information too quickly to a new recruit; you may want to establish a little more credibility first. Talking over lunch may help lower coworkers' initial guards.
- How do you prefer to work? Are you an e-mail person, phone person, or a face-to-face person? How do you like to receive and give status updates?
- I'm a newcomer to this group. Is there anything I should know before I start doing my job?
- What are some potential political issues that are already at play between your boss and mine? (Be extra cautious about asking a question like this; you should reserve it for when

you are more familiar with your position and your colleague's.)

- Can you give me the top performance criteria/measures for someone in my role?
- Can we have lunch? Let's get something on the calendar.
- Tell me about your team. Who are the members? Let's get them together to meet my staff at a luncheon.

When in doubt, take the initiative. If your tendency is to avoid appearing pushy, you may need to force yourself to take the first step, but you'll find it easer each time. Being an effective leader may simply mean being the first to initiate an important contact or project.

## SOLIDIFYING YOUR ROLE IN THE COMPANY —

# NO JOB DESCRIPTION, NO TITLE

Tooting their own horn is hard enough for some Asian Americans, but it can be even harder when you are suddenly thrust into a new corporate culture. Dennis Nguyen is an example of someone who changed careers and found himself a fish out of water. He was a known commodity in his Wall Street job, yet at the small start-up that he moved to, he realized how serious was his inability to promote himself and continuously communicate his accomplishments.

### BACKGROUND

Dennis, a Vietnamese American, spent 4 years as an equity research analyst at a large brokerage house. He was very bright, with strong quantitative analysis skills and a knack for the stock market. But he was tired of the long hours on Wall Street and wanted to work at a small high-tech firm. As most of his contacts were limited to Wall Street, he realized he needed to branch out and meet people who

were involved with small companies. After a year of networking—
which he dreaded, being an introvert at heart—he finally landed an
attractive offer at a small Internet company.

### PROBLEM

As soon as he began working at the start-up, Dennis felt that he had
made a huge mistake. As an analyst at a prestigious Wall Street firm,
he had had a title, structure, and the unlimited training resources of
a big company. He found the environment at the new job to be ultra-
political, and the company had a flat (no) organizational structure.
Everyone was jockeying for position (sometimes in ridiculous ways),
and he was never given a clear job description. Dennis had never
enjoyed selling himself at work, but now he found that he had to do
it to survive. In addition, though there had been competitiveness and
politics at his former job, he'd always felt valued as a knowledgeable
contributor. At the new job, he felt that he had to look over his
shoulder every moment of the day.

Dennis was unhappy when I met him. He told me, "I don't
know where things went awry. I was tired of the big firm experience
with all its bureaucracy, and I thought moving to a small shop would
bring increased camaraderie and team spirit. I was mistaken. I grew
up in a very traditional Vietnamese family where we were rewarded
for keeping our mouths shut and not blowing our own horns. I'm
probably the best Confucian son a parent can have! Unfortunately
for me, in my current job, I may get fired if I don't start to brag a little
bit. I guess the larger firm was a better fit for me after all."

Dennis is typical of many Asian clients I have coached. First,
I encouraged him to say at least one thing at every meeting he
attended, even if he felt that what he had to offer was a small
opinion or one vaguely reminiscent of someone else's comments. It
was okay if he failed to volunteer the most original and creative
answer; his role was to be an active, contributing member of the
team! Gradually, he began to get to know the people at his bosses'
level more personally, meeting them over drinks after work and
getting a sense of the direction of the company. At these informal

settings, he was able to keep the managers posted on many of his accomplishments, a hard task, given that his colleagues were often traveling and out of the office. He also asked everyone for feedback on a continual basis, especially right after a client meeting or a marketing pitch.

After 4 months, he felt more comfortable with his newly acquired skills. Today, he's thriving at that small company, and he may make some real money if it goes public.

## KEY LESSONS LEARNED —

- Don't keep your trophies to yourself. Recognize the value of communicating your accomplishments as they occur.
- Once you identify the steps needed to progress in your company, be determined to make the subtle attitude or behavioral adjustments necessary to succeed.
- Cultivate strong vertical and horizontal relationships with senior management and coworkers in different departments.

## GETTING PROMOTED —

## AT A CAREER IMPASSE

### BACKGROUND

Kelly Hirada, a Japanese American, came to the United States at age 10, was educated there, then returned to Hong Kong and Tokyo to work with Asian markets for 6 years before returning to the United States. Extremely bright and without a trace of an accent, she was successful in her early years at a large accounting firm. However, when the partner title eluded her after 2 years of being considered, she wanted to know why her career had suddenly stalled.

When Kelly attended school in Japan as a young girl, she was an excellent student. But the educational system in Japan was very different from the American system: She learned a lot of things by rote memory, and she rarely had the opportunity to challenge her teachers or parents. Docile, bright, and easygoing, Kelly was always considered a "model Japanese girl." Later, in the small Midwestern suburb her family moved to, she did well throughout middle school. It wasn't until she went to high school and the structure of the classes changed that she started getting grades that didn't reflect her abilities. She evolved into a B student, and teacher feedback was always along the lines of "Kelly doesn't verbalize her opinions in class very often. Even if she disagrees with the theory or opinion of someone else, she backs down, often without a question or a defense."

Kelly had moved up all the way to manager in her Big Four accounting firm but consistently had trouble politicking with her seniors throughout her career. She handled herself well with more junior employees and same-level colleagues but never felt very comfortable dealing with the senior partners except to give them routine updates on her work. Recalls Kelly: "I knew I could make partner. I definitely had the skills to do it, and feedback from my clients was always stellar. However, in the deep recesses of my mind, I knew I didn't know how to brownnose and play the game with my seniors as well as some of my peers did. It just didn't come as easy for me. My peers are such great storytellers, while I'm always too busy just trying to do a good job and get along with everyone."

## CULTURAL ISSUES

Kelly adds:

> Eric, another guy I started out in training with, does politicking so naturally and makes it look so easy. I actually think I may be

better with detail and problem solving than he is, but at our level it looks like it's more important for us to know how to play the corporate game. Sure, he's Caucasian, but I refuse to attribute my shortcomings to my ethnic background or Asian heritage. I know I am naturally a reserved, detail-oriented person and don't love to schmooze for the sake of schmoozing. However, I know that the constant reinforcement I received as a kid growing up in Japan and later, as a professional in Asia, to conform and to obey my teachers, parents, and people in authority left an indelible mark on the way I behave in corporate and business settings. It's not easy to change that kind of behavior overnight, but awareness definitely helped.

## ACTION STEPS

Kelly realized the importance of carefully drafting a self-marketing statement. To be visible to senior managers and have them consider you for special projects, internal transfers, and promotional opportunities, you need to be in their line of vision constantly. If you hesitate to step outside your boundaries for fear of not knowing how to present yourself, then a strategic marketing statement can help you. Similar to a marketing pitch that you create for an external job search, this marketing statement will introduce you to your colleagues succinctly and clearly.

Kelly created a marketing statement for herself. She often had trouble being spontaneous when networking, so we made sure that she had four different versions memorized (until they became second nature) so that she could use them in different settings. Also, I told her that she needed to be better at storytelling. We created four stories from her personal experience that she could use, two for cocktail parties or spontaneous meetings and two that she could use in various internal corporate settings. Whenever she went to networking meetings, industry association gatherings for health care, or even social events, she practiced using her new marketing pitches.

After a few months, Kelly was a pro at storytelling. Only she and I knew that her anecdotes weren't quite as spontaneous as they sounded. Because she already possessed superb interpersonal skills, we were just adding to her arsenal. Granted, she still did not *love* networking and she certainly wouldn't call herself naturally gregarious, but she no longer dreads picking up the phone and calling a senior-level person because she has an internalized script she can always depend on.

### KELLY'S MANAGER'S VIEW

After Kelly had acquired these new skills, her manager said:

> Kelly is aggressive about marketing herself now, not just dependent on her accomplishments to speak for themselves. She's not the loudest member of my group, but she's a lot more vocal about her new deals in her own reserved manner, and clients just love her. I really see a difference. She's still Kelly and isn't someone who'll run you over like a freight train, but if she continues to grow and develop in this direction, she will be a star here.

## KEY LESSONS LEARNED —

- Be sensitive to the American emphasis on participation, and be aware that when you approach a new environment, speaking out is likely to be valued as a sign of engagement and as a way of establishing your presence.
- Develop a few good scripts for yourself. Obtain feedback from trusted advisors or a career coach. Practice using them in a variety of scenarios, including social gatherings. Customize the scripts for each purpose—one script for a promotion, one for an internal transfer, and another for serving on cross-functional task forces.
- Be knowledgeable about the internal transfer protocol

202 | BREAKING the BAMBOO CEILING

in your firm—the same strategies that work for seeking promotions can apply when seeking to work in another department. Abide by the rules as much as possible; you don't want to alienate your current boss by having him find out through the wrong communication channels that you are ready for a change.

■ Become active on special project committees, corporate task forces, and other high-profile initiatives with plenty of senior management involvement.

---

### Practical On-the-Job Tool 1: The Personal Marketing Pitch

See Chapter 7 on networking for more examples.

DO'S

1. Review your résumé, previous performance evaluations, and other assessment exercises to extract highlights of your accomplishments.
2. Draft a three- or four-sentence pitch for yourself that effectively answers the request "Tell me about yourself" while marketing your qualifications and appropriately conveying your seniority or level.
3. Review the marketing statement, deleting any awkward phrases that may sound too canned.
4. Ask a trusted advisor or mentor to critique your new pitch.
5. Continue to revise your pitch as your career needs evolve.

DON'TS

1. Don't make your pitch longer than 1 or 2 minutes. You don't want to bore your networking contacts.
2. Don't use a chronological play-by-play of every single job you have held. Instead, make your pitch crisp and compelling so that it makes people want to know more about you.

# PREPARATION COUNTS

How effectively you answer the questions or requests "Tell me about yourself" or "Why should I hire you?" or "What sets you apart from other candidates with similar credentials?" can make or break the deal.

EXAMPLE A, FOR INTERNAL TRANSFERS  Gail was interested in transferring from one function in advertising to a very different function. Her first attempt at a pitch ("Before"), something she quickly pieced together for a luncheon, wasn't a bad marketing statement, but it lacked a few important ingredients. It provided her entire corporate history and the details of her accounting experience but didn't adequately focus on the target of her career interest. The "After" statement incorporates the do's listed earlier and expertly provides an informative skill-based rationale for a move to the marketing department without repeating the contents of her résumé. It is crisp, easy to understand, and to the point. Quite frankly, it also sounds more interesting than the first.

**Before:**

I started out my career at ABC Partners, a small market research company, and after five years, I made a move to XYZ to get into the advertising business. I started out in the accounting department; then the VP of the finance group pulled me into a financial analysis function. I've been in this role for a few years now. I am really interested in your marketing group because I've always felt that I had an interest in developing more marketing skills to round out my career. I was intrigued to hear about your group and the expansion efforts that you are planning.

**After:**

I work in the finance group of XYZ Advertising Company. There, I interact regularly with marketing, product development, and accounting to ensure that the profit-and-loss statement and related financial reports are captured accurately. I provide not only the quantitative results but also the anecdotal feedback that can be used by senior managers in the firm to make business development decisions. One of my latest interests has been the marketing end of the business. I find myself looking at new ways of presenting this information, and I understand that the marketing group is often under-staffed. Can I ask you a few questions about the direction and focus of your group over a coffee break?

EXAMPLE B, FOR CAREER CHANGERS    Steve developed his first pitch in preparation for an information technology job fair. Though the "Before" pitch clearly states his career change objective, it doesn't distinctly link his background to the types of skills required by a potential employer. As you can see, the "After" pitch discusses his obvious aptitude and enthusiasm for the stock market and demonstrates his in-depth knowledge about the field.

**Before:**

Hi, I'm Steve Kong, and I will be graduating this fall from business school. I started my career at ZD Capital as a programmer. After one year, I moved on to MJT, doing similar work but with fixed income products. In addition to my technical skills, I have good interpersonal skills and can work in a team. I would like to make a switch to a smaller environment, and your company seems to be a great fit, based on what I've read.

**After:**

I'm Steve Kong, with five years of experience in the applications devel-opment group at MJT Financial Services. I am eager to transfer some of the process management and technical expertise I've gathered to a smaller envi-ronment, particularly in the dot-com world, where I can make an impact. One of the things I've heard about your company is that you look for entre-preneur types. While at MJT, I put together an innovative way to process trades in a much faster time frame, and I was able to sell the idea to senior management. Later, I was able to lead a cross-functional team of people in the global implementation of that effort.

*Practical On-the-Job Tool 2: Internal Networking Questions for Career Advancement*

■  If you had an unlimited budget and resources to accomplish your objectives for your department, what would be the top three initiatives you would launch?

- What is the preliminary succession plan for your group? Are you looking to groom your current staff for senior roles, or are you looking for different skill sets?
- What are the hot-potato items on your to-do list that are not getting accomplished? What other projects could you focus your attention on if these were taken off your plate? (This question will help the manager to think more strategically about her group, a big plus for you.)
- What are some of the skills you look for in your ideal employees? Are they naturals, or are they groomed?
- Would it be possible to work on some projects together in the future? I can speak with my manager about the possibility of sharing resources.

## LEADING AND MANAGING A MEETING —

## BACKING DOWN TOO EASILY WHEN CHALLENGED

### BACKGROUND

As a senior financial analyst in the controller's area for a top pharmaceutical company, Jeanne Eng enjoyed her job. It allowed her to use her interest in finance and her CPA and have an impact on the daily operations of the business units she supported.

### PROBLEM

After 5 years at the firm, Jeanne had a staff of accountants for whom she was responsible, and she was often required to lead meetings to resolve issues with other departments and to manage project deadlines. But she continued to get feedback that she was ineffective in managing meetings. Conversations with her manager revealed that she had an issue with being confronted or challenged. Says her manager:

Jeanne is so accurate with her reports, and we always have great talks about her work. However, when she is faced with defending her case and numbers to senior management or her internal clients in the business units, I see a completely different side of Jeanne. She freezes up, or rather she becomes this silent person who doesn't defend her work, even if it's totally accurate. If someone challenges her figures or says something is wrong on her report, the most she says is "I'll look into that. Maybe I missed something." I could have said something at some of the meetings, but I didn't want her to think she should depend on me if I weren't there.

I spent time with Jeanne distilling her issues. She had great instincts, and her work was almost always 100% accurate. However, as she recalls:

I know my work is always impeccable, and I should always be able to stand behind my numbers. But when I'm faced with a direct confrontation from a really strong personality, I totally shut down. Instead of going logically through my backup numbers and reviewing the facts, I simply want to make peace at the table and I back down. It's a terrible habit, and I know I need to break it.

## CULTURAL ISSUES

As we discussed her cultural upbringing, Jeanne said:

My parents were doting, supportive people. I was born in the U.S., but at home we were raised the "Chinese way." During family dinners at home, we would have discussions about various things that happened that day. If a contentious topic came up and I disagreed with my parents, I was usually told to obey them because they knew better and that I should respect their authority. We might have had different opinions, but we tried to keep them to ourselves if they flew in the face of the established way. We weren't punished for disagreeing with their views, but there was an understood sense of disapproval if I openly showed rebellion. I suppose this was also probably true of my non-Asian teenage friends at the time, but my family was definitely a subscriber to the true Confucian order, where filial piety and respecting authority was and is very important.

## ACTION STEPS

Jeanne and her manager came up with a game plan: learning to stick to her guns in meetings, periodically working with an executive coach, and taking some assertiveness training courses offered by her company. If these resources are not readily available to you, you can still use the questioning techniques that Jeanne used when her numbers were challenged during heated discussions from internal clients. She now has a focused strategy for standing firm. Instead of cowering at the first negative comment, she responds to these unexpected challenges with a question that allows her time to regain composure, such as: "What numbers are you referring to exactly? The sales figures were tallied according to the profit-and-loss sheets that your group double-checked and approved, so it would be helpful to have more specific information."

This questioning strategy has helped Jeanne tremendously. Moreover, her manager has been very supportive of her fight against her tendency to back down. In the beginning of her coaching sessions, he attended many of the meetings with her. When she became more comfortable, Jeanne attended some of the meetings alone. However, because she knows her tendency to back down, she still likes to bring her manager to the *really* tough meetings that are fraught with conflict. In a later status update with her manager, we observed some remarkable improvement. Her manager recalls:

We had a great conversation about how I can show support with my presence in some of these meetings. Jeanne told me that even though she is pretty confident about her work, she loses that confidence because culturally she has always been brought up to respect and obey her elders, not answer back to them, even if she feels they are wrong. She wasn't blaming her upbringing, but she wanted to acknowledge that it was there and that she wanted my help in dealing with it.

At the next big meeting, I made sure that I supported her views if she stuck her neck out. It was as simple as saying, "Jeanne has reviewed these reports with me, and they look top-notch." That gave her the confidence to continue to stick to her guns. In about two or three months, her ability to push herself to defend her views and support her statements and reports improved, and I did not need to attend many of the meetings with her.

Remarks Jeanne: "When I recognized that I could do something about my inaction at these meetings, I was able to take concrete steps to improve. Having these good comeback statements give me the confidence to stick my neck out even if I am only reasonably sure about my opinions."

## KEY LESSONS LEARNED —

- Be persistent and assertive in a style that is comfortable for you. Use questioning techniques to probe challenges during meetings. By asking others direct questions to clarify the problem, you'll divert attention away from yourself long enough that you can think through a good response.
- Stick to your guns to show your confidence in your work. If you've done your homework already, there shouldn't be too many surprises. Self-confidence in the face of adversity is a critical skill for corporate survival, and the earlier you master it in your career, the better.

ASSERTING YOURSELF AND HAVING FUN
WITH YOUR COLLEAGUES —

## HESITANCE ABOUT REVEALING YOUR ASIAN SELF

If you look at some of the most successful executives in corporate America today, you'll find that most of them are not afraid to be themselves on the job. However, if you ask Asians to name a barrier to success in corporate America, they often report feelings of needing to be someone else in the workplace. They operate one way at home (very respectful of their elders, not talking back or going against the tide, speaking in softer tones, and so on) and then are challenged to behave a different way at the office, where they are rewarded for their assertiveness, creativity, and uniqueness.

### BACKGROUND

Suresh Singh, an Indian American, found himself on a work team with two Caucasian men at a midsize software consulting company. Suresh speaks with a slight accent, has lived in the United States since the age of 3, and was educated at the best U.S. universities. Though he had retained much of the Indian culture of his parents, he feels more American than Indian. Everyone on his team seemed friendly and good-natured, but Suresh found himself being excluded from social interactions. He often felt that the other men were cutting him off in meetings or not taking him seriously. As the project progressed, this affected his ability to contribute to the team, and he felt slighted by his coworkers.

   In the third week of the project, Suresh approached his team about the issue. Surprisingly, the two men who seemed to be giving him the cold shoulder were unaware that Suresh felt this way. During the encounter, David, one of the two men on his team, confessed that Suresh was the first Indian professional with whom he'd had any contact. Though David wasn't consciously distancing himself, this feeling of "unfamiliarity and awkwardness" stopped him from socializing with Suresh. Of course, this seriously affected the dynamics of the team. As a result, David dealt more with Tom, the other team member, and failed to include Suresh in impromptu social gatherings after work, simply because he felt more comfortable with Tom.

David remarked: "Suresh seemed to contribute only minor statements during meetings and never provided his opinions with confidence." So, often, one or both of the other team members felt that he should assist and support Suresh in completing his statements. They perceived his lack of assertiveness as a lack of understanding about the subject matter. Apparently, these disruptive behaviors were actually attempts to "help" him.

When we sat down to discuss Suresh's dilemma, I made two observations: (1) Suresh was extremely uncomfortable and self-conscious sharing his cultural heritage at work. He felt reluctant about standing out beyond what was already physically apparent to everyone. (2) Because of his tendency to keep his Indian heritage to himself, his confidence level had plummeted, and it was affecting his assertiveness at work. No wonder, because his Indian background was such a significant part of his identity.

I encouraged Suresh to initiate a candid discussion with his colleagues after he determined how he could share a glimpse of his Indian heritage with them. After some thought, he decided that he would introduce them to Indian cuisine, and then, once his colleagues became more comfortable with him socially, he would share some of his cultural background and its impact on his professional demeanor. I asked Suresh to speak with conviction during meetings no matter how self-conscious he felt.

He took all of these suggestions to heart and had a follow-up meeting with his colleagues over drinks one Friday afternoon. He told them about how, growing up in his traditional South Asian family, he would never interrupt anyone if they were speaking and was taught to always think through a question before shooting off an answer. After learning about Suresh's tendency to be thoughtful before speaking and his concern about not "having an empty mouth," his colleagues became more sensitive to the issue.

Says Suresh: "Since I left the company last year for a better position, I have gained a lot of ground with my new employer, a pharmaceutical company. They are a demanding group, yes, but I've actually been able to practice some of the things we discussed. It's unfortunate that I couldn't use these techniques more at ABX Company, but they didn't go to waste, and I still keep in touch with Dave and Tom."

Those who come from a majority background most likely don't have a problem fitting into the mainstream culture. When they walk into a new situation, there's a strong chance that someone of their ethnic background will also be present. But most Asians have often experienced being the only Asian in the room and too often feel as if they represent every Asian in America. Being "too ethnic" or different can sometimes hurt you in corporate America. No matter how many diversity awareness task forces exist, most non-Asians in corporate America still don't know a lot about Asian Americans and the cultures from which they originate. Change takes time. And sometimes, non-Asians may lump all Asian Americans (be they Chinese, Japanese, Korean, Vietnamese, Thai, Asian Indian, or Cambodian) into one big group. When something is foreign to a person's experience, there is often less trust. Though you don't want to stamp out your cultural leanings in the workplace, it's also not smart to be "too ethnic," isolating yourself from others in your group.

## ACTION STEPS

It's important to showcase your sense of humor and the value of your culture at work. Diversity means more than having ethnic representation—it also means being inclusive about different ways

212 | BREAKING the BAMBOO CEILING

of relating and behaving. Suresh's "Indianness" always made him feel as if he were in a fishbowl, being watched because he sounded different. Instead of trying to be a unique professional, he'd wasted energy trying to fit in and be as Westernized as possible, socially and professionally. The pressure he put on himself this way had caused him a great deal of stress.

Later, after Suresh changed careers, I followed up with him to discuss his career mobility since the coaching period. Suresh had again used his idea to introduce his coworkers to different aspects of his Indian culture. One of his clients reported:

> Suresh is a great guy, but early on in our working relationship, I felt like he never really revealed his true self to me. He always treated me well, of course, and was always well mannered in his dealings. On top of that, he seemed to have a very successful career at the firm, but whenever he took me to lunch, he never talked about his personal life or family much. Lately, though, that's changed dramatically. I hope he continues to open up to me, because sometimes when you don't feel like you know someone well, you are reluctant to give him your trust, because you're just not familiar with what they're all about. The more I see the personal side of him, it's like I'm getting to know him in a different way. I am now a big Indian food fan!

## KEY LESSONS LEARNED —

- Don't be afraid to stand out or be different. As long as you are ethical and acting within the bounds of acceptable corporate behavior, sharing your heritage with your colleagues can enhance and provide an interesting dimension to your career, not hurt it.
- Be yourself within the confines of your own industry. One of the keys to success in corporate America is to add value.

If you can add value to your work by maximizing the positives of cultural influence and managing the negative impact of some cultural baggage, you'll be well on your way to success.

## CHALLENGE TO MANAGEMENT

When you, as a member of management, see a person on your team not fitting into the mainstream corporate culture, make an effort to engage that person and discuss the issue with him one-on-one. Make sure that the after-hours events are inclusive of everyone in your group, not just one type of person. If you believe that there are behavioral changes that can be made, draft a development strategy with your Asian employee.

## Superior Mentoring Strategies

Mentor: *a trusted counselor or guide.*

—*Merriam-Webster's Collegiate Dictionary,* eleventh edition

*Give a man a fish and you feed him for a day. Teach a man to fish and you feed him for a lifetime.*

—Chinese proverb

*Giving people self-confidence is by far the most important thing that I can do. Because then they will act.*

—Jack Welch

Mentoring is an age-old tradition. An effective mentoring relationship, with an informal, friendly exchange of ideas and advice, can pave the way to your career success and give you the tools to navigate corporate politics. As Brad Johnson and Charles Ridley write in *The Elements of Mentoring*, "Research consistently demonstrates the following benefits for mentored protégés: enhanced promotion rates, higher salaries, accelerated career mobility, improved professional identity, greater professional competence, increased career satisfaction, greater acceptance within the organization, and decreased job stress and role conflict."

But despite its virtues, many people simply don't bother to do mentoring correctly. I hear more often about failed mentoring relationships than fruitful ones. Both mentoring and being a protégé require understanding a set of relational rules. Yet I continue to encounter hundreds of professionals, mentors and protégés alike, who are unaware of the rules, because no one has defined them. And in mentoring relationships, as elsewhere in the workplace, cultural influences (particularly issues of hierarchy and authority) may get in the way.

Sam, a Chinese American marketing executive, shares: "In my experience, when a fellow Asian colleague approaches me to be a mentor, I typically see one of two extremes—the distant, respectful protégé or the dependent little sibling. The first protégé is hesitant to call when he's struggling because of his sense of respect for my title and rank, and the second type is completely dependent on me to be his caretaker in the company and takes little ownership over his own career development. I find both variations ineffective.

"In the first case, as an 'upper' middle manager in a large company, my plate is almost always full. If my protégé doesn't take the initiative to pop up on my radar screen every once in a while and instead waits around for me to reach out to him, I am unlikely to know what is going on in his career. In the latter scenario, it's difficult to work with a protégé who is unwilling to do anything to manage his own career. Both are ineffective because neither is driving his own career development. I can't say enough about the importance of knowing how to manage a healthy mentoring relationship. Busy executives need protégés that know how to drive the mentoring process. I'm not saying that I would never initiate contact with someone my junior, but it goes a long way when a protégé helps maintain the momentum."

Protégés shouldn't need to be spoon-fed everything, but they need to be pointed in the right direction so that they are encouraged to courageously pursue their own career objectives. Because there may be some underlying issues of hierarchy and authority at play with Asian protégés and mentors, any mentoring relationship should be carefully examined to ensure that it is effective.

Many of the professionals whom I meet report that they have mentors, but when I probe to determine the topics they cover during their mentoring meetings, many of them report mostly social conversation that produces little impact on their careers. So, what is not happening to make these meetings productive? Sometimes it's because the relationships never get below the surface. These close professional relationships, when used effectively, can help break down formalities and should help people get down to the "heart of the matter" so that important concerns are brought to a level where real decisions can be made. When you can break through the formalities of a work relationship and know someone well enough to get down to the tough issues, you can make some important changes. I have always had at least two or three mentors at every stage of my career. My mentors have also served as sponsors because they were in a position to consider me for high-profile opportunities and special projects in other business units that would otherwise be unavailable to me. But as with any relationship, it takes time and effort to cultivate strong mentoring relationships.

Not all mentoring relationships are the same. And you shouldn't expect that one person can fulfill all of your career knowledge and skills needs. Many people find that it is helpful to have at least two or three mentors at any given point in time who play different roles and can help you in targeted, focused ways throughout your career. At the very least, you should aim to identify three mentor candidates at work shortly after you start a new job. You may not be able to identify them on day 1, but within the first 4 to 6 months is fine.

## TYPES OF GUIDES: SPONSORS, MENTORS, CAREER BUDDIES, ROLE MODELS —

A *sponsor* is someone who, because of her senior position or her seat on a selection committee for senior-level leaders or on a succession planning committee, has the ability to toss your name in the ring for consideration and be your advocate. She can vouch for your work and abilities. But you must be known as a player to be put in the game. You can have a mentor who's also a sponsor, but it is absolutely critical if you want to move up that you have a sponsor inside your company.

A *mentor* is someone who coaches you throughout your career or a portion of it. He should be someone you meet with on a regular basis, but he doesn't have to work at your firm. He provides you with periodic guidance about workplace issues such as office politics, maneuvering techniques, and resolving conflicts.

A *career buddy* is only 1 or 2 years ahead of you in the firm and is someone you can contact to get the scoop on how to fill out the self-appraisal section on your performance evaluation form, how often to expect raises, the protocol for writing interoffice memos, and so on. He can help you identify the small things that can turn out to be big things if you get them wrong. You can never have enough buddies. If you know the right people, you'll always know where the minefields are.

An inspirational Asian *role model* (ARM) is someone in your industry or a related industry who can serve as your inspiration. It's always helpful to have an ARM even if the two of you don't meet on a regular basis. Even young Asian professionals who don't have an ARM with whom they meet regularly report feeling inspired whenever they see another Asian person in their field who has made it. Your role model should ideally be senior to you, but if it's difficult to identify one, remember that peer mentors have proven to be effective as well.

One colleague of mine came to admire a female executive who worked at a high-tech company. Though they actually never met, my friend continued to follow this executive's career and was inspired by her skill at breaking through gender and racial barriers. That alone was enough to spur her on to achieve similar heights in her own career.

You can be an ARM yourself. Extend yourself when you see a junior Asian person who works at your company. I saw this modeled very clearly by an African American colleague in sales. A few years ago, he took me, a client, to a baseball game along with his protégé. His protégé was a new African American recruit at his company who had attended his alma mater. I was amazed at how much time and interest he was investing in her. He explained to me, "If I don't bring her along and help her navigate in my company, which has virtually no African Americans in sales, no one at the top will help her! It was hard for me as a black salesperson without a mentor, and I want to try to save her some of the headaches I had to deal with." He spent lunch coaching her at least once every 2 weeks. He was definitely not just a token mentor; he had taken complete ownership over the responsibility of advising this new recruit.

## AN ASIAN MENTOR OR NOT? —

Does your mentor have to be Asian for the relationship to work? Certainly not. For one, the demand far exceeds the supply of Asian mentors in some industries and occupations. Although the numbers of Asian professionals in certain disciplines are growing, there are still very few Asians on corporate boards or in executive suite positions. In fact, Johnson and Ridley say, "Because junior professionals from minority groups often have limited opportunities for same-race mentorships, white mentors should establish as a priority the mentoring of protégés from diverse groups."

It's important that there be chemistry between you and your mentor. Just being Asian and in a senior position doesn't mean that a particular person is the right mentor for you. But when you pick up an annual report and see the lovely photograph of the management team on the inside cover, do you see someone who looks like you—or not? Subconsciously, the low numbers of Asians in top positions send us the message that it will be a difficult climb—not an impossible climb, but one that will be a workout. Sometimes it's just helpful to talk to someone in your firm or industry who understands what it's like to be in the minority. With an ARM you can discuss cultural values issues and brainstorm on how to handle conflicts over diversity/inclusive leadership issues.

Remember, though, that not all Asians in leadership positions have a strong sense of their Asian cultural identity or feel an affinity with other Asians. Because you can't know in advance where the senior Asian professional in your organization stands on these issues, be sure to proceed carefully and avoid making assumptions about her receptivity to you just because you share the same skin color. You can use the grapevine to get an idea of how this person is perceived, but eventually you'll have to approach her yourself. It's been my experience that as Asian American professionals move up the ladder and attempt to climb past middle management, they find that their Asian ethnicity could play a more significant role than it did earlier in their careers as junior professionals. So don't be quick to dismiss an Asian executive as being uninterested in the Asian professional community at your company. When I worked at a large corporation, I was very excited about the new member of senior management who was just hired into my business unit. Not only was she female but she also was a Chinese American with a successful track record. I took the opportunity to speak with her during a recruiting trip.

## YOUR MENTOR DOESN'T HAVE TO LOOK LIKE YOU —

"There are no Asians at the top! If no one has done it, I don't think my chances of moving up into a senior role are very high."

That's a sentiment shared by many Asian professionals. It implies that Asian employees can benefit only from another Asian as their mentor. That couldn't be the further from the truth. There's nothing wrong with seeking a non-Asian mentor, and in fact, you should be looking for more than one mentor/advisor/sponsor. And you won't necessarily lead only other Asians, either. You may need to remove some cultural misperceptions of your own to get the coaching you need.

## MENTORING/PROTÉGÉ PROTOCOL —

What if the perfect mentor fails to walk into your life? Eric Liu, author of *Accidental Asian* and *Guiding Lights* and a former speechwriter for President Clinton, states: "If someone arrives and says 'I want to be a mentor for you,'—you're lucky! For most of us, the challenge and opportunity is to make your own mentor—a composite—out of the many people you encounter in life."

For the majority of you who may be in the market for a mentor, here are some guidelines to facilitate the process!

### *How to Find a Mentor*

1. Look around in your company or in your industry for people whom you respect and who have the qualities you want to acquire. Mentors do not have to be identical to you. In fact, when personalities are complementary, both parties can benefit.

2. Approach the candidates. Explain to them what you are looking for.

3. Establish meeting times and frequency. Also discuss what you want to accomplish.

4. During the first meeting, introduce yourself and get to know your mentor.

5. Set guidelines early on in the relationship, including when you'll reevaluate progress. Nobody wants to be stuck in a relationship that's going nowhere.

### *Five Tips for Being a Great Mentor*

■ *Encourage your protégé to communicate openly.*

If he happens to be of Asian descent and sees you as a formidable authority figure, it may take time for him to open up to you. If after your third or fourth meeting you still feel that your protégé is hesitant about speaking up, try asking him some tough questions to encourage breakthroughs in conversation, such as "If you could change one thing about your relationship with your boss, what would it be?" or "How do you think your Asian culture may have affected the way you work with your colleagues and clients?" If you ask the latter, be sure to proceed with sensitivity whenever you bring up issues of race and culture.

■ *Set firm guidelines and expectations from the beginning.*
Determine how frequently or infrequently you will meet. Ask the protégé to explicitly state what he would like from the mentoring relationship; tell him clearly what you are hoping to accomplish. Find out what skills your protégé wants to develop.

■ *Provide clear performance measures.*
This way, your protégé can chart his career progress. Follow up with him each time you meet.

■ *Practice active listening.*
Don't dominate the conversation; be an engaged listener and respect what your protégé has to say.

■ *Take mentoring seriously.*
If your current workload is overwhelming and you find it difficult to devote time to your protégé, it may be better for you to bow out until a later date.

### Five Responsibilities of a Protégé

■ *Take the initiative and approach your potential mentor.*
You can't start a mentoring relationship without asking someone to be your mentor. Look inside your company and industry to identify people whom you admire or would like to emulate, regardless of ethnicity or gender. If you have trouble finding Asian role models at the senior management level (a likely problem because there is a scarcity of Asian American executives in some industries), seek out high-performing non-Asian executives who take an interest in your development. Be explicit with your mentor about what you hope to accomplish.

■ *Don't be overly deferential.*

If you know you have a tendency to be too deferential with your elders and you hesitate to approach your mentor with what you think is frivolous talk about the daily ins and outs of your workplace, you must get over this hurdle and reach out to him. Many mentors report that their best protégés were the ones who were pleasantly persistent about pursuing the relationship. They never gave up, despite busy travel schedules, packed calendars, and missed appointments. Says one mentor: "My protégé and I met in the strangest places. One time, because she needed to meet with me in-between my flight change, my protégé came to the airport and we had a great twenty-minute conversation at the airport Starbucks! She always looked for ways to connect with me, even when it was inconvenient for her." You are the one looking for guidance, so the onus is on you to be proactive.

"My mentor, who is Caucasian, never used to ask me questions about my Asian background, because he was afraid to offend me," says one young Korean American stockbroker. "We were both being very politically correct and were not digging into some important workplace issues. Six months into our relationship, we are now talking very candidly about my Korean upbringing, including the emphasis my parents place on respect for authority and other cultural issues."

■ *Do your homework.*

If your mentor asks you to do some follow-up work to help you develop your professional skills, do it. There has to be accountability in the mentoring relationship for it to be effective.

■ *Don't expect your mentor to fulfill every career need.*

You may need more than one mentor for different aspects of your career. Draw different things from different people. Not everyone will be an expert in every area.

■ *Respect the time that your mentor invests in you.*

Prepare for your meetings and report the progress you've made since the last meeting. Follow through on things you've promised to deliver. If your mentor has helped you find a new position, make sure you keep him apprised of how his assistance has helped you develop. As an Asian American professional, you can play an active part in helping people understand the differences among Asian nationalities. If your mentor is not Asian American, you can be a critical link for him to Asian cultures. The more that non-Asian businesspeople know about the diversity within Asian cultures, the less likely they will be to make inaccurate assessments of you.

### When Protégés Don't Hold Up Their End of the Deal

Recently, Miles, an Asian senior vice president of a large global financial services organization, expressed his frustration about his attempts to mentor junior recruits in his firm:

> As a relatively visible Asian manager in the firm, I have always been asked to share my views on numerous diversity panels and speak as a member of senior management to various diversity councils and minority constituencies. Invariably, many of the young Asian recruits would approach me at the end of these meetings and ask me if I would mentor them or help them with their careers. With high hopes, I started taking some of them to lunch and spent quite a lot of time explaining how the firm works and deliberately investing in the relationships. In the ten years I have been in this firm, I can count over one hundred separate lunches I have had with these guys. I can tell you honestly that very few of them have ever really taken a proactive stand and earnestly pursued the mentoring relationship. In fact, it got so bad that with a few people, I actually had to go and pursue them to find out what was going on with their careers. I was hoping that the junior Asian professionals here would find me a resource. In reality, they didn't know how to cultivate a mentoring relationship. They didn't understand the mechanics of building a networking relationship for the good of their career development.

They started out right—identifying Miles as a potential mentor—but they didn't know where to go from there. Miles and I decided that we needed to put together a targeted training program for the junior protégés because it was obvious that they didn't know the rules. In addition, I conducted a few focus groups that discussed the issues that arose from a pro-

tégé's point of view. The techniques that follow are intended to help protégés cultivate more productive mentoring relationships.

## POOR MENTOR–PROTÉGÉ MATCH
### Problem:

They assigned me to a mentor the first week I finished my training program. My mentor took me out to lunch once, but during the lunch we never really hit it off. We didn't have a lot to say during our lunch conversation. I tried to ask a lot of questions, but I never got much more than a few short responses. He was nice enough, but I could sense that he was there more out of obligation than a true interest in helping me to navigate my career. I didn't sense the warm fuzzies at that meeting, and though we met once or twice after that, he never really followed up with me.

### Proposed improvement:

Mentoring relationships tend to work out best when mentor and protégé come together of their own accord. But organizations can also provide forums in which potential mentors and protégés can successfully come together. After all, without a lunchtime presentation or a mentoring mania cocktail hour, how would you ever meet a senior person who works in an entirely different business unit? In these relatively unstructured forums, potential mentor and protégé can determine who they are naturally drawn to and can later approach each other about entering into a mentoring relationship.

## CULTURAL ISSUES
### Problem:

My mentor was a member of senior management and a mover and shaker. She served on three corporate boards, served on the merger integration task force, and was constantly traveling internationally. Though she expressed to me during our first few meetings that I could call her anytime I had a question, I really felt that I needed to show respect for her as my senior and not become a burden to her. Weren't they supposed to contact me if I was their protégé? Culturally, I was raised to try to not be intrusive and be polite, especially with my seniors. It would be insulting to call someone on her cell phone while she was traveling internationally.

**Proposed improvement:**

If the protégé feels uncomfortable approaching his mentor about certain work issues because of fear of being intrusive or annoying, it would be better to have the meetings set up and structured ahead of time. A good start would be for the protégé to tell his mentor about his culture's influences on his behavior, something like this: "Sometimes, I can be a little too polite for my own good. I was raised in a home where harmony was everything. If something didn't happen, or if something bad happened, you just learned to deal with it and not raise a red flag. Because of your busy schedule, I tend to think twice before calling or e-mailing you to get on your calendar again. I think I need to be really deliberate about putting you on the calendar more frequently." For example, establish early on that you will meet once a month for lunch at a designated place and that the protégé will send an e-mail update to the mentor once every 2 weeks about any issues that arise. The protégé should be careful not to put in writing any confidential information that may come back to haunt him in the future. E-mails can be forwarded to anyone at the touch of a button, so it's better to be safe. Save those hot-potato topics for phone conversations or meetings.

## LACK OF MENTORING TRAINING AND STRUCTURE
**Problem:**

When the mentors were assigned to the summer interns at a large consumer goods company, they got the names of their protégés, along with a copy of their résumé, which helped to introduce their backgrounds. However, we never received any guidance about what we should expect for the 2-month period. Given the brevity of that mentoring period, it would have been helpful to establish that everyone who elected to serve as a mentor should meet with their assigned intern at least once every 8 to 10 days. There were two protégés who actually met their mentors only once during the entire summer because of all their busy schedules.

**Proposed improvement:**

Put together a 1-day kickoff event for all the summer interns to meet with their summer mentors. Prior to that, provide two profile books for each group: one book with photos and departmental roles/responsibilities of the mentors and another book with the students' highlights. During the kickoff, have each mentor team up with his or her protégé and work in teams during some icebreaker games. Have the summer intern program manager deliver a short 1-hour mentoring training session. Divide up the group, give the mentors a list of guidelines for managing the mentoring process, and give all the new protégés a summer intern handbook that tells them about the resources of the firm, as well as contact information for the resources. The interns should also receive some training about how to sustain mentoring relationships and how to be proactive in pursuing mentors.

### Qualities of a Great Protégé

It isn't enough to find a mentor. The onus is on you to develop and maintain the momentum of the relationship. Too many people assume that the senior person is supposed to be the one making room in her schedule to meet with them. You need to reach out to her. Once you do, your mentor can walk you through the tough situations in your career—dealing with that sensitive political problem in your office, managing a tough client who constantly gives you new deadlines, and working with an ineffective boss. Don't be afraid to get personal. As long as you are not being unethical, there's nothing wrong with asking each other a few personal questions to get the conversation rolling.

---

# Staying in the Succession
# Planning Pipeline

---

## VISIBILITY: YOU CAN'T BE SELECTED IF NO ONE
## KNOWS WHO YOU ARE OR WHAT YOU DO —

No matter how strong a performer you are, no matter how many superlatives appear on your performance evaluation, no one can guarantee that you will get promoted. Because of the limited number of senior management titles and a limited budget for salary increases and bonuses, not every-one who performs his job well will get the promotion he might deserve. This might be a difficult reality for many Asian Americans to face as they progress in an organization, especially if they grew up in traditional homes where study and diligent work were the only things deemed necessary for success.

If you want to be considered for high-profile roles that lead to promo-tional opportunities, the right people at your organization must know who you are and the extent of your capabilities. Be visible by showing up at cor-porate functions and learning to introduce yourself in situations where you don't know anyone. If you're not being selected to be part of recruiting trips, consultant meetings, diversity discussions, or other high-profile proj-ects, you may be able to volunteer for some.

In addition, you must verbalize your desire to move into a more sen-ior role or a different function at your firm or to be considered for an early promotion. No one will assume that you want a title. Says a managing di-rector at an international investment banking firm:

Find ways that work within your demeanor to make sure that the right people know what you are doing. Constantly look for ways to show, by ex-ample, model innovation and creativity, because when you do this, you are being a trailblazer, and even if you are a modest person by nature, no one can take that pioneering example away from you. Demonstrate change and that you can add value to existing functions. Be innovative and different from others.

## HOW TO STAY IN THE SUCCESSION PLANNING PIPELINE —

Find out the criteria for moving into certain positions. Take this assessment:

■   *Are you included in discussions about strategic initiatives for your com-pany? If you are merely a worker bee and not actively engaged in the overall direction of the company, you might find yourself left behind.*

■ *Do you get asked to go on campus recruiting trips to represent the firm?*

■ *Are you often tapped to replace or sit in for a senior manager who is unable to attend an industry association meeting or conference?*

■ *When unexpected positions are vacant in the firm, are you on the slate for potential consideration? Internal staffing decisions don't happen accidentally. Selection committees and recruiting teams try to make deliberate decisions about who should fill key positions in a company.*

■ *Before a decision is made in your business unit, are you someone who is called for various project deliverables (a new system implementation, a new client marketing project, a focus group session, a business development summit)?*

## KEY LESSONS LEARNED—

■ Invest in mentoring relationships. Many professionals of color report a lack of key professional relationships as the major barrier to their career advancement. If you don't have a mentor, take the time to find at least one person who will invest in you at your company.

■ When it's time to end mentoring relationships, be honest about doing it. Get to know the mentor first before suggesting that you enter into a mentoring relationship. When it's a natural time to move on, say so. You don't drop the person like a hot potato, but you may no longer need to meet your mentor as frequently for updates. It may be enough to meet every few months for lunch to maintain contact.

■ Be a good protégé. Make it easy for a mentor to enter into a mentoring relationship. Time is of the essence for most senior-level professionals, who have busy personal lives as well. Prepare an agenda for each meeting; open yourself up to learn something new each time you meet with him or her.

# Getting Your Voice Heard:
# Saying No . . . and Pushing Back
# with Diplomacy

*I was taught to never talk back to my parents. If I didn't obey, I faced punish-ment. There was no sense of negotiation or dialogue about an issue. They were my early authority figures, and now, they're my career guides. With few or no role models to pave the way, I have been a pioneer in my own career develop-ment. Growing up, I lived this crazy bicultural existence—Asian at home, more Westernized at school. Now, as a working professional, I still find it hard to firmly say no to my boss, even when I know I don't completely agree with his point of view.*

—Sharon Rodriguez, Filipino American

Managing work relationships is a critical skill for any professional. Manag-ing the boss is a challenging task for even the most assertive professionals. At an important meeting, how do you walk the fine line between being on your boss's team by supporting her statements and standing up to her in a nonoffensive way when you have an opposing viewpoint? Even the most capable senior executives report having a difficult time when they need to make the hard calls or to make their personal opinions known in front of their bosses and other colleagues. The best way to handle such sensitive sit-uations is to prepare ahead of time and to approach your boss about a po-tential conflict prior to the big meeting. Waiting until a meeting to bring up an opposing viewpoint can be politically dangerous because your boss has no idea what you are about to say.

There are a few scenarios (such as if the meeting is a large-scale, open-ended brainstorming session where there are no wrong answers) in which you can bring up your opinions without warning and without potential for negative consequences. For most business meetings, however, it is impor-tant that you prepare your boss for what is to come. An informal meeting with her a day or two before the actual meeting may be the best forum for sharing your opinions. Even if she doesn't agree with you, at least she knows your stand on the matter and won't be surprised in front of a room full of people.

## SPEAKING UP IN ONE-ON-ONE OR PUBLIC SETTINGS WITHOUT COMPROMISING WHO YOU ARE —

Reports that Asian Americans aren't vocal in meetings and other public settings are common in my consulting practice. One of my clients, a Chinese American woman, reports: "When someone questions or challenges me in a public meeting room setting, I feel like I'm losing face, and I feel myself melting down. Before I can even say a word, I know defeat must be written on my face." Peggy Klaus, communications coach and author of *Brag! The Art of Tooting Your Own Horn Without Blowing It*, agrees: "I've seen it on numerous occasions. Whereas with other cultures they become defensive and strident, Asians tend to just freeze and back down without a fight at times." But it is possible to question or challenge your boss without feeling as though you've just betrayed him.

When Tracy Yoon, 26, a second-generation Korean American and a star performer in her business unit, realized she was being underpaid for her level of experience and educational credentials, she approached her manager about it casually. The response she got was "Oh, okay. I'll have to check into it." One month later, she still hadn't heard back from her manager. Instead of following up within a week of her request, she decided to wait for her manager to get back to her. The response never came. Tracy says, "In the Korean language, there is the word *han* that basically means 'unresolved feeling, bitter feeling, and resentment,' and some people endure years of it without any resolution. I was raised for years to *chahm uh*—a Korean term that basically means enduring long periods of suffering, or going through a hardship of some sort. There is an understanding that you can withstand long periods of sadness and injustice for the sake of the good at the end." Unfortunately, she never told her boss that she was unhappy about the way that he dropped the ball. Finally, after 6 more months of

230 | BREAKING the BAMBOO CEILING

sticking it out, she decided to leave the firm for a competitor. Though it may sound tough, *han* is a common sentiment known by many in Korea and perhaps some Korean Americans. It's not just Korean, either. In Japanese it's called *gaman*. If you watch any of the Chinese or Japanese television melodramas that are broadcast in Asia, you will see countless people hurting quietly and enduring years of suffering because self-restraint is held in high esteem in the culture.

Saying no and taking a stand in a public setting can be difficult for some Asians. Klaus says:

> When put in stressful or confrontational situations, Asian Americans tend to suffer what I call a "communication meltdown" faster than people from other cultures. Where they need to take command and speak up, they often become softer in vocal volume, make declarative sentences into questions ("I think this is a good budget? I think this is a good budget!") and avoid asserting their opinions even if they are the expert or running the meeting. The fear of being wrong, offending someone or showing off is tantamount in their communication and will keep them from "taking the stage."

To be effective, you need to develop your own style of speaking up—a style that's gracious, yet firm and effective.

Some of you may be thinking, *Oh no! Do I need to change my personality and undermine who I am just to be more assertive in the workplace?* No, you don't need a personality makeover. You simply need to learn some new skills for doing your job well. You can look at it as learning to speak a new language; if you speak an Asian language, you already know the advantages of being fluent in more than one language. But you can use this new language in the style and manner most comfortable to you.

If you tend to be soft-spoken, your speaking volume at work doesn't necessarily have to be 10 times louder than your normal voice. But you should try to stretch beyond your comfort zone (perhaps going a few levels louder) in situations where you need to be heard. Even so, keep in mind that although many high-level decisions are often made *outside* of the meeting room in informal meetings and one-on-one discussions, you can still influence decisions and get buy-in for your projects.

Patrice Hall, a managing director and director of diversity at JPMorganChase, relates crossing cultural barriers to her experience in her bowling league in high school: "If you want to hit all the pins, you figure out where you want the ball to go, then adjust yourself on the lane to make sure you hit the right pins." Carefully calibrate the way you communicate to be most effective within each particular situation. Sometimes you need to be more expressive to have your voice heard, as when you're showcasing your product to a new client or pitching a new idea. To do this smoothly, you should first rehearse at home.

On the other hand, if you are presenting in a boardroom to the top seven senior management team members, you should wait for your cue to present your research. In this kind of setting, you don't need to be so vocal; using a moderate, engaging, professional tone while presenting your material is the best way to go.

When you're talking with your client on the phone to deliver news that a product launch is being delayed, you need to be extremely cautious about your choice of words.

Note that you are still the same person in all of these scenarios. You're just making full use of your range of expressiveness to execute important work tasks; you're not overhauling your personality. The ability to communicate in diverse work scenarios will be extremely important as you move up the ladder.

## TAKING A STAND

**Q:** *I work as a manager for a telecommunications company. In an upcoming meeting, I may have to stick my neck out to save a business unit from being overlooked in a major business reorganization plan. There are definitely some politics going on here, but I know that if they make the decision without the two managers, they may meet the deadlines but overlook some important issues. What would you suggest?*

**A:** This sounds like a political landmine. As such, I would suggest speaking to the parties involved one-on-one, instead of in a group meeting. Rather than responding to a decision that you don't like with "I don't know about this decision. It doesn't seem fair to everyone involved. Can we look at this a different way?" you may want to say, "We are excluding two of the unit heads by making this decision when they are away on business. I propose that we wait for their return in two days so that we can get their input. Deciding to downsize the entire technology unit without discussing this with two very critical line managers seems potentially litigious. There may be other alternatives here." The second statement will lend you a sense of authority, and you'll come across as a thinking person who doesn't just look at the numbers. It will also show how effective you are as a people manager.

## PREPARING FOR THE TOUGH QUESTIONS —

Rehearse your responses to objections you may get in a meeting. I find that people do everything they can to prepare for a closing on a house or to take care of other personal matters, but when it comes to their careers, they often don't invest time in diligent preparation for their meetings, relying on their ability to handle it spontaneously. If you have an important meeting coming up where your reputation is at stake, you should definitely have your story together.

- Research your audience: Who do you know in the audience? Who is a definite supporter and who is a naysayer?
- Prepare answers to potential objections.
- Ask good questions.

## THREE WAYS TO RESPOND TO A TOUGH CHALLENGE

Challenge from a senior business unit vice president: "Where in the world did you get the raw material for that budget? The numbers from last year don't seem right."

### Safe Response

"Is that right? Let me see those numbers again and get back to you. I thought I had looked at everything."

You can also have your manager available to support your numbers in a few early meetings. This has to be done with caution, as others may always perceive you as a junior person who can't handle herself. Having your boss there to support you might give your numbers credibility but won't add to your self-confidence. However, if this is an early-stage scenario and you are new to being assertive in the face of opposition, this response is better than not asserting yourself at all.

### Better Response

"I know these numbers are right; if you need to see support documentation, I can easily get the information that you need once I go back to the office."

This is a better response because you stuck to your guns this time.

### Best-Case Scenario: Assertive Response

"Well, let me see where you're confused here. I checked this over with the head of marketing and head of research [and name the people you checked with if that would help your case] and double-checked it last night before loading the presentation, but if you have a question about a specific section, you can point out to me where the issues are and I can address them right here."

You must *really* prepare for these potential objections that people have. You are bound to run across a devil's advocate or two at some point in your career. Make the necessary phone calls *before* the meeting, so that you're ready for the toughest daggers that may be thrown your way. Sandra Gréné Bucklin, Women's Initiative

Strategy leader at Dell, agrees: "If you know you may be going into a contentious situation, you need to be prewiring the stakeholders early." It is critical that you "prewire" the people who influence the major aspects of the decision ahead of time. This means you should meet with these colleagues early to give them a heads-up about what to expect and to obtain buy-in about your proposal.

### *Good Questions to Ask Yourself When You're in Meetings*

Monitor your assertiveness in meetings:

- Do I make opportunities to speak?
- Am I sensitive to everyone in the meeting room?
- If I'm running the meeting, do I make sure that everyone gets to say his or her piece?

### *When in Doubt, Ask the Right Questions*

Knowing what questions to ask and understanding how to prepare for challenging meetings will be even more important as you get into higher levels in the organization. Sometimes, it's by knowing what type of questions to ask that you actually arrive at the right solution. Don't feel pressured to execute too quickly if you aren't satisfied with the available data. When in doubt, learn to ask probing questions that get to the heart of the problem. Being assertive isn't about being difficult or saying no all the time. Sometimes pushing back and asking questions just allows you to be more effective at finding the best solution.

## FREQUENTLY ASKED QUESTIONS ON
## STANDING UP TO YOUR COLLEAGUES

Here are some scenarios in which my clients developed skills to enable them to stand up to their bosses and other individuals in authority.

**Q:** *For the longest time, I have found it difficult to challenge my superiors. It wasn't so hard to deal with this in school because my grades were always based on my individual performance. As I move up in the ranks as a middle manager, I find that I am constantly placed in meeting settings where I need to express my discontent about something to senior managers, or push back on my boss so that I can speak up for my subordinates. It has been really difficult for me to do this, and it makes me seem like a weak and spineless manager to my subordinates. How can I overcome this?*

**A:** As with any deeply ingrained culturally influenced behavior, your tendency to avoid conflict with superiors is difficult to change overnight. However, now that you recognize it as an issue, you can come up with a game plan that may be effective. Though you may find it difficult, you should consider discussing it with your manager. Tell her about your tendency to back off when she asks you to do something, and explain that when she challenges you, you don't know how to respond because you feel that you should be supportive of her in front of the team and her peers. Next, prepare for the meeting agendas ahead of time. If you foresee an item with potential for conflict, attempt to speak with your boss about it beforehand. If you already know that the meeting will be fraught with conflict, you may also want to have one-on-one conversations with others who will be present to strategize your approach. There is no excuse for not preparing.

**Q:** *I had to deliver some really bad news to a client last week, and I couldn't do it. I didn't know how I was going to disappoint him. It got so bad that right before I had to call him, I chickened out and left the office. I find it really hard to directly tell a client we can't* *deliver on his request. Raised in a traditional Asian home, I was taught to always strive for harmony in every situation, so no one loses face. We rarely expressed feelings of discontent openly in our family. You just felt what you felt, and you learned to deal with it. An irate client could upset that sense of harmony any day! What should I do?*

**A:** The best thing for you to do in this case is to have the full details of the situation in front of you when you call your client. This is actually a wonderful opportunity for you to practice assertive communication. Try to contact the client as soon as possible; people dislike when you are dishonest with them, and you are bordering on being misleading by not confronting him with the facts as soon as you have them. Also, don't assume that your client's reaction will be negative. He may be fine with your answer. Instead of thinking about how this might upset your client, spend time thinking of other ways to provide him with better alternatives. If you can deliver a piece of good news with the bad news, that can ease the blow. Regardless, tell him the news, sooner rather than later. If you tell him quickly enough he may be able to come up with plan B without much effort.

## KEY LESSONS LEARNED—

- *Putting your head down for too long may only keep you in your seat, not move you up on the corporate ladder.*

In the work world, the rules of the game are entirely different than those for school or home. It is no longer sufficient for you to do your work, do well on tests, and get A's. You need to be sensitive to the American emphasis on participation, where speaking out is likely to be valued as a sign of engagement and as a way of establishing your presence. It is important that you communicate frequently about your work projects. *Overcommunicate* if you know that you have a tendency to keep your accomplishments to yourself.

■ *Acknowledge your culturally influenced work behaviors.*

The better you understand your cultural tendencies, the more easily you can modify your behavior and manage others' expectations of you. Too often, Asians who are unaware of their cultural biases ignore their own problematic work behaviors or chalk them up to a personality quirk. I'm not advocating that you blame your modesty, for example, on your culture, but that you recognize any harmful impact it may have at work and develop the skills you need to get the credit you deserve.

■ *Invite your manager, coworkers, clients, and subordinates to partner with you in your career management.*

Professionals often mistakenly assume that asking for assistance is a sign of weakness. Not necessarily. Sometimes the only way to enable change, especially in repeated patterns of behaviors, is to ask one or two trusted advisors at your firm to hold you accountable. Ask them to give you regular—perhaps weekly or even daily—feedback about your performance and your interactions with others, not just positive pats on the back. When you do get constructive feedback, don't take it personally. Use it to grow and develop professionally.

■ *When you start a new job or take on a new function, set up meetings with as many people as you can.*

Don't isolate yourself, especially if you work in a smaller, flatter organization where you need to be very entrepreneurial and aggressive about meeting new people. During the first week or two of your new job or project, meet with each person with whom you will be working. Ask them questions. Let them get to know you and your work style.

■ *Build your own network—with the long term in mind.*

One of the perceptions that people have of Asians is that they can be insular and not fluent in corporate political language and that they don't care enough about the company. You must dispel this perception by building a broad and deep network of personal and professional contacts with whom you circulate on a regular basis. If you've always felt more comfortable around other Asians, move out of your comfort zone and build new relationships with more non-Asians. Once you build this network, maintain it by keeping in touch with your contacts and keep the relationships reciprocal.

■ *Create a marketing pitch, whether you are conducting an active job search campaign or not.*

Develop a marketing statement that you can use in social or professional settings. You have only one opportunity to make a first impression. If you, like many Asians, are uncomfortable talking about yourself and grew up being taught to be modest, a pitch can help you when you meet new people.

■ *Be prepared to defend yourself in meetings with strong statements and/or questions.*

Stand firm if you know you have the right answer. Your opinion is just as valid as a senior manager's. Take on a partner mentality in a meeting setting, especially if you are the expert in the room. Keeping in mind the corporation's political climate, state your opinions nonabrasively but firmly. Soon you will soon be known as a force to be reckoned with, not someone who goes along with what the group decides. Prepare for any potential objections that may be thrown your way; never go into a potentially contentious meeting without preparation.

■ *Don't be afraid to stand out or be different.*

The loudest duck won't get shot! There are positive aspects of Asian cultures and traditions that many non-Asians are eager to know more about. As long as you are within the bounds of acceptable corporate behavior, sharing your heritage and values with your colleagues can help your career, not hurt it.

■ *Above all, be yourself within the confines of your own industry.*

To succeed in corporate America, you must add value. You can do that by maximizing the positives of cultural influence and managing the negatives.

■    *Determine what skills you lack so that you can add them to your career tool kit.*

Determine the critical success factors in your job function and your industry at large. Create a long-term skills development plan for your career and follow it.

# NINE

# EXTENDING YOUR REACH: PROFESSIONAL ASSOCIATIONS AND AFFINITY NETWORKING GROUPS

*Consider our potential for learning and advancement if, instead of coming together only in times of strife, we were able to bridge distance when there were no fires to put out. Think of the possibilities if we could stay focused on what we have in common.*

—Phoebe Eng, *Warrior Lessons*

## THE NEED FOR UNIFIED CORPORATE ASIAN NETWORK GROUPS —

Why get involved with the Asian organization at your company? Asian affinity networking groups, or advocacy groups, can serve as important forums for meeting other Asian professionals at your company. They can be a critical tool for breaking down stereotypes at your company and for unified communications with the CEO and members of the senior management team. They also provide a platform for Asian employees to discuss issues of concern in the workplace. They can sponsor and facilitate mentoring programs and leadership training to help Asians breaking into the management ranks.

Despite the virtues of being involved with these networking and advocacy groups, I've often heard such complaints as "Why do we have to be lumped in together in a group with all the other Asian nationalities? I'm Chinese, and most of the group is Korean." And "I'm from India, and South Asians have very little in common with the East Asians." And "There aren't any Vietnamese in my company." Though there is plenty of ethnic diversity within our separate diversity networks, we need to come together as Asian Americans because for the most part, that's how non-Asian executives in our companies still see us. And that is still how most organizations categorize us in terms of race and ethnicity breakdowns. There is an unmistakable strength and unity in approaching senior managers as one voice. If we approach them as six to seven smaller Asian groups, each representing a distinct Asian nationality, we will be less likely to be heard and run the risk of appearing fragmented. It might take longer for us to achieve the visibility in the organization to move things forward.

### Diversity Within Asian Groups

A recommendation that I've made to companies that want to be inclusive of all Asian nationalities is to have a focus group or subcommittee for each of the Asian nationalities with adequate numbers, with each subgroup having a chairperson who will represent their nationality to the broader Asian network. This way, the group will have both the strength of numbers and the distinct personalities of the different nationalities represented. The small groups can also meet and then come together with the larger group periodically. As an example, the small groups can be in charge of organizing cultural celebrations, such as Chinese New Year, Asian American Heritage Month, and Diwali (aka Deepavali, Divali, Dewali). Employees can also organize organically, perhaps informally in smaller group forums, then have board meetings where all the group heads come together to form one voice. Subgroups may not be warranted in companies where the Asian employee population is small.

## Why Start a Group for Asians?

Why have a group for Asians? First off, it helps insulate Asians from discrimination. There is something powerful about an active, vocal organization. Also, what CEO or vice president of diversity wants to receive hundreds of separate e-mails from members of a particular ethnic group? It is more efficient to respond to a single organized group. If a group of 50 Asian employees expressed a desire to get increased exposure to senior management or additional leadership training in an organized proposal, it would be taken more seriously than a disgruntled Asian employee who sends an emotionally charged e-mail to senior management. Additionally, the group can provide opportunities for professional networking and camaraderie.

"When you have the weight of a community or group behind you, you have more power and authority to make a difference. They will have to listen," says Dale Minami, founder of the Asian Law Caucus and NAPABA (National Asian Pacific American Bar Association). If all the Asians are isolated and working only in their little cubicles, employers won't take their needs seriously.

If you don't have such a forum at your company and you want to start one, talk to people in the firm. You don't have to reinvent the wheel, either. Many companies are doing innovative things to reach out to their diversity subgroups, and you can contact these groups for information. For example, IBM has an Asian Diversity Task Force/Steering Committee, Citigroup has over 12 different networking groups, and Deloitte & Touche has developed innovative programs for its Asian network.

### Reasons for Getting Involved

BOOSTING YOUR CAREER    Meeting other people can help expand your professional network. Whether you are actively looking for a job, seeking mentors and colleagues who come from Asian backgrounds, or want to meet others in your industry, one of the easiest ways to make new contacts is to join a professional association or a networking group. Your involvement with a committee can expose you to others in the industry and give you the kind of leadership experience and exposure that you may need. You may even be able to show a potential employer that you know something about a new industry without actually having been employed in it. To a potential employer, any relevant experience is valid, whether it's gained through a paid position or a volunteer one.

Here's an example: Chris, a colleague of mine who was interested in moving into finance after having spent time in operations management, became active with his MBA alumni association. He worked very closely with Tom, the association president, as the treasurer for 1 year. Chris's involvement with the organization paid off. Tom happened to be the corporate controller for a firm that was one of Chris's top five target companies. Not only did he get some good financial management and budgeting experience, but he impressed Tom enough that Tom took him under his wing. When Chris decided to actively look for other opportunities, Tom introduced him to others in his industry who worked in different areas of finance—16 other finance directors and CFOs at medium-size fast-growing companies in his target market. He was able to make the career switch within just 6 weeks.

OVERCOMING CULTURAL ISOLATION AT WORK    Being part of an Asian networking group can also ease your cultural isolation at work. For Esther Flora, a Filipino American who lives in a state with a minuscule Asian population, getting involved with a local NAAAP (National Association of Asian American Professionals) chapter gave her the opportunity to meet other Asian professionals near her city. Being one of three Asian employees in her company, she often felt that her manager never fully understood her Filipino culture, and non-Asian employees often confused her with a Chinese coworker and saw her as representing all Asian ethnicities. Soon, she found herself withdrawing from social interactions at work. Says Esther:

> Oftentimes, they would make some stereotypical comments about Japanese and Chinese people, expecting me to go along with it and not take it so seriously. I wished I had a few other Asian colleagues to share this experience with, but since there was virtually no one in my business group, going outside the company to join this organization helped me to get the perspective that I needed. Instead of figuring out how to get out of my company, I am

going to stick it out and try to do something about it. Don't get me wrong; my coworkers have not changed overnight, but after hearing what other Asian American colleagues had done to open up communication lines with senior management about diversity and sensitivity training, I am planning to approach my firm about it as well.

As a direct result of her positive experience and the camaraderie she felt with members of the NAAAP, she started to engage more with her coworkers and regained her sense of self-confidence because she no longer felt that she was the only one trying to change things in her office.

## A PERSPECTIVE ON FORMING ALLIANCES

Dale Minami, partner of Minami, Lew & Tamaki, is the winner of the American Bar Association's 2003 Thurgood Marshall Award; he is also the founder of the Asian American Bar Association and cofounder of the Asian Law Caucus. He has been cited on numerous occasions for civil rights leadership for Asian Americans. Dale is a cofounder of the the Asian American Bar Association of the Greater Bay Area, the Asian Pacific Bar of California, and the Coalition of Asian Pacific Americans.

**Q:** *What made you start the Asian Law Caucus?*

**A:** In the late '60s, when I graduated from law school, my generation began to recognize the injustices rampant in society, which spawned the anti–Vietnam War movement, the race riots, and a heightened awareness of a need for social services and social justice. Justice was not being served in the late '60s for Asian Americans in America. So we tried to provide low-cost or free legal services (similar to Legal Aid) for Asians who could not obtain legal services, and we undertook impact litigation to highlight issues and educate both our communities and the larger American public. Additionally, we hoped to inspire our communities to fight for their *own* rights.

**Q:** *How did you and your colleagues start the Asian American Bar Association of the Greater Bay Area?*

**A:** Once we started practicing law at the Asian Law Caucus in the '70s, we began to encounter discrimination in the court system. The idea that all Asians came from one country was a common problem. For example, some judges pretended to not know the difference between Chinese and Japanese people, to the point where they would request me (a Japanese American) to interpret for a Chinese American client.

At times, they would even question why they needed interpreters: "Can't he speak English?" Moreover, they couldn't believe that we were attorneys, and we often got the question "What are you here for?" There would be looks of surprise when they discovered that we were attorneys representing the other side. We understood that politics determined who became judges and decided to organize to lobby for Asian American judges as well as provide a political and emotional support system to combat discrimination in the courts.

**Q:** *What forces were effective in gelling the group?*

**A:** A few things: (1) A need for political power and influence in the legal community at large, (2) a great sense of emotional support for each other, and (3) it provided a social outlet for us. We helped each other with job opportunities and other professional connections.

**Q:** *It's amazing to see how that original group has multiplied. How many people were in the original group, and how many are there now?*

**A:** About sixty to seventy original members, and now, over five hundred! The Asian American Bar Association and other local Asian Pacific American Bar Associations provided the critical mass for the formation of a national organization, the NAPABA, with forty-five local chapters representing over forty thousand attorneys.

**Q:** *Can you offer additional suggestions for forming an effective networking group at a corporation or an Asian community organization?*

**A:** Active participation in organizations is key. If you are isolated and not perceived as part of a larger, organized group, you are vulnerable. Your boss or CEO will take you more seriously if they perceive that you have the power of an organization behind you.

What impressed me most about Dale's comments about the Asian Law Caucus was that in the early years, he found a lot of camaraderie among his Asian peers because of the hardships they experienced. They really seemed to be able to band together as a family during difficult times. I believe that we should continue to reach back and remember how, in the not-so-distant past, we were so easily discriminated against. Although the biases in corporate America in the politically correct, diversity-sensitive twenty-first century tend to be less blatant, in some ways, we are still at a disadvantage, no longer because we are so small in number but because our lack of cohesiveness as a community can make us vulnerable when crises occur. Perhaps this can be the "fire" we gather around and use to make a difference in our careers and for the Asian American community.

## GUIDELINES FOR GETTING AND STAYING INVOLVED WITH AN ORGANIZATION —

■ *Be an advocate for change by initiating discussion.*

Realize that most people, including many Asians, are not aware that even "positive" stereotypes may not always be good for the Asian population. Whenever possible, inform your boss, coworkers, colleagues, and clients of the fact that Asian Americans in the United States represent a wide range of countries of origin and varying levels of acculturation. Each comes with a unique set of cultural traditions and values. You can combat stereotypes by opening up a dialogue between you and your non-Asian colleagues and creating a safe environment to talk about issues of race and ethnicity. Many are afraid of even bringing up these issues, so you may have to take the first step.

- *Be sensitive to others when talking about issues of race/ethnicity.*

You may be comfortable with issues of race and culture because you have grown up dealing with them, but there are still many others (your fellow Asian American colleagues included) who are not as comfortable discussing them in the context of the workplace. When you're engaging senior management in diversity discussions, keep in mind that tone and delivery is as important as the content of your statements—make sure that you don't come across like the diversity police.

- *Have patience.*

All organizations go through growing pains. People tend to get excited about starting up something new, and when immediate change is not seen, they get frustrated and see no point in pressing on. It's only through perseverance and continued hard work that you will see results.

- *Model active participation for others in the networking group.*

Nothing energizes others and gets people more fired up than one or two committed people. Instead of looking for hundreds of people right away, start with a few very active people who genuinely care about the issues. With a committed core group, you can go very far, and once you have a well-run organized core, you can recruit others who buy into a similar vision.

- *Incorporate your company's vision and business objectives when you are developing your diversity strategy.*

When you are ready to engage HR or senior management about diversity issues, couch your passion for pursuing new diversity initiatives in terms of your company's corporate vision. If your firm has never had affinity groups before, you may need to provide some statistics or information on best practices implemented by competitors that demonstrate the effectiveness of affinity networking groups.

- *Solicit feedback about the effectiveness of the networking group.*

Once every 6 to 9 months, ask the members of your networking group if the organization is meeting its objectives. Feedback will help you improve the group's programs.

- *Get one or more committed senior management members to champion the networking group.*

The right senior manager can communicate the group's importance to the rest of the organization and solicit help from the top to provide funds for its events.

One transportation company, after having seen so much attrition among its minority employees over 5 years, started a networking group for its professionals of color and women. Eventually diversity efforts started to take on a life of their own. People were taking the issue seriously. "Women's groups are not so unusual, whereas even ten years ago," says one female banker, "the guys looked at us with suspicion whenever we would leave our desks for an hour to attend one of our women's networking lunches. Today, it's just accepted as an important meeting." A senior vice president at a large financial organization says, "Our male bosses provide funding for our women's executive mentoring lunches now! We have come a long way in this area. Hopefully, Asian groups and the other affinity groups can also achieve that in the near future."

# TEN

# GETTING AND MAINTAINING YOUR WORTH: SHOW ME THE MONEY . . . AND A PROMOTION!

*As a Chinese American, I grew up believing that good work would be rewarded and merit recognized. Playing the game of politics and learning to read between the lines of social banter were never part of the picture. So when my boss fired me, she also killed off something inside, my belief that I could rise as high as my potential would allow, my faith that the rules of the game were fair and would be enforced.*

—Claire S. Chow, *Leaving Deep Water*

*You must do the things you think you cannot do.*

—Eleanor Roosevelt

## "How Am I Doing?": Acing Performance Management Discussions

Before you can approach your manager about compensation, you first need to have a dialogue about your work performance. Be mindful of this chapter's basic tips about handling performance evaluations, which provide the foundation for salary, bonus, and promotion discussions. Most organizations use some type of performance management program to document their employees' contributions and track their performance. Yet, many people tend to view the annual performance review season with fear and disdain. But if you manage it correctly, it can actually be a pleasant, enriching experience. In the ideal world, you should be asking for performance feedback on a regular basis, especially as you finish a transaction, close an important deal with a new client, or complete a major portion of your project. However, the annual evaluation is *not* the time to find out that you should have done something differently in the previous year or that your manager is dissatisfied with the quality of your performance. In addition to receiving appraisals from supervisors, at some companies you may get appraisals from peers, clients, and subordinates. Some organizations may even ask you to also conduct self-appraisals. This type of performance management system is similar to a 360-degree feedback method that is commonly used in executive coaching programs. As the phrase suggests, the 360-degree method allows you to obtain a mini review from the variety of people who are affected by your work.

## WHY PERFORMANCE DISCUSSIONS ARE IMPORTANT —

Performance reviews serve several purposes:

■   They document your performance. They can support future promotions by tracking your work performance over time. In one company, if an employee is interested in a transfer to a different business group, the previous two performance evaluations are sent to the new department for review.

■   They provide a means of differentiating your performance from others who are performing comparable job functions.

■   They provide a basis for measuring performance so that pay practices can be differentiated. Companies want to reward the best performers with the right incentives. It would be difficult to justify awarding a large bonus or a higher raise to a lower-than-average performer.

## "SO HOW DID I DO?" OBTAINING REAL-TIME PERFORMANCE FEEDBACK

I remember hearing with fascination how Joe, a new analyst at an investment banking firm, made use of external feedback from Paul, a senior banker. Instead of waiting for feedback to be given to him, Joe solicited it from Paul immediately after a client presentation. When Paul said that Joe needed to improve his ability to deliver client reports with strong conviction, Joe learned to get back on the horse to try again. Then, after refining his presentation style, he went in and presented his piece to another client. He then asked Paul for additional feedback and continued to do this for 3 months. He was relentless in his pursuit of excellence. He took no offense at the sometimes harsh feedback; Paul was often direct and rarely minced words. By his third meeting, Joe was quite effective at presenting his recommendations.

I give kudos to both Joe and Paul in this situation. Joe did a great job of asking for feedback, not waiting for it to be given. When the constructive feedback came, he developed a plan for altering his approach and then took action without hesitation. And Paul always took Joe with him to every client meeting that wasn't restricted. Because Joe had done all the number crunching and the financial modeling, Paul considered it important to include him in all meetings that involved client interaction, even if it meant that Joe didn't always have an opportunity to present at the meeting. Other senior bankers tended to go to client meetings on their own and didn't always think about providing exposure for their junior analysts. This informal real-time performance feedback proved to be some of the most valuable pointers Joe received in his banking career.

## Preparing for Performance Discussions —

Early on in your job, ask for a written job description, or, if one is not readily available, sit down with your manager and write down the main responsibilities of your job. It is important that she specify what she wants you to accomplish over the next review period. Later, during performance discussions, make sure you refer to the same list and talk about how many of your objectives you've accomplished. If you have taken the time to monitor your performance and have solicited ongoing feedback from your manager, customers, peers, and subordinates throughout the year, you should have a good idea of what to expect during your annual performance discussion. This formal discussion should mostly be a two-way dialogue about your development plan for next year and your personal career objectives in the firm. You should use that time to discuss potential next steps or stretch opportunities within the firm.

But if you haven't already had such discussions with your boss and colleagues throughout the year, you'll need to prepare extra carefully for the annual discussion. Take time to prepare a list of your key accomplishments for the previous year and an accurate self-evaluation of your strengths and areas of improvement. In addition, make sure you go into the meeting with your "key accomplishments" list—or what I call a winner's file—of accolades of which you are especially proud.

## Negotiating Your Compensation and Severance Package

Even if you're not seeking a position at a new employer, you can use the information in this section to prepare to ask for promotions and raises at your current company.

## Negotiate the Job Requirements
## of a New Position —

Before any talk of money takes place, make sure you understand what you are negotiating for. Don't answer an ad in the paper or an internal job posting without doing enough thinking. Instead of taking the job description at face value, you should ask yourself, *What unique skills do I bring to this job?* Jobs are created for multidimensional people with different experiences. It's rare to find someone who perfectly fits a written job description. If you have the capabilities and talents to do more than what the job requires, you may be able to negotiate higher pay commensurate with your experience.

> Senior accountant for a major hospital system with over 500 employees. Knowledge of PeopleSoft or Oracle helpful. Strong understanding of month-end processes, budgeting, and financial analysis. CPA required.

Jennifer Hwang, a 28-year-old Chinese American, had all of the experience noted in the above posting, as well as 2 years of managerial experience. She had been the assistant controller for a small retail company. Because of her background, she was able to negotiate and expand the job description to get additional pay. She got some managerial responsibility and additional special project responsibility and offered to fill in for her boss during his vacations. These agreements took place before any discussion of money.

Never take a job posting at face value. If you want to work for the company but the description isn't a good match with your qualifications, there may be a way that you can network or negotiate your way into other functional areas.

## Make Sure You're the One:
## Get a Verbal Offer —

It's usually too early to start bringing up discussions of money until the company is convinced that you're the right candidate for the position.

Make sure that you understand all the components of the offer. If it isn't clear, make sure to contact HR or the benefits manager to get the details. You can't negotiate a package without the complete story. This is the stage when the hiring manager says that he wants to bring you into his team after you go through the interview process and informs you that he will be putting together an offer letter. But if he doesn't bring up money explicitly at this stage, you shouldn't, either.

## NEGOTIATE THE ENTIRE COMPENSATION AND BENEFITS PACKAGE —

It's never just about salary. There are many elements to a pay package. Here are some components to consider: You may also be able to negotiate a faster promotion schedule, an off-cycle evaluation, an additional week of vacation, eligibility for stock awards or an equity stake, a 401(k) plan, or a sign-on bonus if you are leaving a bonus behind at your firm. You may even be able to negotiate your severance up front. In an uncertain economy or a shaky start-up situation, it makes perfect sense to negotiate your severance prior to joining such an organization. It is beneficial to have these details ironed out if you are walking into a volatile situation. They may be very willing to offer the severance details in your hire package but won't do it if you don't ask.

### Setting the Right Tone for Compensation Discussions

During your compensation negotiation process, bear in mind that once you are being offered the position, you are basically already on the other side of the interview table. The company has established that it wants you to join its ranks. Company representatives should be very interested in working with you to come up with a fair and balanced compensation package. If you use a collaborative problem-solving approach to negotiation, you will ultimately reach an agreement. But make sure that you, as the job hunter, take the responsibility to move the process along. Kate Wendleton, author of *Interviewing and Salary Negotiation*, says: "It is your job to keep the conversation open until all of the items you want to discuss have been discussed. . . . Manage the conversation, keep it flowing, and thank the hiring manager for discussing these details when all he or she wants to do is get someone into the job and get on with it."

### Other Components of the Compensation Package

Numerous aspects of a compensation package can be negotiated, especially if the base salary is not negotiable. Also, because base salary is a fixed cost to companies, your potential employer may have a little more flexibility on the other components of the package. Make sure that you do some homework about what the market is paying for your position in your industry. Then do some research across industries as well, to verify that you're getting a comprehensive range for the pay package. You may not need to ask all of the questions below, as not all companies will offer every compensation component. For example, profit-sharing awards are typically paid only in banks, and stock awards are usually reserved for senior-level executives. Once you understand all the components of the compensation package, you'll have the tools to negotiate effectively.

BONUSES    When you're negotiating an offer, here are some questions you can ask the hiring manager or HR:

- Will I be eligible for bonuses?
- How much of total compensation is fixed (base salary) and how much is variable (bonus, profit sharing, stock awards, and other incentives)? (It's likely to be more variable in the financial services industry and in sales functions across all industries.)
- Is the year-end bonus completely discretionary or calculated on a percentage of earnings? Is it based on individual performance or team performance?
- Can you provide a written guarantee of the bonus award? If not, can you provide a floor amount for it? (Even if the company is unable to indicate an exact amount in the offer letter, you may be able to get information on the floor of the bonus range for your position. If you are leaving a lot on the

table at your current employer to move to the new company, you may want to ask for a 2-year guaranteed bonus.)

- Will you give me a sign-on bonus to make up for the bonus I am leaving behind at my current employer?

## STOCK AWARDS

- Will you do a buyout of my outstanding stock awards or options?
- If you give me a stock award, what is the vesting schedule? For very senior executives, do you offer other investment vehicles to invest in?

## VACATION

- Can I take an extra week of vacation?
- How flexible are my hours?

## RELOCATION PACKAGES    If you're being relocated, you may be eligible for a relocation package. Ask:

- How will the relocation benefits be administered? Will you pay for services or give me a lump sum payment to organize my move myself? (Keep in mind that lump sum awards are often taxed up to 50%.)
- Have you accounted for the cost of living differential? (Note: You should probably fight for this differential harder if your compensation is based mostly on your salary, as the cost of living calculation is based on base salary.)
- If I need services, what are you willing to cover?
    - Will you pay for me to fly out to look for new living quarters?
    - Will you assist with the broker's fee or other real estate expenses?
    - Can you provide mortgage assistance?

## PERFORMANCE REVIEWS AND FUTURE PAY INCREASES

- How often is performance reviewed? How often will I be eligible for salary increases? Every quarter? Every year? Every two years?
- When could I be promoted? What will my title be? (Title is important to some people, not as important to others. Sometimes, if you're not given the title of director at time of entry, the company may be willing to consider an

off-cycle promotion after 6 months, when managers feel comfortable that you have the abilities to warrant the title.)

### TUITION REIMBURSEMENT AND TRAINING EXPENSES

- I am already working on an MBA at night and am receiving tuition reimbursement from my current employer. Will you provide the same benefit?
- What type of professional development programs can you provide? Will you pay for professional association memberships (such as Financial Women's Association, American Marketing Association, Society of Security Analysts, Society of Human Resources Management)?

## IMPORTANT COMPENSATION TERMS —

SIGN-ON BONUS    A sign-on bonus is a one-time buyout award that is an incentive for you to join the company. Sometimes it is used to replace a year-end bonus award at your current employer. It can also be a bounty award to show how much they want to hire you.

PROFIT SHARING    Profit sharing is a cash award based on corporate earnings, typically found in banks.

STOCK OPTIONS    A stock option is a grant to purchase stock at a fixed (usually favorable) price.

DEFERRED COMPENSATION    Deferred compensation is the ability to make deposits to a deferred salary plan from your pay on a before-tax basis so that amount of income is subject to taxation in the year you make the deposit.

COMMISSIONS    Commissions are monetary awards based on your total volume or dollar sales in a specified period. They are usually calculated on a quarterly basis but can also be computed monthly or annually.

*Compensation Discussions Should Always Be Tied*
*to Work Performance and Job Functions*

You should never conduct a compensation discussion in the absence of a performance discussion. So if your intention is to go into your boss's office to ask for a promotion and pay increase, your first step should be to prepare for a performance discussion. Compile the highlights of your key accomplishments for the past year. If there are any significant contributions that you have directly made to the business unit's bottom line or if you helped save the firm millions of dollars in expenses, explicitly state the role you played in the successful outcome. You do not have to share your entire performance report with your boss, but prepare a cue card to help guide your discussion.

Once you have spoken boldly about what you have accomplished in the past year, you can help shift the discussion to money quite naturally. You're not asking for a random increase because of greed or pure need. You accomplished quite a lot and should be rewarded for your work. Salary negotiations are another area in which you have to toot your own horn. Salaries and benefits are expensive for companies, so they will make a change only if you make a truly valid case for an increase.

## DEALING WITH DOWNSIZINGS AND LAYOFFS —

In this economy, especially in light of increased merger activity, more companies than ever are downsizing, laying off, and expanding job descriptions as a result of such changes. If you are affected by a downsizing, not only will you have to deal with the blow of losing your job, your head may be spinning with discussions of outplacement packages and severance agreements. Most companies design severance packages based on the employee's level and years of service with the company and may have a formula that they must adhere to for liability reasons.

Joe recalls the day that he was laid off by his employer of 8 years. He was called into his boss's office one day and there sat the head of the business with the head of HR. They explained that the recent merger with another firm created the need to eliminate all the positions in his unit. They then proceeded to review the contents of his severance package, including COBRA benefits and his 401(k) plan. He was caught off guard, and he had no idea how to respond. Will you know how to respond when you are laid off?

# FREQUENTLY ASKED QUESTIONS ABOUT PROMOTIONS, SALARY NEGOTIATIONS, AND NEGOTIATING SEVERANCE

## PASSED OVER FOR A PROMOTION

**Q:** *I got passed over for a promotion again this year. How do I make sure that this doesn't happen again?*

**A:** Don't wait for the next performance evaluation to determine how you're doing. Get performance feedback from your manager, internal or external clients/customers, and coworkers on a real-time basis, as projects are finished, as deals are closed, and as work tasks get completed. In this scenario, you should ask your boss (or boss's boss if that's the person who makes promotion decisions) as soon as possible what targets you would need to hit to get a promotion. Then, state that you *want* the promotion: "I was really hoping I could get promoted this time around. As I look forward to next year and my development plan, I really want to be visible to senior management and be involved in projects that will stretch me, give me more experience, and test what I can do. How can I reach that goal?"

## NEGOTIATING COMPENSATION FOR A BIGGER JOB

**Q:** *I am interviewing for a job that is a lot more senior than my current role. Though I enjoy my current job, I've been at it for so long that I can do it with my eyes closed. The new position at this* *company would provide me with more exposure, supervisory experience, and additional skills that I haven't used before. How do I negotiate the best compensation package, given that my current salary and bonus do not reflect what the new position should be paying in the external market?*

**A:** First of all, negotiate the position. You're bringing to the job unique experience that only you have to offer, and that may mean that you could be upgrading the job. At the same time, your new position will require you to do things you have not done before. If you are switching companies, you should get some sort of a premium to move to the new company. The hiring managers ought to give you some incentive to join their firm. In addition, because you will be doing a higher-level job, that should warrant your getting an increase. Make sure that they want to hire you first, before you start dissecting the ingredients of the compensation package. Then, negotiate all the components. If you are leaving a year-end bonus behind by joining this new company, see if they can make up for it with a sign-on bonus in your hiring package. If you are staying at the same company, they should be able to give you an off-cycle salary increase for a promotion.

## NEGOTIATING YOUR SEVERANCE PACKAGE

**Q:** *My group has just been sold to another company. I know that we will be receiving severance packages and outplacement coaching from an outside firm, but from what people have been saying, the standard package is one month's pay and one month of outplacement coaching. Can I negotiate that? And how can I get a package that is commensurate with my level and experience?*

**A:** Many people are so shell-shocked at the moment of a layoff that they often don't have the mental capacity to analyze their severance package. However, in many cases, you *can* negotiate severance packages on the way out just as you can negotiate a compensation package on the way in. First off, it is unusual for a company to give the same severance package to every single employee in the firm, especially given variables such as years of service, level, and other factors. So one person's package may look entirely different from yours and still be equitable. Reach out to your network to determine what similar positions are paying at competitors. Before you go into the severance discussion, write down the things that are important to you. If the actual cash severance payment is not negotiable, you may want to ask for other components that are very important to you. (Please note that this is not a time to ask for everything under the sun.) For example, perhaps you are going for an MBA at night, with only two semesters remaining. They may be able to extend tuition reimbursement to you even after your last date with the firm. You should also receive your accrued vacation pay in a lump sum. Because your next objective is to secure another full-time position, perhaps they can extend more career coaching time with your outplacement firm. Some people decide to ask for additional career coaching support and outplacement so that they actually have a place to go when they are conducting their search. It may not seem so important to you now, but many job hunters confirm the importance of career coaching after the termination is long past. If your employer hasn't designated an outplacement firm, you can ask if you can identify one of your choosing.

---

Whether you are negotiating a compensation package or severance payment, be sure to do research in your industry and talk to other people at similar levels and length of service. Then look across industries and review comparables with similar years of experience. You can use any of the verbiage provided here, but make sure that you also use your own words. They will sound the most natural and effective.

## PERFORMANCE MANAGEMENT AND COMPENSATION —

### KEY LESSONS LEARNED —

■   *Solicit performance feedback regularly.* The annual evaluation is not the time to find out that you could have worked more effectively in the previous year. Aim to keep a close pulse on your work performance throughout the year. Don't be afraid to ask for constructive feedback.

■   *Before you ask for a raise, initiate a performance discussion.* Discussion of compensation increases should always be closely linked to performance.

■   *Before you can ask for a raise or negotiate a job offer, you have to understand the language of negotiation, compensation discussions, and performance management.* It is inefficient to walk into someone's office and demand a raise without any grounds for it.

■   *When you negotiate your compensation package, know your competitive market salary range, a wish list of compensation and benefits, and the floor amount you are willing to accept.*

■   *Keep in mind that tone and delivery is everything when you're discussing matters related to compensation and benefits.* Be firm but reasonable, professional but pleasant.

# BREAKING THE BAMBOO CEILING

*Be the change that you want to see in the world.*

—Mohandas Gandhi

## REMOVING THE BARRIERS AND EMPOWERING THE LEADER —

At one of my speaking engagements, Elizabeth, an Asian woman at a mid-size technology company, approached me after the presentation and expressed her frustration about the concept of taking the leadership baton. She questioned if it were really possible to have full ownership over your own career. She said:

> I really enjoyed your talk, but it got me thinking about how I would make it work at my present employer. And quite honestly, I don't really feel like a leader at my firm. I was just promoted to the director level, but it took me years of hard work and self-promotion to barely climb up to this level. Now that I've made it this far, I'm pretty happy with what I've achieved. But when I look around the firm, most of my peers have left the firm because they no longer see a promising future. I don't see any professionals of color past the director level around here, and it's pretty depressing to see a lack of Asian role models in the senior management ranks.

It was evident from her countenance that she had experienced hardship during her career, and she seemed on the verge of burnout. We spoke further about how she might start doing something about it, yet her discouragement about her company's limitations continued to be an impediment during our discussion. She felt trapped in her new position.

How do you know if you're an Asian American leader? We're all leaders, no matter what role we play in an organization. Are we going to wait to be appointed vice president before we begin exhibiting senior management qualities? Or will we demonstrate the leadership qualities of a senior executive despite the absence of a title or recognition? In many companies in corporate America, power and authority can be ours for the taking if we act like leaders; unlike in companies in some Asian countries, our years of service and corporate title alone will not automatically give us the influence and skills that we're waiting to attain. In fact, one of the most important criteria for selecting someone for promotion to an executive-level position is whether he or she already plays that role of a partner/VP/CFO/COO/CEO and demonstrates the competencies it requires.

Will you be the one who takes the ball and runs with it? If we let the current state of events in our companies dictate our attitudes and adopt a defeatist attitude, we're not of the CEO mentality; a negative attitude is not going to help us achieve our goals. Elizabeth felt trapped and that she wasn't going anywhere. Because of the limitations she placed on herself, she couldn't see how she might take on additional responsibilities to get exposure and play a leadership role.

Evan, on the other hand, is someone who appears to have broken the bamboo ceiling: He's a senior vice president at a financial services organization. What was his secret for getting to the top? He told me that he had to find a unique way to be effective and that he learned early on in his career the critical leadership skills that he needed to succeed in his company. While he used to be more insular and focused purely on doing the technical aspects of his job, he quickly learned to be more vocal about his work and became fluent in the language of his work environment. He also did a good job of managing others. In his company, it wasn't enough that he was meeting his job requirements. In addition, he deliberately carved out time in his schedule to cultivate relationships with other senior managers. Whereas he used to work through lunch, he began to make it a regular practice to have lunch every day outside the office. He used those lunch meetings as an opportunity to make a personal connection with someone in the firm or with a new client. Because of these strategic relationships, he created an indispensable network of allies whom he could call on whenever a work issue arose that required expertise that he didn't yet have. In other words, he invested time in building alliances and became known as a quick-witted, collaborative decision maker who could solve the most complex business problems.

If you speak to Evan now, he'll say that he hasn't finished climbing. He wants to ultimately serve on the senior management committee, to sit at the table with the CEO. There are still a few layers to get through before he gets there, but he's optimistic about the road ahead. It's exactly this type of attitude and drive that has helped Evan get to his current position and the same resilient, outward-focused disposition that will help him achieve his career goals at his company or elsewhere.

Because Elizabeth felt trapped in her role, she created a vicious cycle. Her reluctance to accept that her position was one of leadership kept her from using it to forge new paths at her company. As a result, not only did she neglect to seek out people who would mentor her or identify junior people to mentor herself, her retreating, defeated attitude signaled to her colleagues that she didn't have an active stake in the company. Her employer held partner qualities in high regard, promoting people who embodied them, who took ownership of the well-being of the firm and acted like an owner. Inevitably, her self-imposed constraints helped build her bamboo ceiling. With the right feedback, though, she might begin to see herself as others saw her and learn to be a leader. If we want to be keepers of the flame, we must get out of our seats and make a difference in practical ways at our jobs. Let's encourage one another to become keepers of the flame.

## EMPOWERING CHANGE AT THE INDIVIDUAL LEVEL —

As demonstrated throughout this book, if diversity programs and corporate initiatives are going to work, the process of transformation needs to occur at the individual level. And this transformation process can be as unique as the individuals themselves. Once you've completed a comprehensive self-assessment, you'll be better equipped to take on leadership roles and stretch assignments, because you'll have identified the personal barriers to success that you must overcome. This includes taking stock of your entire package: skills, personality, communications skills, work style, work values and motivators, cultural values, and cultural influences on your professional and social relationships. You can then share your findings with non-Asian colleagues, including bosses and subordinates, to forge stronger relationships with them. And you can encourage your Asian friends and colleagues to do the same.

## KEY LESSONS LEARNED —

### Know Yourself and How Others See You

Take the self-assessment exercises found in Chapter 5 ("To Thine Own Self Be True: Understanding Yourself, Your Vision, and How to Break Your Bamboo Ceiling"). Ask the trusted advisors in your life how they see you. If you don't have advisors, find some. Understand your skills, strengths, areas of improvement, blind spots, and cultural values. Self-awareness is the first and most important step in breaking your bamboo ceiling.

### Understand How Confucian Values Might Present Challenges in a Socratic World

Asian culture tends to emphasize harmony, collectivism, and self-control, while mainstream Western culture values individual achievement and questioning authority.

### Maintain the Best of Your Asian Values

Don't be afraid to be yourself. Seek to keep the richness and depth of your Asian heritage, and introduce your knowledge to others—food, culture, family values, respect for authority and traditions—while letting them know how fully American you are. Don't let the negatives in your cultural values stand in your way of success, but do take pride in your background. Your ethnicity shapes who you are, and you must lead in a way that is true to yourself. Your unique stamp will enrich workplace interactions.

### Create Your Unique Personal Brand

When you are able to interact with others in a natural way while retaining the best of your Asian heritage, you will have created a unique brand that only you could create. Instead of looking for ways to fundamentally change your personality so that you can fit into one corporate mold, make it your responsibility to create your own brand. Eric Liu, author, agrees: "Growing up, one thing I noticed was that there are plenty of Asian Amerians who are eager to prove the stereotypes wrong. They wind up being prisoners of the stereotypes because they are responding to someone else's judgment of them. I know, because I used to be that way myself."

### Encourage Diversity of Ideas and Model Inclusive Leadership

Encourage diversity in all its fullness and support creative ideas and the unique perspectives of others. No matter what your acculturation level, be inclusive in your professional and social relationships—if your friendships tend to be all Asian or all from another ethnicity, open yourself to new friendships. Get involved with Asian and mainstream organizations to educate, inform, and share the value of different opinions, viewpoints, and ideas.

### Recognize When Not to Reinvent the Wheel: Build Bridges with Other Diverse Constituencies

Continue to build on your public speaking abilities, mentor young Asian Americans, especially those in high school and college, and seek to assist and benefit from other ethnic diversity initiatives (African American and Latino, for example) and women's groups to gain insight and lessons from their experiences. Recognize when *not* to reinvent the wheel.

Think creatively about building alliances and leveraging Asian initiatives with other diversity subgroups. Women's initiatives have made great strides; you can learn how they have mobilized their resources and supported their career development.

*Develop Career Resiliency by Overcoming Odds in the Workplace*

I believe that Asian Americans have resilience in abundance. Many of us have overcome tremendous odds to come to the United States and have dealt with difficulties, including both subtle and blatant prejudice, throughout our immigration history. Use that resilience to bounce back when you make mistakes and whenever others make false judgments about you. Continue to appreciate the universal value of hard work and perseverance, but *don't* be silent when you have an opinion. Jeannie Diefenderfer, a Korean American and a senior VP at Verizon Communications, shares, "Even if I had been discriminated against earlier in my career, I never felt like a victim. If it happened, I bounced back and remained assertive. I never took it home and never took it personally." Indeed, this resiliency, this sense of inner strength, has helped Jeannie weather the storms throughout her career.

## SHOULD I STAY OR SHOULD I GO? DEVELOPING RESILIENCY

You can stay resilient despite unexpected circumstances at work. Layoffs will undoubtedly occur, as will downsizings and mergers. How you respond to these changes will make a difference in your career. Career resiliency is developed and tested over time, and it can often be refined by difficult storms in your career. It takes a resilient person to overcome cultural differences and step out of his comfort zone to do what is required to advance his career.

What will you do when people at work seem less than overwhelmed when they meet you for the first time? How will you respond when your boss tells you that he hired you because he wanted a math whiz to handle the financial models, when your résumé strongly highlights other strengths? If you're resilient, you won't let these circumstances discourage you from running hard after your career goals.

Guy Kawasaki, principal of Garage Technology Ventures and one of the cofounders of Apple Computers, told me during a recent interview: "In Silicon Valley, failure is not necessarily a negative thing. Failure is seen as something neutral. If people fail here after a start-up doesn't take off, it's either 'So what?' or it's a positive, as it shows that you have valuable experience. I have never thought of being Asian American as a negative. I never believed that your race is an excuse to feel that you are a victim."

True, there are times when you will *have* to leave your company, especially if you are working in a no-win situation or one where there is emotional or mental abuse. However, the work environment of the twenty-first century is increasingly becoming a storm to wade through, and those who learn how to survive the tough times will become leaders.

### Give Back to Other Asian Americans and the Broader Asian Community

■ *Be visible. Get involved with networks. It doesn't matter what networks, race/ethnicity based or mainstream—just get involved. Give back to the Asian community by supporting local Asian nonprofits, from social services to educational forums. Serve on a board or get involved with planning an event.*

■ *Become visible in your industry and make sure that your role extends beyond your own company. For you to be known as an industry leader, you must be recognized by others outside your firm.*

■ *Support high schools, colleges, and graduate school programs with recruiting and other mentoring programs.*

Make waves where there are problems and injustices. Come together with others in creative ways, create alliances, and show that you too can foster inclusive leadership—by reaching beyond your Asian enclave.

### Become a Keeper of the Flame

Asian Americans are a diverse group, representing 80 Asian languages spoken and numerous cultures. But no matter our country of origin, we have all experienced a cultural upbringing that can often be at odds with mainstream corporate norms. We have many things in common and should continue to look for ways to build bridges. Satish Gupta, a vice president at IBM and one of four Asian Task Force cochairs, says, "Your Asian heritage is a key asset. Don't neglect it. Instead, use it to build bridges with your own community and with other constituents." If we can first take the step of self-awareness and then claim ownership over the positive aspects of our cultural norms, we will not only be more effective in our jobs but we will enrich the lives of our colleagues and friends in a way that no one else can.

### Create a Balance Between Teamwork and Collegiality

Harness your leaning toward community and collective thinking in a productive fashion. Get away from your natural tendency to follow the group at the sacrifice of your own desires and become a mobilizer of groups. A vice president in HR who has, among other roles, worked in the Asian Pacific region, says:

> The characteristically "Asian" way, the team-based collaborative decision-making process, is actually a great way to build up a team. We don't always have to be so superaggressive about getting things accomplished. At first sight, though the Asian professional may seem meek and mild-mannered, I have seen Asians succeed who have, by virtue of their own styles, managed to perform as well as or better than their non-Asian counterparts. We Americans can be too brash and inconsiderate of our colleagues. We have something to learn from Asian cultures; they can teach us some good principles on respecting authority and creating harmony in work relationships.

## Develop an Action Plan That Works with Your Persona

You don't need to offend people to get your points across. As the corporate world continues to become more diverse, you have something to add to the way that business is conducted. And we continuously rediscover what works for us. Bobbi Silten, a second-generation Japanese American and president of the Dockers® brand U.S., of Levi Strauss & Company says:

> Because my name does not shout "Asian," I have numerous stories of initial face-to-face encounters with existing clients and potential business prospects who have reacted with surprise and sometimes disappointment when they meet me for the first time. After years of experience interfacing with clients, I learned that for me, a petite Asian woman in a very visible position, it is important that I get down to business and talk about the agenda items sooner than later. It is only when I start talking and they realize that I know what I am talking about that I am acknowledged as the expert. In the past, I thought it was more important that I use small talk to build the relationship with a new client. Now, I realize, I earn credibility when I actually start showing what I know!

## Make Use of Your Bicultural and Bilingual Abilities

Biculturalism can be an important business skill. Because you understand Asian cultures, you can act as a bridge to other countries, an important competency for large global companies looking to manage multioffice operations.

## Share What You Have in Common

We understand it. We know, when we talk to other Asian Americans, that they too have been at the receiving end of stereotyping or false perceptions at some point in their lives. Yet instead of feeling dejected about it, we can combat stereotypes and misperceptions by communicating when we feel uncomfortable, allowing others to laugh at themselves, maintaining our own sense of humor, and pointing out those perceptions that are completely false.

This book is a call to action for both Asian Americans and organizations. Effectively managing human capital is a key determinant to a firm's success.

Many Asian Americans' potential remains untapped in the workplace, and a company that can look past cultural barriers to harness the underlying diverse talents will excel in this increasingly complex and global marketplace. As an Asian American, it's your responsibility to take charge of your career, by understanding what you have to offer, determining what skills you need to get ahead, and then learning the skills. Tooting your own horn, speaking up in meetings, asking for a promotion, questioning business decisions, and making your career aspirations known, all in your own style of relating, are examples of developing new skills in the workplace. They have nothing to do with undermining your cultural values and everything to do with operating flexibly in a competitive work environment. Realize that you may need to learn different competencies as you move up in your company—your technical abilities may have taken first place early in your career, but as a more senior manager, you may need to focus more on promoting your and your team's accomplishments by building strong relationships with bosses, clients, and your professional network. Refocus your priorities to reflect the change in your level of responsibility. Learn the different roles that you must play in different segments in your career. Develop the critical qualities of flexibility and resilience early; they will always serve you well. Be creative about leveraging your identified strengths, including your cultural assets, so that you can achieve your career and life goals. And as you achieve successful outcomes, share your inspiring story with other Asian Americans to help them break the bamboo ceiling.

## A Conversation with Andrea Jung, Chair and CEO of Avon Products —

If anyone can be called a ceiling breaker, it is undoubtedly Andrea Jung. Chinese American and a graduate of Princeton University, she is the only Asian American CEO of a Fortune 500 company. Since joining the firm in 1994, she has transformed Avon by creating a new vision and successfully reinvigorating the company's bottom line by expanding its range of products and selling to new markets. With annual revenues of almost $7 billion, Avon calls itself "the Company for Women." Andrea has been the chair of the board of directors since September 2001 and CEO since November 1999. She started her career at Bloomingdale's in the management training program and later held senior management positions at I. Magnin and Neiman Marcus prior to joining Avon Products. Her ability to advance up the ranks in a Fortune 500 company is an inspiration to all who aim to reach the top of their professions.

**Jane Hyun:** *Has a mentoring relationship helped you in navigating your own career? How has he/she been influential?*

**Andrea Jung:** Various men and women have provided insightful advice at critical points in my career. Jim Preston, the former chairman and CEO of Avon, was one such mentor. When I interviewed with Jim ten years ago, a plaque on the wall of his office caught my attention. It showed four sets of footprints: first, the footprint of a barefoot ape, followed by the footprint of a barefoot man, then the footprint of a wingtip shoe, and last, the footprint of a high-heeled pump. The title of the plaque was "The Evolution of Leadership." At first, I wondered if Jim really felt this way, but later I discovered that he was truly ahead of his time, and he always supported my professional growth at Avon. Jim gave me this plaque when I became CEO, and I now keep it in my office. I had another mentor, a woman I admired, who also gave me some solid advice. She said: "Always follow your compass and not your clock." There was one point in my career when I was passed over for the top job, and I struggled with whether to stay at the firm. I decided to follow my compass—my heart—and it turned out to be the best decision.

**JH:** *What are some Asian cultural influences that have impacted you in your career?*

**AJ:** When I entered the retail industry as a management trainee at Bloomingdale's in 1979, my father questioned whether I could succeed because I didn't fit the mold of an aggressive retail executive. My parents raised me to be a respectful Chinese daughter. I was taught to be nonconfrontational and to be especially mindful of elders and others in authority. I used to be more emotionally reserved, perhaps even aloof in the way I came across. I had to learn how to be more assertive because I realized it was a required skill for my work. Through coaching and development tools, such as 360-degree feedback, and the use of formal and informal assessment, I was able to monitor my strengths and my areas for improvement. Eventually I found a way to be more assertive without being overly aggressive and while still demonstrating respect and consideration for others. Leaders come in all shapes and sizes. You have to find a way to be effective that works best for you.

**JH:** *How have you dealt with failures or challenges?*

**AJ:** Through stretch assignments and new opportunities, I've learned the importance of risk taking and using skills that I had not exercised before. It's this courage that has helped me to be effective in my job. I'm not afraid to take risks, and I don't get intimidated by failure. To be successful, you need to be able to fail. There were times when I would tell my mom: "I'm not sure if I want to continue doing this," and my mom would tell me: "You can't quit! You're Chinese!" I had a built-in strength and an inner core of courage. I have also learned to trust my intuition.

**JH:** *Looking back on your career, what has been your greatest obstacle?*

**AJ:** I would say it would have to be my age. I was passed over for the top job when I was 38, and age was probably a factor. But I did end up getting the job at 40—still very young for this type of post.

**JH:** *Networking is an important skill for professionals to learn. What role do you think networking can play in advancing one's career?*

**AJ:** Networking is more than just a job search tool. I see networking as a long-term commitment and an openness to external viewpoints, so that one can keep from becoming insular. Even in my role, I enjoy meeting and talking with other CEOs to continue the learning process and to benefit from the viewpoints of others. It's a constant learning process.

JH: *What should one consider when selecting a career?*

AJ: You should select a field where you have some passion for the work. Too often Asians can be pushed into stereotypical industries or jobs that they don't really love. It's so important to have a love for the work that you'll be doing.

JH: *What are your words of inspiration for a young Asian professional looking to move up the corporate ranks?*

AJ: Maintain the spirit of excellence in everything you do. This is part of your heritage. Also, self-awareness is critical—everyone has blind spots, so find out what yours are by learning from the external viewpoints of others, inside and outside of your company. Look for ways to forge relationships and continue to get a pulse on the market. Learn the skills that you need to be successful.

## THE COMPANY FOR WOMEN

### ABOUT AVON'S DIVERSITY INITIATIVES

Avon has a history of being recognized as a leader in corporate diversity, with women comprising 73% of its employee population. The business case for diversity seems clear here. In addition to career development and succession planning programs that are embedded in its management practices, Avon has the following internal employee networks: a Parents' Network, a Hispanic Network, a Black Professional Association, an Asian Network, and a Gay and Lesbian Network. According to Rosalind Bennett, Avon's director of global diversity and inclusion: "The diversity initiative isn't a new thing here, and the process has now taken a different turn—we now want our networks to regenerate ourselves. Women's networks started originally in the 1980s because we needed more female representation at the top. Now I hear senior women asking: 'What are we doing for the men? They are the minority group now!'"

## How the Avon Asian Network Gives Back to the Community

Shirley Dong, marketing manager and the chair of the Asian Network at Avon, spoke about the network's role in reaching out to the Asian community. She spoke of the importance of having a senior management sponsor who oversees their progress. Bob Corti, CFO of Avon, is the management advisor for the Asian network. Says Shirley: "The effectiveness of our Asian network is attributable to the strong relationship that we've developed with Bob Corti. He has always encouraged us to put our own imprint on the network."

One imprint that the network has made is its impact on the Asian American community. The network sponsors the Day of Renewal and Beauty, in which it partners with the Asian Women's Center (a shelter for victims of domestic violence and a provider of legal and translation services for Asian women) to provide six women from the center with a day of pampering at the Avon Spa. The firm also seeks to provide leadership opportunities for future leaders. By partnering with the Organization for Chinese Americans (OCA), the network awards ten scholarships to ten college-bound female Asian American high school students with demonstrated financial need, strong academics, and an interest in community service. The scholarships are awarded at the national OCA convention each year.

## – APPENDIX A –

# SUMMARY OF CHALLENGES TO MANAGEMENT

### SUMMARY OF SUGGESTIONS TO MANAGEMENT —

1. Ensure that a member of the senior management team is closely involved with the sponsorship of diversity networks in your organization. Encourage the senior manager to communicate the importance of these initiatives throughout the firm.

2. Recruit from a diverse array of sources. Using only employee referrals as a source of new hires may result in the recruitment of people from the same demographics, especially if your employee base is already homogeneous. Include minority networking organizations, industry associations, Asian business societies, and campus organizations when looking to diversify your workforce.

3. Develop an infrastructure in your organization that supports career development. Create a culture that fosters internal mobility and information sharing. Consider holding a job fair day, where every business unit in the company sends a representative to talk to employees.

4. Provide access to stretch assignments and special projects to all qualified people. Encourage minority employees in your organization to take these assignments.

278 | SUMMARY OF CHALLENGES TO MANAGEMENT

5. Invest extra time to work with or support someone who is different from you. Mentor junior minority professionals and discuss cultural differences with them. Be aware of the challenges that Asian protégés may face in their work environments.

6. Organize and sponsor events that foster mentor-protégé relationships. Minority employees may not have access to the informal networks that are so critical to career advancement. Create opportunities for potential mentors and protégés to meet one another. Hold mentor-protégé training sessions. Have a take-your-protégé-to-lunch day in your employee cafeteria.

7. Create an atmosphere that fosters open communication in your team. Set the tone by initiating a dialogue with team members about diversity issues. Solicit feedback about your communication style from your colleagues.

8. Aim to create an inclusive environment where every employee's opinion is valued and appreciated. Share information with all members of your team.

## Summary of Key Lessons for Asian Professionals —

1. Take the time to do a thorough self-assessment. Identify your blind spots and weaknesses. Review your career plan every year to ensure that you are staying on track or to alter its course, if necessary.

2. Recognize your bamboo ceiling barriers, both personal and organizational. Work with your manager, coach, or mentor to develop a plan that will help you break some of those barriers. Understand your Asian cultural values and how they may impact your work relationships.

3. Choose an employer that fits your personal values and interests. It may take extra work in the beginning to identify the right one, but in the long run, you will find more satisfaction and a better overall fit.

4. Develop cultural competency. You do not have to compromise your Asian values to succeed. As you progress in your organization (from entry level to management), you will have the opportunity to play different roles. Identify the skills you need to develop in those expanding roles and get the training that you need to be effective at each stage. Develop an ability to move in and out of your comfort zone as needed. Practice the skills that you need to succeed (i.e., leading a meeting, presenting, negotiating, fund-raising, or marketing) by utilizing them in extracurricular activities or outside your immediate work responsibilities.

5. Find mentors to take an active interest in developing your career. Identify senior-level sponsors in your company who know about your work. Develop a strong peer network in your company. You may need to make yourself visible by seeking opportunities to meet potential mentors at industry association meetings or conferences. Be pleasantly persistent about pursuing these relationships.

6. Commit to building a deep and broad network. Invest time early in your career to build a network. Keep in contact with the people in your network on a regular basis and let them know how you're doing. Use a communications method that works for you (e-mail, holiday cards, letters, lunches, etc.).

7. Make use of your bicultural and bilingual abilities. Don't underestimate the value you add to your organization because of your Asian background. As companies become increasingly global, your job title may evolve from "financial analyst" to "global fixed income research analyst," from "marketing associate" to "marketing coordinator for U.S. and Europe," from "IT project manager" to "implementation manager for the Americas and Asia/Pacific."

8. Get into the habit of asking for and giving honest feedback. Get regular feedback from mentors, bosses, and coworkers. Ask them about your interpersonal skills and management style, not just your ability to get things done. Never stop pursuing excellence in your work. Use the Trusted Advisor Assessment in

Chapter 5 to guide you. Incorporate the feedback into your development plan.

9. Develop resiliency in your career. Don't be afraid to fail. There is no shame in having failed if you have the courage to come back for another round. Have the strength to take a risk in your career. Most high-profile assignments carry a degree of risk.

10. Be politically astute. Understand the political climate of your organization. Be aware of changes in senior management, reorganizations, and business initiatives. Discuss the implications of such changes with your mentor or manager.

# – APPENDIX B –

# ASIAN PACIFIC AMERICAN ORGANIZATIONS

I encourage you to get involved with one or more of these organizations. Not only will they help you to broaden your social and professional network, many of them will provide opportunities for volunteering and community service. Where there is no chapter in your local community, contact the organization and ask if it would support you in launching an affiliate in your city/town. You may also want to consider attending an organization's national conference to meet like-minded individuals. Finally, this is not an exhaustive list! If you have other organizations that you would like to see included in a future edition, please e-mail me at info@janehyun.com.

**NOTE:** The author has not worked with every organization listed here and therefore does not necessarily endorse these organizations. The reader is encouraged to review an organization's Web site and contact the offices directly to determine which would be appropriate for his or her involvement.

## PROFESSIONAL ASSOCIATIONS, CULTURAL ORGANIZATIONS, COMMUNITY GROUPS —

### *Asian American Alliance (AAA)*

http://www.asianamericanalliance.com
Headquarters: Chicago, IL
The Asian American Alliance (AAA) is a small business advocacy organization committed to assisting Asian American, minority, nonminority, women-owned, small, and disadvantaged business owners in Illinois. The alliance was incorporated in 1994 as a result of collaborative efforts by the Chinatown, Korean, Philippine, and Vietnamese American Chambers of Commerce. The mission of the alliance is to increase the economic potential of small businesses by providing technical knowledge to entrepreneurs through training, vendor development, technical assistance, and advocacy.

### *Asian American / Asian Research Institute (AAARI)*

http://www.aaari.org
Headquarters: New York, NY
Founded by the City University of New York, the Asian American/Asian Research Institute (AAARI) is a scholarly research and resource center concerned with issues and policies affecting Asians and Asian Americans. The institute connects and enables academics to conduct nonpolitical cultural research and disseminates their findings to the community.

### *Asian American Bar Association of New York (AABANY)*

http://www.aabany.org
Headquarters: New York, NY
The Asian American Bar Association of New York (AABANY) is a professional membership organization of Asian/Pacific American attorneys and other attorneys concerned with issues affecting the Asian community. Incorporated in 1989, AABANY has sought not only to encourage the profes-

sional growth of its members but also to serve the Asian American community through advocacy.

### *Other Asian American Bar Association chapters include:*

*Asian American Bar Association of the Greater Bay Area* http://www.aababay.com
*Dallas Asian American Bar Association* http://www.daaba.org
*Asian American Bar Association Chicago* http://www.aabachicago.com

### *Asian American Federation of New York (AAFNY)*

http://www.aafny.org
Headquarters: New York, NY
The Asian American Federation of New York (AAFNY) supports the health and social services that serve the Asian American community in the New York metropolitan area. The organization analyzes current policies—and advocates for new ones—that improve the quality of life for the Asian American community, while promoting and facilitating philanthropy within the community.

### *Asian American Journalists Association (AAJA)*

http://www.aaja.org
Headquarters: San Francisco, CA
The Asian American Journalists Association (AAJA) is a national organization dedicated to encouraging and enabling Asian Americans to pursue careers in journalism, in addition to striving for fair and accurate coverage of Asian Americans in the media.

### *Asian Americans/Pacific Islanders in Philanthropy (AAPIP)*

http://www.aapip.org
Founded in 1990, Asian Americans/Pacific Islanders in Philanthropy (AAPIP) is a national membership and philanthropic advocacy organiza-

tion dedicated to bridging philanthropy and Asian Pacific American (APA) communities. AAPIP seeks to increase the leadership and participation of APAs in the philanthropic sector, to connect philanthropy with APA and other immigrant and refugee communities, and to increase resources to these underserved populations. AAPIP currently has eight chapters in six regional areas, including Chicago, Minneapolis, Boston, New York, Seattle, San Francisco, Los Angeles, and the Metro D.C. area.

### Asian American Writers' Workshop, Inc. (AAWW)

http://www.aaww.org
Headquarters: New York, NY
Established in 1991, the Asian American Writers' Workshop, Inc. is a non-profit literary arts organization dedicated to the creation, development, publication, and dissemination of Asian American literature. The workshop publishes *The Asian Pacific American Journal,* the literary magazine *Ten,* and various anthologies on underrepresented Asian American experiences. In addition, AAWW sponsors readings, book parties, and panel discussions and offers creative writing workshops. It also hosts the annual Asian American Literary Awards Ceremony to recognize outstanding literary works by Americans of Asian descent and offers youth arts programs and special initiatives such as *Through Our Eyes* for underserved teenagers and young adults.

### Asian Community Online Network (ACON)

http://www.acon.org
The Asian Community Online Network (ACON) is an Asian American and Pacific Islander community network that connects concerned individuals with other nonprofits and community-based organizations. ACON's network is composed of regional and national Web/e-mail groups along with community organization Web sites. ACON also offers a Web site hosting service that enables organizations with very little technical knowledge to set up and maintain their sites on their own.

### *Asian Diversity, Inc. (ADI)*

http://www.adiversity.com
Headquarters: New York, NY
Asian Diversity, Inc. (ADI) is an organization that seeks to empower Asian Americans in the workplace. ADI assists companies engaged in diversity initiatives in accessing the Asian American talent pool. The organization also serves as a resource for Asian American professionals via career events, job placement, and an online cultural awareness magazine.

### *Asian Law Caucus (ALC)*

http://www.asianlawcaucus.org
Headquarters: San Francisco, CA
The mission of the Asian Law Caucus (ALC) is to promote, advance, and represent the legal and civil rights of the Asian American and Pacific Islander communities. Recognizing that social, economic, political, and racial inequalities continue to exist in the United States, the Asian Law Caucus is committed to the pursuit of equality and justice for all sectors of our society, with a specific focus directed toward addressing the needs of low-income Asian American and Pacific Islanders.

### *Asian Pacific American Heritage Council (APAHC)*

http://www.apahcinc.org
Headquarters: Washington, DC
Established in 1979, the Asian Pacific American Heritage Council (APAHC) is a volunteer-led coalition of over 20 nonprofit organizations, representing over 9 million Asian Pacific Americans. The council seeks to promote awareness, appreciation, and understanding of Asian Pacific American culture, heritage, diversity, and achievements among other Americans. APAHC's primary mission is to provide opportunities for the enhancement of Asian Pacific Islander culture as a necessary and vital part of the greater American society.

## *Asian Pacific American Institute for Congressional Studies (APAICS)*

http://www.apaics.org
Headquarters: Washington, DC
Founded in 1995, the Asian Pacific American Institute for Congressional Studies (APAICS) is a nonprofit, nonpartisan, educational organization dedicated to increasing participation of the Asian Pacific Islander American community in the political process at the national, state, and local levels.

## *Asian Pacific American Legal Center (APALC)*

http://www.apalc.org
Headquarters: Los Angeles, CA
Established in 1983, the Asian Pacific American Legal Center (APALC) provides Asian and Pacific Islander and other communities in Southern California with multilingual, culturally sensitive services and legal education. APALC's attorneys and paralegals have expertise in a variety of areas, such as immigration and naturalization, workers' rights, family law and domestic violence, immigrant welfare, voting rights, and antidiscrimination, and they have also worked toward building interethnic relations.

## *Asian Pacific American Network (APAnet)*

http://www.apanet.org
Headquarters: Los Angeles, CA
The Asian Pacific American Network (APAnet) is a broad-based coalition of community-based organizations that act as a catalyst to develop and promote the application of computer information technologies relevant to the needs and perspectives of Asian and Pacific Islander Americans. APAnet seeks to enhance the service-delivery capacity of community-based, nonprofit organizations using technology. The network accomplishes this by providing opportunities for education and training and by offering technology assistance—affordable computer and Internet services and community resources to help implement various technology solutions.

### Asian Pacific American Teachers Association (APATA)

http://www.apata.org
Headquarters: Stanford, CA
A relatively new organization, the Asian Pacific American Teachers Association (APATA) was founded by a group of K through 12 educators concerned that Asian Americans in the teaching profession, as well as those considering it as a career option, face many difficult challenges. APATA seeks to bring the percentage of Asian American teachers to parity with the percentage of Asian children in schools, create a supportive community among Asian educators, and increase school participation among Asian families.

### Asian Pacific American Women's Leadership Institute (APAWLI)

http://www.apawli.org
Headquarters: La Mesa, CA
The Asian Pacific American Women's Leadership Institute (APAWLI) is a national organization committed to enhancing and enriching the leadership skills of Asian American and Pacific Island women via training programs, the expansion of leadership capacity, and the creation of a support network.

Each year, a group of outstanding Asian American and Pacific Island women are selected to attend training programs designed to nurture their development as ethical, caring leaders. They meet for three 1-week sessions in different U.S. cities for the National Program and the second weekend of each month in one city for the Discovery Leadership Program. Upon completion of the program, each group member is expected to create and implement a Leadership Impact Project that positively changes the lives of at least 25 people for the National Program and 100 people for the Discovery Leadership Program.

### Asian Pacific Islander American Vote (APIA Vote)

http://www.apiavote.org
Headquarters: Washington, DC
The Asian and Pacific Islander American Vote (APIA Vote) 2004 is a national coalition of nonpartisan, nonprofit organizations that encourage civic participation and promote a better understanding of public policy and the electoral process among the Asian and Pacific Islander American community. Its objective is to effectively engage the APIA community in the political process by coordinating outreach and educational activities and programs. Currently APIA Vote is focusing on organizing local coalitions and efforts in nine regions: Nevada, Michigan, New York, Washington, Oregon, Illinois, Minnesota, New Jersey, and California.

### Asian Professional Exchange (APEX)

http://www.apex.org
Headquarters: El Segundo, CA
The Asian Professional Exchange (APEX) is an organization that helps young Asian American professionals to explore new career paths. APEX also aims to create a community among these professionals, in hopes that the collaboration will create innovative projects that can serve the community. APEX is also a chapter of the national umbrella organization called the National Association of Asian American Professionals (NAAAP).
*Not affiliated with Apex-ny.org*

### Asian Professional Extension, Inc. (APEX)

http://www.apex-ny.org
Headquarters: New York, NY
The Asian Professional Extension, Inc. (APEX) seeks to promote the personal and educational development of Asian American youth by providing Asian American adult role models. Founded in 1992, APEX is dedicated to helping underprivileged, inner-city Asian American youth overcome the multiple challenges they face as adolescents and as multilingual and multi-

cultural individuals. Through one-to-one relationships with caring volunteers, youth are able to explore new career options, receive guidance and support in navigating the educational system, and improve their self-esteem and confidence. APEX aims to foster the skills that girls and boys need to become healthy adults.

### Asian Women in Business (AWIB)

http://www.awib.org
Headquarters: New York, NY
Asian Women in Business (AWIB) is a not-for-profit membership organization founded in 1995, which assists Asian women entrepreneurs by providing training, information, and networking opportunities. AWIB has offered innovative training and facilitated networking opportunities for thousands of Asian women entrepreneurs. It collaborates with other organizations, such as the Coalition of 100 Black Women and 100 Hispanic Women, to maximize opportunities to share, learn, and make business connections.

### Asian Women Leadership Network

http://awln.org
Asian Women Leadership Network (AWLN), a national professional network, was founded in 2004. Its mission is to promote the career development and advancement of Asian women professionals.

### Asia Society

http://www.asiasociety.org
Headquarters: New York, NY
Founded in 1956, the Asia Society is a national, nonprofit educational organization focused on promoting awareness between Asians and Americans. The Asia Society represents over 30 countries in the Asia-Pacific region through art exhibitions, performances, films, lectures, seminars, and conferences for students and teachers.

### Burmese American Professionals Society (BAPS)

http://www.bapsusa.org
Headquarters: San Francisco, CA
The Burmese American Professionals Society (BAPS) is a nonprofit organization of professionals and students from Burma. BAPS organizes events and activities to foster professional and social cooperation among its members. The society seeks to provide networking, career development advice, and guidance to its members; promote and encourage communication and flow of information among members; assist new immigrant professionals from Burma in their job searches; hold regular meetings to discuss ideas; and create career opportunities.

### China Institute in America

http://www.chinainstitute.org
Headquarters: New York, NY
Established in 1926, China Institute in America is a nonprofit, nonpartisan educational and cultural institution that promotes the understanding, appreciation, and enjoyment of traditional and contemporary Chinese civilization, culture, and heritage. It provides the cultural and historical context for understanding contemporary China. The organization carries out its mission through classroom teaching and seminars, art exhibitions, public programs for children and adults, teacher education and curriculum development, lectures and symposia, and business programming.

### The Filipina Women's Network (FWN)

http://www.ffwn.org
Headquarters: San Francisco, CA
The Filipina Women's Network (FWN) provides educational resources through publications, lectures, activities, and programs to further the professional and personal development of its members. FWN enhances public perceptions of Filipina women's capacities to lead, changes biases against Filipina women's leadership abilities, and fosters the entry of Filipina

women into positions of leadership in corporate, government, and non-profit sectors.

Membership includes Filipina women from corporations and government and nonprofit sectors, including organizations that support FWN's mission.

### Hmong National Development, Inc. (HND)

http://www.hndlink.org
Headquarters: Washington, DC
Founded in 1993, Hmong National Development, Inc. (HND) is a national nonprofit organization that works with local and national organizations, public and private entities, and individuals to promote educational opportunities, increase community capacity, and develop resources for the well-being, growth, and full participation of Hmong in society.

### International Association of Korean Lawyers (IAKL)

http://www.iakl.net
Headquarters: Korea
Chapters:
*Korean American Bar Association of Hawaii (KABAH)*
*Korean American Bar Association of Northern California (KABANC)*
*Korean American Bar Association of Southern California (KABASOCAL)*
*Korean American Lawyers Association of Greater New York (KALAGNY)*
*Korean Canadian Bar Association (KCBA)*
The International Association of Korean Lawyers (IAKL) is an organization that brings together lawyers from Korea and of Korean descent and other interested persons from around the world. The IAKL has held a number of international conferences that have attracted attorneys, judges, and law professors from throughout the United States and Korea, as well as Canada, Brazil, Argentina, Panama, Australia, and other countries.

### Japanese American Citizens League (JACL)

http://www.jacl.org
Multiple chapters
The Japanese American Citizens League (JACL) is a civil rights organization, founded in 1929, originally dedicated to addressing discrimination targeting Japanese living in the United States. Today, the organization is committed to protecting the legal rights of all Asian Pacific Americans. It is one of the oldest national Asian American organizations.

### Japan Society

http://www.japansociety.org
Headquarters: New York, NY
The Japan Society is a private, nonprofit, nonpolitical institution offering programs in the arts, business, education, and public affairs. Founded in New York in 1907, the Japan Society promotes greater understanding and cooperation between Japan and the United States, and in recent years it has reflected a broader Asian and global context in U.S.–Japan relations. The Japan Society offers educational resources to the community in the form of special programming in language, arts and culture, and U.S.–Japan relations.

### Korean American Coalition (KAC)

http://www.apanet.org
Headquarters: Los Angeles, CA
Chapters:
*Washington, DC* http://www.kacdc.org
*Los Angeles* http://www.kacla.org
The Korean American Coalition (KAC) is a nonpartisan community-based advocacy organization. Established in 1983, its mission is to facilitate the Korean American community's participation in civic, legislative, and political affairs so that it can contribute to and become an integral part of the larger American society. The coalition offers a college internship pro-

gram in addition to sponsoring a national college student leadership conference.

### Korean American League for Civic Action (KALCA)

http://www.kalca.org
Headquarters: New York, NY
The Korean American League for Civic Action (KALCA) is a nonprofit, nonpartisan education and community advocacy organization. KALCA is dedicated to promoting the active participation of the Korean and Asian American communities in the civic process; educating community members about their rights, duties, and responsibilities as American citizens; and encouraging community members to contribute to the broader American society. KALCA strives to accomplish its goals through leadership development, education, and advocacy programs on behalf of the community.

### Korean American Network (yKAN)

http://www.ykan.org
Headquarters: New York, NY
The Korean American Network (yKAN) is a nonprofit, nonpartisan organization of one-and-a-half- and second-generation Korean Americans who strive for the advancement of all Korean Americans in mainstream American society. The organization holds monthly meetings.

### Korean American Society of Entrepreneurs (KASE)

http://www.kase.org
(Has chapters in Southern California, Silicon Valley, and New York)
The Korean American Society of Entrepreneurs (KASE) is an organization founded by corporate professionals—including entrepreneurs, venture capitalists, and engineers—that seeks to create and maintain a network of Korean Americans in high-growth industries in the United States. KASE sponsors seminars that facilitate professional development among its members.

### Korea Society

http://www.koreasociety.org
Headquarters: New York, NY
The Korea Society is a private, nonprofit, nonpartisan organization with individual and corporate members that is dedicated solely to promoting greater awareness, understanding, and cooperation between the people of the United States and Korea. In pursuit of its mission, the society arranges programs that facilitate discussion, exchanges, and research on topics of vital interest to both countries in the areas of public policy, business, education, intercultural relations, and the arts. From its base in New York City, the society serves audiences across the country through its own outreach efforts and by forging strategic alliances with counterpart organizations in other cities throughout the United States as well as in Korea.

### Leadership Education for Asian Pacifics, Inc. (LEAP)

http://www.leap.org
Headquarters: Los Angeles, CA
Leadership Education for Asian Pacifics, Inc. (LEAP) is a national nonprofit organization that serves other nonprofits, federal and state government agencies, colleges and universities, and Fortune 500 companies. LEAP has steadily grown from its roots as a volunteer organization offering community training in Los Angeles. LEAP's mission is to empower the Asian Pacific American community by offering leadership training, public policy research, and community education initiatives.

### National Asian American Telecommunications Association (NAATA)

http://www.naatanet.org
The National Asian American Telecommunications Association's (NAATA) mission is to present stories that convey the richness and diversity of the Asian Pacific American experience to the broadest audience possible. NAATA accomplishes its goal by funding, producing, distributing, and ex-

hibiting films, videos, and new media—which support and encourage Asian Pacific American artists working in film, video, and other electronic media.

### *National Asian Pacific American Bar Association (NAPABA)*

http://www.napaba.org
Headquarters: Washington, DC
Chapters:
*New York* http://www.aabany.org
*Washington, DC* http://www.apaba-dc.org
*Los Angeles* http://www.apabala.org
*Silicon Valley* http://www.sccba.com
Other chapters can be located by conducting an Internet search on Asian Pacific American Bar Association.
The National Asian Pacific Bar Association (NAPABA) is one of the few national associations specifically comprised of Asian Pacific American (APA) attorneys, judges, law professors, and law students. Formed in 1988, NAPABA now represents over 40,000 attorneys in 45 local APA bar associations, whose practices include work with corporations, legal service organizations, nonprofits, law schools, and government agencies. NAPABA uses its network of committees to promote APA political leadership, advocate for equal opportunity in education and in the workplace for APAs, and to serve as a watchdog for anti-immigrant backlash and hate crimes. NAPABA publishes a quarterly newsletter, *The NAPABA Lawyer,* for its members.

### *National Asian Pacific American Legal Consortium (NAPALC)*

http://www.napalc.org
Headquarters: Washington, DC
Founded in 1991, the National Asian Pacific American Legal Consortium (NAPALC) works to advance the human and civil rights of Asian Americans through advocacy, public policy, public education, and litigation. In accomplishing its mission, NAPALC focuses its work to promote civic engagement, to forge strong and safe communities, and to create an inclusive society in communities on a local, regional, and national level. NAPALC

has expertise on specific issues important to Asian Americans, including affirmative action, race relations/anti-Asian violence prevention, census statistics, immigrant rights, immigration, language access, and voting rights.

### National Association for the Education and Advancement of Cambodian, Laotian, and Vietnamese Americans (NAFEA)

http://www.searac.org/nafea.html
The National Association for the Education and Advancement of Cambodian, Laotian, and Vietnamese Americans (NAFEA) is a not-for-profit organization serving professionals who are Southeast Asians or who work with the Southeast Asian community in the fields of education, social services, and community development. NAFEA's mission is to promote and support the advancement of Cambodian, Laotian, and Vietnamese Americans through education, advocacy, networking, and cross-cultural exchange.

### National Association of Asian American Professionals (NAAAP)

http://www.naaap.org
The National Association of Asian American Professionals (NAAAP) is a national, volunteer-based, not-for-profit organization where professionals of varying Asian descent represent Asian American professionals in North America in over 24 metropolitan areas, including Atlanta, Boston, Chicago, Houston, New York, San Francisco, Seattle, and Toronto. NAAAP strives to empower Asian Americans to pursue excellence in all professions, from executives in Fortune 500 companies to government officials in federal, state, and local agencies, from Hollywood personalities to local community leaders.

### National Association of Vietnamese American Service Agencies (NAVASA)

http://www.navasa.org
The mission of the National Association of Vietnamese Service Agencies (NAVASA) is to empower the Vietnamese American and refugee commu-

nity across the United States and to facilitate the transition of refugees and immigrants from dependency to self-sufficiency. The member agencies work with refugees and immigrants at the local and regional level, while NAVASA coordinates and develops national programs, initiatives, and resources.

### *National Congress of Vietnamese Americans (NCVA)*

http://www.ncvaonline.org
Headquarters: Washington, DC
Founded in 1986, the National Congress of Vietnamese Americans (NCVA) is a nonprofit community advocacy organization working to advance the cause of Vietnamese Americans by participating actively and fully as civic-minded citizens engaged in the areas of education, culture, and civil liberties. The organization serves to defend the rights of not only Vietnamese Americans but all Asian Pacific Americans against prejudice, as well as promote economic development and foster youth leadership.

### *National Council of Asian Pacific Americans (NCAPA)*

http://www.ncapaonline.org
Headquarters: Washington, DC
Founded in 1996, the National Council of Asian Pacific Americans (NCAPA) is a coalition of Asian Pacific American organizations nationwide. Based in Washington, D.C., NCAPA serves to represent the interests of the greater Asian Pacific American (APA) community and to provide a national voice for APA issues. NCAPA supports efforts to recognize the contributions of APAs to American society; to promote understanding and appreciation of APA cultures, traditions, customs, and heritage; and to promote multiracial, multi-ethnic, and multicultural unity and coalitions.

### *National Federation of Filipino American Associations (NaFFAA)*

http://www.naffaa.org
Headquarters: Washington, DC
The National Federation of Filipino American Associations (NaFFAA) is

an organization dedicated to act as the voice for Filipino Americans and those of Filipino descent. It is recognized by Washington policy makers, private industry, and national advocacy groups. The organization functions as a nonpartisan, nonprofit, national affiliation of more than 500 Filipino American institutions and umbrella organizations. Its 12 regions cover the continental United States, Hawaii, Guam, and the Marianas.

### Network of Indian Professionals of North America (NETIP)

http://www.netip.org
The Network of Indian Professionals (NETIP) is an organization dedicated to advancing South Asian American professionals via career development, political participation, and community service. NETIP provides networking opportunities, conducts seminars pertaining to professional development, and facilitates fund-raising and community service to the disadvantaged. It was founded in Chicago in 1990.

### Organization of Chinese Americans, Inc. (OCA)

http://www.ocanatl.org
Founded in 1973, the Organization of Chinese Americans, Inc. (OCA) is a national nonprofit, nonpartisan advocacy organization of concerned Chinese Americans. OCA is dedicated to securing the rights of Chinese American and Asian American citizens and permanent residents through legislative and policy initiatives. With 44 chapters across the United States, OCA's objectives include the promotion of active participation of Asian Americans in both civic and national matters.

### Philippine American Bar Association (PABA)

http://www.paba-dc.org
The Philippine American Bar Association (PABA) is very active in professional, political, cultural, and social enrichment for Filipinos—not only those residing in the United States but also those in the Philippines. The organization seeks to gather and unite Filipino and American legal minds to focus on the protection, promotion, and preservation of the legal rights and interests of Filipinos in the United States.

### *Philippine–New York Junior Chamber of Commerce Inc. (Jaycees)*

www.philnyjacees.org
Headquarters: New York, NY
The Philippine–New York Junior Chamber of Commerce (Jaycees) is one of the first ethnic chapters granted a charter by JCI in the 1960s. The Jaycees started with the purpose of serving the social and civic needs of the then small but growing Filipino American community. In recent years, the Jaycees has acted as the primary supporter of the formation of other ethnic Jaycee chapters in New York City. The Jaycees is a strong network of young men and women from 21 to 39 years of age focused on community development and leadership training of its members and the community through speak-up, financial management, personal dynamics, public relations, communication dynamics, team building skills, time management, write-ups, and numerous community projects.

### *Philippine Nurses Association of America (PNAA)*

http://www.pnaa03.org
Headquarters: Cerritos, CA
The Philippine Nurses Association of America (PNAA) is a national organization with chapters across the country whose purpose is to uphold the image and foster the welfare of Philippine nurses in the United States. PNAA seeks to promote activities that will unify Filipino American nurses, network with professional organizations and agencies to implement educational programs relevant to the nursing practice, and play an active role in influencing legislation and public policies that will affect Filipino nurses.

### *Project by Project (PbP)*

http://www.projectbyproject.org
New York, NY
Headquarters: Los Angeles, CA
Project by Project (PbP) was founded in New York City in 1998 by young Asian American professionals committed to effecting social change by developing innovative methods for raising awareness, volunteerism, and capi-

tal for the nonprofit community. PbP is now a national organization of so-cial entrepreneurs who forge partnerships with community-based organiza-tions and help to serve their needs. Working on a volunteer basis, the PbP team uses a diverse network of public, private, and community resources to achieve its partner's goals. Every year, each PbP chapter partners with a dif-ferent nonprofit community-based organization and tailors an 8-month campaign according to the partner's specific needs. These objectives are ac-complished through three main campaign goals: fund-raising, community outreach, and public awareness.

### Singapore American Business Association (SABA)

http://www.saba-usa.org
Headquarters: San Francisco, CA
Founded in San Francisco in 1992, the Singapore Business Associa-tion (SABA) is an organization dedicated to promoting business relation-ships between Silicon Valley, Singapore, and the rest of the Pacific Rim. Recognizing the significant economic potential of the Asia Pacific region, SABA works to provide its members with a networking forum and to facil-itate access to business opportunities in the United States, Singapore, and throughout Asia.

### South Asian Bar Association of Northern California (SABA)

http://www.sabadc.org
Headquarters: Washington, DC
The South Asian Bar Association of Northern California (SABA) is an organization of legal professionals who practice in public interest organiza-tions, in government legal departments, and in private law firms through-out Northern California.

### South Asian Journalists Association (SAJA)

http://www.saja.org
Headquarters: New York, NY

Established in 1994, the South Asian Journalists Association (SAJA) is a professional networking group that is focused on fostering ties among South Asian journalists in North America and improving standards of journalistic coverage of South Asia and South Asian Americans. Each year SAJA hosts a national convention in New York in addition to its Journalism Awards Ceremony. The organization has chapters in New York, Washington, D.C., the Bay Area, and the Midwest and is currently establishing chapters in Atlanta, Boston, Los Angeles, Philadelphia, Toronto, and Texas.

### Taiwanese American Citizens League

http://www.tacl.org
The purpose of the Taiwanese American Citizens League is to enhance the quality of life for Taiwanese Americans. Its work is largely devoted to building an understanding of Taiwanese American heritage, encouraging pride in Taiwanese American identity, developing a strong Taiwanese American community, and advocating issues pertinent to Taiwanese Americans.

### Thai American Young Professionals Association (TAYPA)

http://www.taypa.org
The Thai American Young Professional Association (TAYPA) is an organization dedicated to creating a nationwide community of Thai American young professionals. TAYPA is an up-and-coming organization of young, Thai American professionals seeking to establish a strong community that will give them a presence and identity in America.

### US Pan Asian American Chamber of Commerce (USPAACC)

http://www.uspaacc.com
Headquarters: Washington, D.C.
The US Pan Asian American Chamber of Commerce (USPAACC) is a 20-year-old national nonprofit business organization representing all Asian Americans and Asian American–related groups in business. Founded in

1984, USPAACC is based in Washington, D.C., but also has regional chapters in New York, Texas, Illinois, and California. Through business colloquia, information sessions, educational programs, and advocacy efforts, USPAACC opens doors for Asian American businesses to grow by building relationships with their business partners in corporate America, federal government agencies, and with other Asian American businesses.

### Vietnamese American Professionals Alliance (VAPA)

http://www.vapaonline.org
Headquarters: Sunnyvale, CA
The goal of the Vietnamese American Professionals Alliance (VAPA) is to create an environment where different professionals can come to socialize, encourage, network, and understand one another through social activities, community service, and leadership opportunities. The organization seeks to educate and foster the professional and personal development of Vietnamese American professionals, and to disburse contributions, gifts, grants, scholarships, real or personal property, bequests, devises, and other funds collected through fund-raising events to provide relief for the poor. It also coordinates with and supports the efforts of other organizations with similar goals.

### Vietnamese Professionals Society (VPS)

http://www.vps.org
Headquarters: Carmichael, CA
The Vietnamese Professionals Society (VPS) is a nonprofit national organization of Vietnamese professionals. VPS membership comprises hundreds of professionals from various fields such as education, law, medicine, dentistry, pharmacy, accounting, physical science, engineering, computer technology, and business. Since its inception in January 1990, VPS has grown in support both in the United States and internationally. As of 2000, VPS had 25 chapters throughout North America, Europe, Australia, and Asia. As a worldwide organization, VPS is a forum for Vietnamese professionals to meet and extend their social and professional networks.

# STUDENT ORGANIZATIONS AND CONFERENCES —

### Asian Pacific American Law Student Association (APALSA)

http://www.apalsa.org

*At Harvard Law School* http://www.law.harvard.edu/students/orgs/apalsa

The Asian Pacific American Law Student Association (APALSA) is a political, academic, community service, and social group dedicated to fostering a supportive atmosphere for Asian Pacific American students at Harvard Law School. APALSA strives to promote a greater understanding of Asian Pacific American issues and culture, serve as a vehicle for Asian Pacific American political activity, and provide a support network for Asian Pacific Americans and the Harvard Law School community. Every year, APALSA hosts a National Asian Pacific American Conference on Law and Public Policy, which invites prominent jurists, public interest advocates, corporate partners, and government policy makers to participate in panels and meet with law school students from around the country.

### Bay Area APALSA Conference (Asian Pacific American Law Students Association)

http://www.baapalsa.org

Headquarters: Bay Area, CA

The Bay Area APALSA Conference was created in 2001 to promote education, leadership, and community awareness and service, as well as foster communication and interaction among Asian Pacific American law students, attorneys, and community leaders. Each year the conference provides a unique opportunity for participants to discuss legal, social, and various public policy issues affecting our communities. Participants are able to enhance their legal education and develop the necessary skills to further their own careers and serve as advocates for their community.

## *Chinese American Intercollegiate Conference (CAIC)*

http://www.caic2004.org
The Chinese American Intercollegiate Conference (CAIC) was founded in 1998 by students who recognized the need for an intercollegiate dialogue about issues pertinent to the Chinese American community and then sought to fill that void. CAIC is an entirely student-organized conference that includes a full range of workshops, panels, performances, and exhibits.

## *East Coast Asian American Student Union (ECAASU)*

http://www.ecaasu.org
The East Coast Asian American Student Union (ECAASU) hosts an annual conference aimed at increasing awareness of Asian American discrimination, promoting activism, and uniting Asian American students among campuses in the East Coast region. A different college hosts the conference each year.

## *Intercollegiate Taiwanese American Student Association (ITASA)*

http://www.itasa.org
The Intercollegiate Taiwanese American Students Association (ITASA) was established by a group of students from the East Coast and Midwest. ITASA is a national organization staffed by students and recent graduates to serve their peers and their respective campuses. Over the years, ITASA has reached campuses from coast to coast and has brought thousands of students together to learn about and address Taiwanese American issues. ITASA provides the facilities for networking, community building, leadership training, and identity forging that are critical to the future of the Taiwanese American generation.

## *Korean American Student Conference*

http://www.kascon.org
Founded in 1986 at Princeton University, the Korean American Student Conference is held annually at a different college campus each year. It is a national forum for discussion and debate on the most pressing Korean Ameri-

can issues as they pertain to business, politics, academia, culture, entertainment, media, and the fine arts.

### Midwest Asian American Students Union (MAASU)

http://www.maasu.org
Founded in 1989, the Midwest Asian American Students Union (MAASU) is a network of Asian American students throughout the Midwest that seeks to facilitate dialogue about issues pertaining to the Asian American community. The organization seeks to promote Asian American awareness via programs that support Asian American student leadership and the collection and dissemination of information that addresses race-related problems. It holds an annual fall leadership retreat and a spring conference.

### National Asian Pacific American Law Student Association (NAPALSA)

http://www.napalsa.org
The National Asian Pacific American Law Student Association (NAPALSA) was founded in 1981 to promote education, leadership, community awareness and service, communication, and interaction among the various Asian Pacific American law students across the country. Each year NAPALSA hosts an Annual National Conference on Law and Public Policy. The annual conference provides a unique opportunity for participants to discuss legal issues and public policies affecting Asian Pacific American communities as well as allows member chapters to establish ties with one another and network for the future.

### SALSA (South Asian Law Students Association)

Chapters:
*Harvard* http://www.law.harvard.edu/students/orgs/salsa
*Seattle* http://www.law.seattleu.edu/salsa
The South Asian Law Students Association (SALSA) was founded in 2003 in order to aid in the organization and hosting of the National South Asian Law Student Association Conference, held in February 2004.

The goal of SALSA is to provide a forum for addressing the issues of the current state of affairs worldwide and their effect on the South Asian community while concentrating on legal aspects and solutions.

### Sponsors for Educational Opportunity (SEO)

http://www.seo-ny.org

Sponsors for Educational Opportuniy (SEO) is a nonprofit organization that was founded in 1963 as one of New York City's first mentoring programs for high school students of color. Over the past four decades, SEO has assisted some 3,000 students and their families. Its programs have benefited a wide age range of students, helping them develop throughout high school, college, and their careers.

The SEO Career Program is the nation's premier internship program for talented students of color (black, Hispanic/Latino, Asian, and Native American) leading to full-time job offers. Since its inception in 1980, the Career Program has placed over 3,200 undergraduate students of color in internships leading to opportunities in exciting and rewarding careers in the most competitive industries worldwide.

### Toigo Foundation

http://www.toigofoundation.org

The Robert A. Toigo Foundation focuses on the development and mentoring of minority business degree students and alumni within the finance industry. It provides support through scholarships, mentoring, internships, and assistance in job placement. The Toigo Foundation works as a bridge between the nation's leading academic and financial institutions, with the goal of fostering greater diversity in the global marketplace.

# – BIBLIOGRAPHY –

*Advancing Asian Women in the Workplace: What Managers Need to Know.* New York: Catalyst, 2003.

Broussard, Chris. "Rockets Seek to Uncover Yao's 7 Foot 6 Mean Streak." *New York Times,* p. D1, January 8, 2004.

Chan, Sucheng. *Asian Americans: An Interpretive History.* New York: Twayne, 1991.

Cheng, Cliff. "Are Asian-American Employees a Model Minority or Just a Minority?" *Journal of Applied Behavioral Science,* Volume 33, Number 3 (September 1997).

Chow, Claire S. *Leaving Deep Water.* New York: Dutton, 1998.

Committee of 100. "The Committee of 100's Asian Pacific American (APA) Corporate Board Report Card." New York: Committee of 100, 2004. Available at http://www.committee100.org/News/engc100high lights_files/2004.04.23%20Formal%20Report.pdf (last accessed July 27, 2004).

Connor, John. *Tradition and Change in Three Generations of Japanese-Americans.* Chicago: Nelson-Hall, 1977.

Daniel Tatum, Beverly, Ph.D. *"Why Are All the Black Kids Sitting Together in the Cafeteria?"* New York: Basic Books, 1997.

Eng, Phoebe. *Warrior Lessons.* New York: Pocket Books, a division of Simon & Schuster, 1999.

Goleman, Dan. *Working with Emotional Intelligence.* New York: Bantam Books, 2000.

*Good for Business: Making Full Use of the Nation's Human Capital.* Washington, DC: Federal Glass Ceiling Commission, 1995. See http://

www.dol.gov/asp/programs/history/reich/reports/ceiling.pdf (last accessed August 6, 2004).

Hymowitz, Carol. "Why Women Professionals Miss Great Opportunities." *Wall Street Journal,* online, February 4, 2004.

Johnson, W. Brad, and Charles R. Ridley. *The Elements of Mentoring.* New York: Palgrave Macmillan, 2004.

Johnston, William B., and Arnold E. Packer. *Workforce 2000: Work and Workers for the Twenty-First Century.* Indianapolis, IN: Hudson Institute, 1987.

Kanter, Rosabeth Moss. *Men and Women of the Corporation.* New York: Basic Books, 1977.

Kim, Audrey U. *Counseling American Minorities: A Cross-Cultural Perspective,* 6th ed. Edited by Donald Atkinson. New York: McGraw-Hill Humanities, 2004.

Kim, B. S. K., D. R. Atkinson, and P. H. Yang. "The Asian Values Scale: Development Factor Analysis, Validation, and Reliability." *Journal of Counseling Psychology* 46(7): 342–352, 1999.

Kitano, Harry H. L., and Roger Daniels. *Asian Americans: An Emerging Minority,* 3rd ed. Upper Saddle River, NJ: Prentice Hall, 2001.

Klaus, Peggy. *Brag! The Art of Tooting Your Own Horn Without Blowing It.* New York: Warner Books, 2003.

Lee, Elisa. "Silicon Valley Study Finds Asian Americans Hitting the Glass Ceiling," *Asian Week,* October 8, 1993.

Liu, Eric. *The Accidental Asian: Notes of a Native Speaker.* New York: Random House, 1998.

Loehr, Jim and Tony Schwartz. *The Power of Full Engagement.* New York: Free Press, a division of Simon & Schuster, Inc., 2003.

Nisbitt, Richard. *The Geography of Thought.* New York: Free Press, 2003.

Patton, Forrest H. *Force of Persuasion: Dynamic Techniques for Influencing People.* New York: Prentice Hall, 1986.

Population Resource Center. 1725 K St., NW, Suite 1102, Washington, DC 20006. www.prcdc.org.

RoAne, Susan. *How to Work a Room: The Ultimate Guide to Savvy Socializing in Person and Online.* New York: HarperResource, 2000.

Takaki, Ronald. *Strangers from a Different Shore: A History of Asian Americans.* Boston: Little, Brown, 1989.

Takamine, Kurtis. "Asian-Pacific Americans and the Glass Ceiling: How Far Have They Advanced?" *The Diversity Factor.* Winter 2001, A Publication of Elsie Y. Cross Associates, Inc. Philadelphia, 2001.

Tan, Amy. *The Joy Luck Club.* New York: Putnam, 1989.

Tang, Joyce. "The Model Minority Thesis Revisited: (Counter)evidence from the Science and Engineering Fields." *Journal of Applied Behavioral Science* 33(3): 291–315, 1997.

Thomas, David A., and John J. Gabarro. *Breaking Through: The Making of Minority Executives in Corporate America.* Boston: Harvard Business School Press, 1999.

Thorndike, E. L. "A Constant Error on Psychological Rating." *Journal of Applied Psychology* IV (1920): 25–29.

Tokunaga, Paul. *Invitation to Lead: Guidance for Emerging Asian American Leaders.* Downers Grove, IL: InterVarsity Press, 2003.

U.S. Census Bureau. "Educational Attainment in the United States: March 2002 Detailed Tables" (PPL-169). Washington, DC: U.S. Census Bureau. Available at http://www.census.gov/population/www/socdemo/education/ppl-169.html (last accessed July 27, 2004).

——— "United States Census 2000." See http://www.census.gov/main/www/cen2000.html (last accessed July 27, 2004).

U.S. Department of Education, National Center for Education Statistics. Digest of Education Statistics, 2002. Washington, DC: National Center for Education Statistics, 2003. Available at http://nces.ed.gov/programs/digest/d02/index.asp (last accessed August 1, 2004).

Wendleton, Kate. *Getting Meetings.* Franklin Lakes, NJ: Career Press, 1999.

———. *Interviewing and Salary Negotiation.* Franklin Lakes, NJ: Career Press, 1999.

———. *Job-Search Secrets (Five O'Clock Club).* New York: Five O'Clock Books, 1996.

Wendleton, Kate, with Wendy Alfus Rothman. *Targeting the Job You Want,* 3rd ed. Franklin Lakes, NJ: Career Press, 2000.

Wu, Frank. *Yellow: Race in America Beyond Black and White.* New York: Basic Books, 2001.

Zia, Helen. *Asian American Dreams: The Emergence of an American People.* New York: Farrar Straus and Giroux, 2000.

# – Index –